SHORT VOYAGES

Forays along the Littoral

STEPHEN JONES

Illustrations by RICHARD BROWN

Maritime matters connect and blend with shore transactions; thus
the concept of "maritime concern" must shade off at the edges.

—Grant Gilmore and Charles L. Black, Jr.,
The Law of the Admiralty

W·W·NORTON & COMPANY·NEW YORK·LONDON

FIRST EDITION

The text of this book is composed in Baskerville, with display type set in Garamond Oldstyle. Composition and manufacturing by the Maple Vail Book Manufacturing Group. Book design by Marjorie J. Flock.

With the exception of "Stand Up for Short Voyages," "The Man Who Bought McGugan's," and "The Scattering of Belle," all the essays here appeared, in somewhat different form, in *Northeast Magazine.*

The lines, "The easy motion of his supple stride,/which turns about the very smallest circle,/is like a dance of strength about a center/in which a mighty will stands stupefied./Only sometimes when the pupil's film/soundlessly opens . . . then one image fills/and glides through the quiet tension of the limbs/into the heart and expires," quoted in "The Evening Read," are from Rainer Maria Rilke's "The Panther," translated by C. F. MacIntyre, from *Rilke: Selected Poems,* copyright 1964 by the University of California Press, Berkeley.

The lines, "And I will cry with my loud lips and publish/Beauty which all our power shall never establish/It is so frail," quoted in "The Evening Read," are from John Crowe Ransome's poem, "Blue Girls," reprinted from *Poems and Essays* by John Crowe Ransome, copyright 1955 by Alfred A. Knopf, New York.

The line, "I shall wear white flannel trousers, and walk upon the beach," quoted as epigraph to "Getting It Together By the Sea," is from T. S. Eliot's poem, "The Love Song of J. Alfred Prufrock," reprinted from *The Complete Poems and Plays 1909–1950* of T. S. Eliot, copyright 1952 by Harcourt, Brace and Company, New York.

The lines, "His breath stops in his throat/And he stands on the cliff, his white/Panama hat in hand,/For he is Monsieur le Poete./Paul Valéry is his name,/On a promenade by the sea,/so/He sways high against the blue sky,/While in the bright intricacies/Of wind, his mind, like a leaf/Turns. In the sun, it glitters," quoted in "Getting It Together By the Sea," are from Robert Penn Warren's poem, "Paul Valéry Stood on the Cliff and Confronted the Furious Energies of Nature," reprinted with permission from *Selected Poems 1923–1975* of Robert Penn Warren, copyright 1976 by Random House, Inc., New York.

The lines, "Here are the foods of the old ceremony," quoted as epigraph for "The Man Who Bought McGugan's," are from Robert Fitzgerald's translation of Catullus' poem, "CI," reprinted from *Spring Shade,* by Robert Fitzgerald, copyright 1971 by New Directions Publishing Corporation, New York.

The lines, "Work while you can/his hopeless spirit thrived to him to say,/along those treacherous coasts," quoted as epigraph for "Winter," are from John Berryman's poem, "Dream Song 178," reprinted from *The Dream Songs* by John Berryman, copyright 1969 by Farrar, Straus and Giroux, New York.

The lines, "Lord, they closin down the corner music store/Lord, they is closin down the corner music store/I don't know where I'll get/My rainy weather lovin anymore," quoted as epigraph for "Blues For Oliver," are from Blind Jelly Falorp's "Music Store Blues," and are reprinted by permission of the composer from *Blind Jelly Falorp's Greatist Moanin',* copyright by the Metz Music Corporation.

Library of Congress Cataloging in Publication Data
Jones, Stephen, 1935–
    Short voyages.

    1. Mystic Region (Conn.)—Description and travel.
2. Long Island Sound (N.Y. and Conn.)—Description and travel.   3. Boats and boating—Connecticut—Mystic Region.   4. Boats and boating—Long Island Sound (N.Y. and Conn.)   5. Jones, Stephen, 1935–
I. Title
F104.M99J66   1985   917.46'5   85-7142

ISBN 0-393-03303-1

W. W. Norton & Company, Inc., 500 Fifth Avenue, New York, N.Y. 10110
W. W. Norton & Company, Ltd., 37 Great Russell Street, London WC1B 3NU

1 2 3 4 5 6 7 8 9 0

To Jessica Jones,
who, though she likes the voyages short,
always insists that they be made.

ACKNOWLEDGMENTS

I WOULD LIKE to pay homage to the memory of five men who did their best to educate me in matters maritime: Antonio Pezzolezzi, Artie MacDonald, Ed Chapin, Major William Smyth, and Lawrence Brustolon.

Thanks also to the members of the Sambonia Brass who introduced me to the joys of music over water: Edward Jones, Arthur Jones, and Roy Allen.

Lary Bloom of *Northeast* was a continual inspiration. Many of these pieces found their first home in his magazine in slightly different form.

Dennis Horgan and Jim Mehan were helpful in different ways.

Barry Thomas contributed the scantlings of the Block Island piano player's last voyage.

Geoffrey Jones is the author of the paragraph that opens the book.

Susan Preston was first reader.

CONTENTS

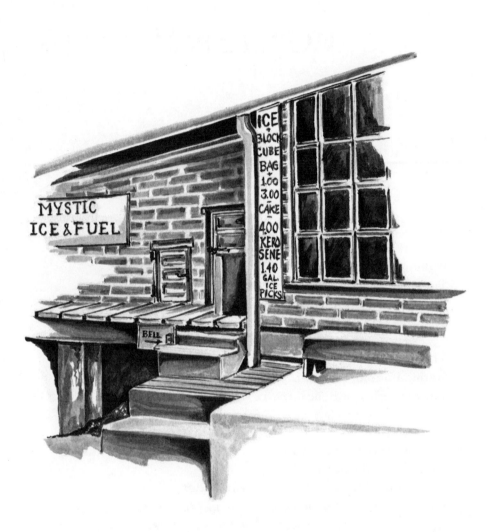

GETTING UNDERWAY
Mystic Ice and Fuel

THE VOYAGE would begin with the ice house.

Back in the memory of people still living, there were a number of such places within a mile or two along this stretch of the Boston Post Road. Each roll in the land had its stream and each stream its pond and dam with the ice house hard by. The only one to survive, however, was on the last hill overlooking the Mystic River, and it manufactured its ice by electricity.

Coming from inland, you got there up a curving, high-crowned road that offered one of the last shady spots before you descended to the river. There was usually a breeze and it was good to stand under the trees by the pile of snow made by the ice saw, for as much as you wanted to get going on your voyage, you remembered that in the low river yards it was often muggy enough to make you pass out.

As prelude at home, we had already dug out one of the big, two-handled canvas bags that smelled like an old sail and were known interchangeably as "ice bags" or "coal bags." The ice house, of course, also sold coal, which was lugged aboard in those bags for the Shipmate stove.

The ice house itself was a brick structure that looked old even forty years ago. It featured a loading stage of worn, wet wood buckled to the building by a band of heavy iron, painted park-bench green. It was at the edge of this stage that the saw had built, cut by cut, the comic snow pile. When I was young, this pile seemed, even on the hottest August day, to stand January high. It was part of the job of getting the ice to bring back snowballs to heave at unsuspecting crew members.

The first time I went there, however, it was almost dusk. It was back in the early forties, and they kept the place open late on Friday nights. We'd come there a long way and run into a brooding thunderstorm. It was the kind of storm that simmered for an hour to let you smell the lightning gather and when it let loose, the trees reeked of electricity, and my mother said dark things. After all, didn't the ice house make its product out of electricity, all those great machines back there generating the water and air? But we had to load the boat and they were closing the ice house, so we went up there anyway under all those dangerous, hilltop trees, and the thunder cracked and in the flash there was a man dancing on the platform, cursing and waving tongs.

Even in sunny weather, there always seemed to be some character on duty: a three-day beard, cigar stump, all fumes and damp. A bit larger than life he was, away up there on the stage with his pick and his tongs and his doors that banged open into gusty inner chambers so at odds with the present weather below. It was a scene to make the simple business of buying a forty-pound block of ice a magical transferal of occult power. "Penny a pound," the man would say, and there was his open, wet hand.

Penny a pound?

For a show like that?

It was amazing to me that all the cars passing at my back had not stopped.

When one did pull in, it seemed as if the people in it were unaware that something special was going on. There were angry faces of impatience, or the set jaw of resigned boredom. For them the voyage had not yet begun.

Yet, no matter how humdrum the vehicle or how unpromisingly domestic the gear inside, there usually was at least one person who would show a flicker of conspiratorial joy. Most often it was, of course, the one who took the trouble to get out with the bag or box. We'd exchange looks.

It was kind of an ice house wink.

We were underway.

PART ONE

Early Summer

I like our language, as our men and coast.
— George Herbert

STAND UP FOR
SHORT VOYAGES

"TODAY is the 8th day out. Yesterday we passed through the Azores. The water is dark green when left alone and lighter than a swimming pool in the prop wash. I have found time to sun. (It doesn't take much out here.)

"Today is the 13th day out. We passed through the Straits of Gibraltar. The rock was the least spectacular sight. I am doing fine."

Thus runs the entire report of my maritime son bound for Genoa, that port of all ports of departure for long voyages. I suppose long voyages have a way of encouraging conciseness, as if time caves in on one, just as the ship's wave spills back on the hole one's passage makes. "The water is dark green when left alone and lighter than a swimming pool in the prop wash."

So there is nothing further to do in the realm of long voyages until he gets back, and I am free to expand upon on the matter of short voyages.

Just how long is a short voyage? Is it a matter of time or the miles logged? And how about intentions, those ETAs and rhumb lines navigators are so fond of announcing as if they were part of the real world? There have been, after all, ambitious voyages interrupted early, not so much aborted as suspended. In some instances these suspensions have lasted for hundreds of years. In such cases shall the voyage back be involved somehow in the calculation? If so, do you count the time actually underway? Or do you figure the elapsed time from home port mooring to home port mooring, including the several-hundred-year suspension (which, among other disturbing hints of discontinuity, would no doubt include a radical change in personnel)? Should there be credit for what might be called "The Ponderous Factor," a voyage made top-heavy by ceremony?

The Ponderous Factor, as I understand it, is a recognition that a voyage ought to consume a respectable proportion of miles in respect to the amount of effort put into it prior to its commencement. If this preparation swells to compete with the effort put into the actual voyaging, then some sort of figure should be applied to reduce the total distance covered and thus make the trip eligible as a short voyage.

An example which seems happily made for a discussion of both the long-time / short-distance voyage and the Ponderous Factor is the case of the 64-gun warship *Vasa* (or *Wasa*), custom built at Stockholm in 1628 for Gustavus Adolphus. Apparently custom built meant loading this vessel up with statues and other kitsch dear to the mantelpieces of Scandinavians at the time. Granted most of this stuff was to be removed as soon as the tour of the harbor on August 10 was completed. The gust that sprung up was not included in the plans and over *Vasa* went, filling just off the dockyard, where she lay in richly preservative Swedish harbor ooze until April 1861. She is now in a special dock in Stockholm, having traveled less than a mile in over three hundred fifty years, seemingly a record for making a short voyage in the longest possible time.

The record was challenged, however, by the six-hundred-ton HMS. *Mary Rose.* Built by Henry VIII, named after his sister, Mary Tudor, this great short-voyager carried a complement of four hundred men. Unlike *Vasa*, however, *Mary Rose* exhibited good sailing qualities and so took part in two relatively long voyages involving wars with the French, serving as flagship. The admiralty, however, not content to leave well enough alone, rebuilt her in 1536, installing a lower deck for guns. On July 19, 1545, the French were lurking off Portsmouth Harbor. How more logical than to dispatch their old playmate *Mary Rose* to frolic with the French? Within sight of land she opened her gun ports, partially, some reports indicate, to show off to those ashore. To the alarm of the spectators, she simply filled and sank, drowning nearly all souls including the ostentatious captain. She was rediscovered in 1968 and after years of further effort on the part of a large group of salvagers, including the Tudor Prince Charles, was raised to return to port.

If we remember that the British vessel was the pet of Henry VIII, Ponderous Factors between her and *Vasa* surely cancel each other, and while *Mary Rose* did travel a few miles further, the short voyage prize should surely go to her because it took her well over half a century longer.

Some short voyages are less tragic than merely despicable. In *Lord Jim*, Conrad, ever the moralist champion of the long voyage, wishes to show how his protagonist is getting soft. Jim is hanging around a bad crowd:

They loved short passages, good deck-chairs, large native crews, and the distinction of being white. They shuddered at the thought of hard work, and led precariously easy lives, always on the verge of dismissal, always on the verge of engagement, serving Chinamen, Arabs, half-castes—would have served the devil himself had he made it easy enough. They talked everlastingly of turns of luck: how So-and-so got charge of a boat on the coast of China—a soft thing: how this one had an easy billet in Japan somewhere, and that one was doing well in the Siamese navy; and in all they said—in their actions, in their looks, in their persons—could be detected the soft spot, the place of decay, the determination to lounge safely through existence.

Conrad was speaking out of a tradition that went back to 1530. Richard Hakluyt, that great chronicler of *The Principal Navigations, Voyages, Traffiques and Discoveries of the English Nation,* puts the case in sonorous Elizabethan:

Old Mr. William Hawkins of Plymouth [father of Sir John], a man for his wisdom, valour, experience, and skill in sea causes much estemmed, and beloved of Henry the Eight, and being one of the principal sea-captains of the west parts of England in his time, [was] not contented with the short voyages . . .

I began noticing short voyagers in the harbor over which my father had the responsibility of harbor master. In the day he had a job working in construction and before I was old enough to join him, he told me to "keep an eye on the harbor" during the hours when he had to be away.

Right out from our house, moored fore and aft between two piles, was *Jumbo,* a twenty-five-foot motorboat that even in the 1940s looked old. A chalky white with the brown trim of old kitchen dado, she had a raised cabin with a rounded front that stopped only a few feet shy of her skinny bow. The raised cabin had two round portholes on each side and ended amidships in a straight up and down windshield. From the windshield aft a wooden canopy took over, supported by iron stanchions, halting just as the cockpit ended in a delicate fantail. "Looks like something you'd expect to see up on the Connecticut River back in the Depression," said my father, who thought that by being down on Long Island Sound in the forties, he'd left both behind.

There were two elderly men who came each day to *Jumbo.* They lived with their sister in a house on the point a half mile from the harbor jetty. Because the wind blew right onto that point, there were no trees, but there was a big flagpole stuck in the stony lawn and a front porch spattered with spume.

To get to their boat, the two old men rumbled down to the harbor alley next to us in a black roadster and parked right up against the short wall. The smaller man, dressed in white jacket and yachting cap, always was behind the wheel. They'd creak out over the running board, each carrying a brown paper bag. The bigger man, always dressed in blue, fetched a galvanized bucket from the jump seat.

Down at the bottom of the wall, nodding on a trolley rig, was a flatiron skiff. The two men would stand there on the wall for a moment, slightly bent, as if waiting for the skiff to come up to them. When it didn't, they stooped to it, the big, blue man first, his red suspenders straining until he got both feet safely aboard. Tugging his blue, peaked cap, fanning his big, black, handlebar mustache, he'd welcome the smaller man, who'd fall through his arms to do a jig until the bilge was steady. Then, adjusting his bow tie, the white-clad man would sit in the stern.

Sometimes, of course, there would be rain water in the skiff and the blue man would employ a long-necked galvanized pump which he would fetch from the roadster's jump seat while his partner pulled on his already small, white mustache.

After much squeaking of trolley lines, the two men would disentangle themselves from the rope and head out into the harbor. The big, blue man, suspenders and handlebar flexing, neck open, rowed. In the stern, clipped mustache and bow tie peeping over a lap full of brown papers bags and the galvanized bucket, sat the other, who, in spite of his baggage, always managed to gesture at least once to correct the course so they would be certain to reach *Jumbo*, which was maybe fifty yards out.

He usually made this correction just as the sister appeared at the harbor wall. She had evidently walked all the way from the house out on the point. Whether this was from her preference for exercise or not, we never knew. In any case she did not wave, nor did the two old men who were, of course, busy with going to sea.

Alongside *Jumbo*, the big, blue man would hold the skiff with both hands.

At this moment the sister began her walk back to her stony point with its flagpole.

Once aboard *Jumbo*, the big, blue man would disappear below. This left the white-clad man at the helm. In a moment there was a cough and a roar. Exhaust spat from the pipe under the fantail. The blue man emerged from the cabin. Then commenced an elaborate performance that for some reason never failed to hold those of us ashore.

While his partner stood patiently at the helm beneath the canopy, the big, blue man danced about him with the various lines that needed moving. It was much the sort of thing I'd seen old priests do in dark churches: a kind of mumbling and dancing about the ancient pathways, familiar routes that, however, sometimes betrayed the celebrants into a slap-handed lurch or inadvertent counterbalancing benediction.

Sometimes it was necessary for the blue man to step up onto the deck alongside the cabin, and then *Jumbo* heeled toward him, burying her waterline, canting her canopy so you could see the smattering of white gull droppings on the brown roof and the darker squares where patches had not yet faded into the rest of the roof. Catching sight of these intimations of mortality one afternoon, my father sighed, "She's an old girl."

"Shhh," my mother said, "voices carry over water."

"Well," my father said, "they're old men."

Nevertheless, shuffling his heels sideways, the big, blue man made his way along *Jumbo*'s raised cabin side, slapping a pipe rail that ran the length of the cabin top, making little thumps audible to us on the shore.

Freed at last from all concern with lines, the blue man stepped up to the bronze lever that rose out of the cockpit floor and pulled it aft. The sound of the engine deepened, and there was a white throb under the fantail that brought the bow of the skiff up tight on its trolley. The captain turned the spokes to port and *Jumbo*'s skinny bow faded away from the piling.

They swung around and headed out of the harbor like that, the big, blue man at the shift lever, the small, white-haired man at the helm.

And even after the boat had gone around the bend, you could hear the exhaust rattle the harbor awnings.

Toward the end of the afternoon they would return and reverse the process, but each man yet in his accustomed role.

And where had they been?

They had merely gone out of the jetty, run the beach a half-mile until they'd gotten right off their house, maybe forty yards of water between them and the big flagpole set in their stony yard. The small man would put *Jumbo*'s skinny bow up into the southwest wind and the big man would toss over an old stock anchor from the fantail, then walk the line forward to the Samson post in the bow. As soon as they had satisfied themselves that the anchor had taken, and indeed it was hardly the best of anchorages—a cobble bottom off a prevailing lee shore of boulders—they would stop the engine. It was time to break out the brown bags and also see if they could fill the galvanized bucket with fish. From the front porch, forty yards away, their sister watched them and kept an eye on the weather so that if it began to blow up she would hoist a red flag on the big pole.

When the flag went up, the short voyage would be over.

Granted some short voyages depend upon their being the residue of long voyages, as when Tu Fu, a notorious short-voyager, comes upon:

> Anchored to the pilings are
> Boats from Eastern Wu
> Three thousand miles from home.

In the case of Tu Fu, it is perhaps the infinite sipping at the backwater, but there is also the short trip tacked onto the long trip: the voyage in an Irish drizzle out of Dalkey Harbor to the island in a modified curragh run by an old Irishman in a long, brown wool coat; the rowboat trip along the Main beneath Wurtzburger castle; the trip to eat dinner on the far side of Poros in the little boat with the stripped awning and the Briggs and Stratton engine just like the lawn mower's at home.

There are certain pictures that suggest short voyages to dream on. These sorties would be exquisite miniatures. Logging only a few meters, they would be distillates of civilization's juicier moments: a snapshot of the archaelogist's rowboat in the Well of Virgins at Chichén Itzá; an oil of the lily-tender's batteau in Monet's pond at Giverny; an etching in the background of Whistler's painting of his mother in which bargeman's wherry is caught in a pool behind a jam of lighters at Black Lion Wharf.

As the Whistler painting houses the engraving, so some long voyages contain short voyages.

One thinks of the Spanish Armada, that ponderous yard-sale collection of galleusses and urcas moving for months up from Lisbon to Portsmouth and beyond. The whole time that flotilla was rotting away more or less on its rhumb line, like some galaxy bound for oblivion, there were little pinnace voyages, interstellar missions, taking place within the formation.

The pinnace was a fore-and-aft rig capable of going to windward and so could overtake the square-riggers and maneuver among them.

The Duke of Sidonia sent them forth as an avant garde to scout for Drake and Frobisher and Hawkins. He had them run ahead up to the Netherlands to see if the Duke of Parma was about to embark on his never-to-be-sailed short voyage out from Holland. Mostly, however, he used them within the fleet, employing them in the manner of sheep dogs to herd the Armada, whose vessels were capable of such widely divergent speeds. Once, when a too ambitious captain took off from the fleet, a pinnace was dispatched to retrieve him. As a warning to others the Duke, formerly a mild enough man who'd spent his life ashore growing oranges, hung the offending captain from the mast of the pinnace. To make sure the message was not lost, the Duke commissioned surely one of the grimmest of short voyages on record, parading the dangling captain about the fleet.

An even shaggier series of short voyages was made within the fleet by a number of Portuguese water dogs. Black, sometimes with white vests and feet, these dogs were about the size of a standard poodle. Like the poodle, they were intelligent and had dense, curly hair. Unlike the Parisian poodle of the boulevards, however, they were closer to the old Baltic Sea retriever, the "Pudel" *(canis familiaris aquatius)*, and their broader feet, slim hindquarters, and barrel chests were originally bred to aid them in retrieving seine nets off their native coasts. The breed has been kept alive in severely limited numbers. You used to be able to see one guarding a gas station on the Connecticut-Rhode Island border. The Armada used the dogs to short-voyage well-corked messages between nearby ships.

Military maneuvers, of course, account for some of the most famous short voyages in history. There is a comic formula lurking here somewhere, for no matter how serious the historical event, if the trip seems fewer in feet than the number of men involved, the effect is always ludicrous. There is no better example of this than George Washington's courageous winter crossing of the ice-choked Delaware in Durham boats. Even the evacuation of Dunkirk comes down to us in the cheerful family-outing atmosphere of *Mrs. Miniver*.

Some women, of course, help to make even a long voyage shorter, so while the Nile is long, Cleopatra's trip is of great duration only in the sense that its afterimage shall linger as long as the English language:

> The barge she sat in, like a burnish'd throne,
> Burn'd on the water: the poop was beaten gold;
> Purple the sails, and so perfumed that
> The winds were love-sick with them; the oars were silver,
> Which to the tune of flutes kept stroke, and made

> The water which they beat to follow faster,
> As amorous of their strokes.

The more important the person, it would seem, the shorter the voyage. Henry VIII visits neighbor Thomas More by barge and leaps, if Mr. Robert Bolt is to be trusted, from prow to mud. Thomas More floats off to visit neighbor Wolsey, a man whom we do not see water-borne in this era of his life, but who surely, at one point, at least entertained thoughts of short voyages and how they might, upon a gust of ill fortune, turn long:

> . . . I have ventured,
> Like little wanton boys that swim on bladders,
> . . . .
> But far beyond my depth

There is much controversy over just how out of control George I was during his famous short voyage at the premiere of Handel's *Water Music*. It is perhaps no wonder that a man who was alleged not to be trusted to sit in a concert hall through a whole performance of the *Messiah* would spawn rumors which have him but a few years earlier growing antsy with Handel out in a boat. Some say that shortly after eight o'clock on July 17, 1717, George's barge fell out of earshot of the vessel upon which Handel was conducting, so the whole thing ("*viz.*, trumpets, hunting horns, oboes, bassoons, German flutes, French flûtes à bec, violins, basses") had to be cranked up again.

Others say that Handel had previously fallen out not of earshot but favor, and so crashed the royal water picnic with his trumpets, hunting horns, oboes, bassoons, German flutes, French flutes a bec, violins, and basses. "His Majesty, equally surprised and pleased by their [the waterborne compositions'] excellence, eagerly enquired who was the author of them . . . [and after much courtly backing and filling] Handel was restored to favor."

There is a third version that merely says Handel was invited to play his water music both before and, because it was enjoyed the first time, again after dinner. However, since each run through the piece took about an hour and the dinner presumably took at least that, we are bordering on something which in time, if not distance, is approaching a long voyage.

Ceremonial short voyages are, of course, a key part of many cultures. This custom seems to have gotten started in Venice which, in spite of Marco Polo and other long-distance travelers, might well be called the capital city of the short voyage. Though a gondola is used, the short voyage I have in mind, however, is not from San Michele to

Harry's Bar, but from the Salute out toward the Lido. This is an annual voyage by the Doge to throw a ring of flowers into the sea (or at least lagoon). The wreath (ring) symbolizes the city's wedding with the sea. There are, of course, fishermen in Venice, but the Venetian trip seems more in the spirit of a merchant paying his protection fee so that his goods will not be hijacked at sea. Other Catholic, Mediterranean countries and the fishing communities of Portugal put the bishop aboard, not a special vessel, but one of the regular fishing boats, albeit "the queen," and the litany has as much to do with making a memorial to those fisherman lost the previous year at sea as insuring the future catch, a custom transplanted by Portuguese fishermen to New England at Gloucester and Stonington, Connecticut.

Even purer than the ceremonial short voyage, some would say, is the short voyage of exploration. Perhaps one's own first voyages are of this sort, the bare foot out from under the sheet into the cold night, a toe wave into the darkness, then a scurry home to the anxious inquiries of the other foot which, like any stay-at-home, is always a bit repelled by the traveler's altered state:

> And I alone have escaped to tell thee.

or:

> By thy long gray beard and glittering eye,
> Now wherefore stopp'st thou me?

Some of the greatest voyages of discovery were hardly longer than these out-pokings of the naked foot. Prince Henry, who himself never got past Morocco, sent his men out to round the capes of Africa one at a time, and much like our cold foot out of the bed, he wanted them to hurry home with the news. Gil Eannes was a favorite:

> "Yes, my Prince, there was another one, another cape."
> "Keep going."

All around Africa, like that, but short voyages all.

Short voyages may not only extend one's space, but add to one's time. There was a man in one of our harbors who was told by his doctor he had six months to live.

He went home and said to himself, "Then I must hurry and get that old boat in the yard next to the house rebuilt."

It had been sitting in his yard for twenty years since his own father had died.

But he went to work immediately and kept working on it every

day, trying to remember how it had looked when his father first had
it built in 1927 in Crocker's yard down in New London. She was a
twenty-foot launch that looked like a catboat without a mast. Her cockpit
was mahogany, vertically sheathed and curved at the stern end. Up
forward was a two-bunk cabin with an icebox and round portholes on
each side. The Palmer engine was in the cockpit in a raised box and
went *dunk-dunk-dunk*. She was steered at the starboard after end of
the cabin just outside the doors that lead below, and she had a bronze
clutch lever in the cockpit floor and a bronze throttle quadrant on the
cabin face by the wheel that connected by an ancient bell crank
system.

The six months passed and he hadn't finished the restoration,
but he hadn't died either, so he kept at the boat. Three years later he
had her completely restored, better than new, and the next summer
he took her out every evening. We'd watch him chug around the harbor, *dunk-dunk-dunk*, steering her, sitting on a stool in his stocking cap
and waving to people on the shore.

I suppose in some ways he reminded me of my favorite short-
voyagers, the two old men in *Jumbo*, though his boat had no canopy
like theirs and he was alone with no big, handlebarred engineman to
assist him or sister to put up the flag when it got rough. Like *Jumbo*,
though, this boat was fine-hulled and left no ripple in her wake, so he
could tear around the harbor. When everyone cheered, he doffed his
stocking cap.

That fall he sat in her cockpit on the stool in his stocking cap and
sweater and baggy flannel pants while they took her up in the hoist
and set him and his boat ashore. I rowed over, and when he climbed
down from his boat I told him how much we'd miss his sundowners.

"Hey, I'm going moose hunting this fall," he said, "not that I
expect to shoot anything, but in moose hunting you get way up there."

"Way up there," I said, "where the doctor can't get you."

"You got it."

He didn't die until later that winter.

That, apparently, is the ultimate short voyage of them all. According to the literature, death seems a bit like a Prince Henry trip,
an installment, that is both a little excursion in itself and part of the
Big Voyage of Discovery. For this kind of voyage, Dante, of course,
has the reputation of being the great cartographer. However, he has
only a thwartwise notion of navigation, and of his four crossings, he's
passed out in the bilge on one and two are mere fordings. True, the
Egyptians and the Norse saw the transport over into the other world
as requiring a boat, but judging by the provisions discovered in tomb

excavations, these journeys were expected to be long ones.

Still, for final voyages, be they short or long, I prefer my old moose-hunting friend on his restored launch. This was the voyage he always took. It was around the harbor, counterclockwise: the home dock; the creek with the swans; the right-field fence of the softball field; the old white, wooden CPO club; the Coast Guard pier with the bell buoys up out of the water lying on top, their roots exposed; the long, low rock with all the cormorants; the sou'west surge at the mouth of the inlet; the crumbling concerete pier on Pine Island; the pillbox up in the poison ivy; the tail of the island; the east breachway where the lobstermen go out; the pine trees on Bushy Point where the deer hide their young; the lagoon at the far end of which hangs the osprey; the mouth of the river where the scallop channel begins and where once he saw nine blue herons watching him, their eyes, as the sun set, glittering in the tall, blond grass.

THE EVENING READ

... and thus it is that he becomes the founder of a family.
— Thoreau, "Reading," *Walden*

COME the bad weather and after supper, my father would take a mild swipe at me with a book and say, "Come here and sit down." He'd point to the couch. "We're going to have a yarn." And he would begin to read to me.

He was a builder then and his hands were big and I was glad to listen.

His father, he explained once, had read to him and so had his father's father. These were men whose education had been in the building trades. They spent their days framing roofs, turning bannisters, laying bricks. Yet all my academic lessons would not have been worth a footnote to a footnote if it hadn't been for the Evening Read.

Before my father inaugurated the evening sessions, however, he employed the Morning Bellow. He would recite . . . or perhaps the word is "declaim," a fine, old nineteenth-century tradition and one my father got from his mother. She was on the old parasol-and-trolley circuit up in Unionville, Connecticut, where she did what were called "pieces"—animated dialogues and monologues featuring such turn-of-the-century favorites as Pat & Mike, from her own Irish tradition, and Hans & Fritz, Ephraim — Rastus, and Olga & Sven, thrown in with patriotic poetry and a piano rendition of "Under the Double Eagle."

But here comes her son, my father . . . It is morning and he's stalking out of the bathroom, face lathered like a clown, straight razor in hand. I don't know how old I am, but I'm looking away, up at the razor, when the lathered face bellows (that is, declaims): "Thy name and purpose, Saxon stand!"

I say nothing. Maybe I cannot even talk at that point, much less parry with Roderick Dhu. (These passages float distorted by time. Sometimes I think he altered them, in the manner of eighteenth-century editors of Shakespeare, to suit his taste.)

The razor flourishes overhead. The lather cracks.

. . . Lay on, MacDuff,

And damn'd be him that first cries, "Hold, enough!"

Indeed, what was my name and purpose? Was I, for instance . . .
MacDuff?

He would block the door to the bathroom, crying,

> Lars Porsena of Clusium
> By the Nine Gods he swore
> That the great house of Tarquin
> Should suffer wrong no more.

And then we would have—before anyone could get into the bathroom— the whole galloping story of Horatius defending the bridge.

Sometimes he would not have the razor, but merely announce,
"Sparticus' Address to the Gladiators at Capua," this usually at dusk,
armed perhaps now with a beer.

"Ye call me chief, and ye do well to call me chief . . ." There followed something about a long time in the meadows, or maybe it was
the galleys.

Or I'd be pretending to be asleep in the dark and he'd come in
and put his face close down and moan,

> Abou BenAdheim (may his tribe increase!)
> Awoke one night from a deep dream of peace

The reading, as opposed to the declamation, came a little later
and involved a prop different from the razor or the beer. This was a
box-shaped object full of papers sewn together. I found it comforting,
though I could not read, because there seemed to be some connection
between this object he called a "book" and my father's behavior, a
connection I could figure out and in some ways predict.

He'd sit me down after supper and we'd have *Paddle-to-the-Sea,*
one chapter a night. On the left-hand page was a painting on the
right, just enough text for a squirming kid to put up with.

And here I put you on this snowy hilltop that may melt in the spring sun and
you will flow down through the great lakes to the sea and be my paddle-
person.

And there was the paddle-person, an Indian's wood carving of a person in a canoe, making its way through each of the Great Lakes, through
sawmills and iron ore sludge and vile backwaters and forest fires and,
finally, over Niagara to the sea.

Kipling's *Jungle Book* was harder. The drawings were smaller and
snuck in unexpected places, and a number of things had to be explained.

Indian plumbing, for instance. (Not the paddle-person's kind of

Indian, but "Ind-jaa," very exotic, though, ironically, Kipling wrote the book within a hundred miles of where we read it, up in Vermont with three feet of snow outside the window). Not that at that age I knew much about plumbing in West Hartford. "The pipe," my father explained, "went from the bathroom out through the wall of the bungalow and into the yard where the water was just supposed to . . ."

"Yes?"

"Spread. . . . The water was supposed to spread. But the snakes, two big cobras named Nag and Nigaina, got to come into the house through the pipe."

"We will come for the man with the thunder-stick," said Nag. "We shall strike when he least expects it," said Nigaina.

All this back-and-forth in the pipe and then here they come up through the tiles one night, their hoods folded flat for the journey, when the man least expects it. But Rikki-Tikki-Tavi is there. A waif of a mongoose originally swept out of his burrow and sent "kicking and clucking" down the storm gutters of Segowlee cantonment by the summer rain, he had been befriended by the man with the thunder-stick and the bathroom (All these connections by watery concourse . . .)

Everybody in the story now meets in a marvelous bit of narrative plumbing, there in the bungalow's bath. The big hood of the cobra rises and spreads. The mongoose bares his teeth. The man with the thunder-stick . . . Having gotten past Horatius at the bridge, it is a wonder I was ever relaxed in that room.

There was poetry, too, as if that hadn't been poetry: Longfellow, usually in outrageous parody:

> The smith, a mighty man is he,
> With large and cinnamon hands.

(My father would demonstrate with his bricklayer's hands.)

Or:

> By the shore of Kitchee-Goomie,
> By the shining big sea water
> Stood the wigwam of Nicko'muss . . ."

Or it was off-shore Longfellow, which in his version went:

> It was the schooner Hesperus,
> That sailed the wintry sea;
> And the skipper had taken his little daughter,
> To bear him company.
> The wind she gores like an angry bull
> Ah-ha, the breaker's roar . . .

One of our favorites was Anonymous, who had written a poem on the milk jug we used each night at the table. (My son Geoffrey has never seen this jug, but knows the poem so well from my father that he has suggested an emendation in line four.)

> The man doomed to sail
> With the blast of the gale
> Through billowous Atlantic to steer
> Thinks of the wave (emended by Geoffrey to
>   "as he bends o'er the wave")
> Which may soon be his grave
> He remembers his home with a tear.

There was also, on cold days, Robert Service:

> A bunch of the boys were whooping it up
> In the Malamute Saloon.

Or, Sam McGee (that prospector) *from Tennessee where the cotton blooms and blows* . . . Poor Sam could never get warm, so he sat in the roaring boiler room of the old derelict "barge on the marge of Lake Lebarge."

These were my father's books, ones he had been given, in some cases, by *his* father.

My grandfather was a man who, when not moonlighting from his carpentry as a side-arm country fiddle player, liked to sit down of an evening with a good book. What he enjoyed was "running across something . . . well-written, something you can chew over, and savor." With me, he used to chew over and savor things like "The Bremen Town Musicians," a story I always thought was really about him, because of the way he acted when he read it. And wasn't his old fiddle right there on the piano the whole while?

One Christmas, I got a beautiful illustrated edition of *Treasure Island* and read for myself, "I take up my pen in the year of grace 17—, and go back to the time my father kept the Admiral Benbow Inn."

Most of it was too hard, however, so as in *Paddle-to-the-Sea,* I'd content myself with the pictures by day, waiting for my papa's voice at night. . . . Pew's green eye shade, Billy Bones' sallow complexion and apoplexy . . .

A strange story, *Treasure Island,* to have your father read to you, he more the Long John type, anyway, than the somewhat wimpy tavern keeper who conveniently, like Peter Rabbit's father, disappears early. *Them that dies is the lucky ones.* And even more ominous, perhaps,

"Mr. McGregor was on his hands and knees in the garden planting out young cabbages . . ."

Later, we did *Black Beauty*, but I did not like that story as well.

"Maybe he's getting too old to be read to," said Mother, "or maybe this book's too old for him. Or maybe it's a little too old-fashioned." (My mother was not a "chewer reader." She had been to college and learned speed reading, and survived one winter of the Depression in a flat in Pawtucket, reading all the Dickens that the Westerly Library could hold while my father shingled a roof at Watch Hill. In any case, she was the one, because of the speed reading, who helped us "keep up" with contemporary articles—articles on education, for example, many of which then were beginning to mention things called "stages.")

When my father came back from World War II, I went to a very old-fashioned school where the curriculum was, whether or not I was, at the "Lady of the Lake" stage. Fortunately, my father, despite a grim encounter in Iwo Jima with an enemy officer and a Samurai sword, was still capable of *the "Lady of the Lake"* stage, too, which is why I suspect he sent me to this particular school. The edition of Scott's poem we used had no glossary or notes. We were expected to make do in seventh grade just as it was:

> The stag at eve had drunk his fill,
> Where danced the moon on Monan's rill . . .

The poem's music was exciting, but I was having a tough time passing the tests that demanded to know whose rill was on whose poniard. Having been away in the war, my father did not know he was supposed to go to the school board and get the English teacher fired. Instead, he offered to read the poem to me and try to piece out the dialect. We all agreed, however, that it was time I learned to read by myself, at least geographically. In other words, when the hard part of reading came: "Go to your room."

We solved the problem with some of my mother's technology.

She read the Sunday *Times* from cover to cover. (It took until Tuesday.) This was when, on the back of the sports section, there were those wonderful war surplus ads for things like tackle that could fit in your glove compartment and lift up your car; parachutes ("ideal for gathering autumn leaves"); horse gas mask bags . . . and surplus "trench telephones."

My father had already used his World War II Seabee experience to employ a flame thrower to melt driveway ice, and a flare pistol to call me home on Halloween. So it was no problem to interest him in the trench telephones as a way to announce Walter Scott.

After supper, I would go up to my room and open the musty old *Lady of the Lake*.

> Effsoon she swart her golden tart
> The burn she knew too well . . .

And down to my father's red chair, I'd send a message:

"Charlie company, this forward observer, sighted golden tart, linea niner tha-ree zeee-row, please identify 'swart.' "

There would be a cough on the other end, "Say again."

" 'Swart,' " I would say again.

"I think . . . it's a small dagger," he'd say. "The kind you carry in your belt on the other side from your saber, so that when your opponent falls off his horse, you get down yourself and then go over to him and open up the earpiece in the helmet and stick it in."

There would be a cry from my mother.

"Or, I think it's a small gate in the back of the castle that the duke can slip out when everybody's at the front door."

We also had Summer Reading lists in those days, including items like Michael Pupin's *From Immigrant to Inventor* and *John Brown's Body* by Stephen Vincent Benêt. We lived at the shore in the summer and the only books I could find on the list were the works of Carl and Mary Jobe Ackley about Africa.

These I read in the Mystic-Noank library, just down the road from where they were written in Mary Jobe Ackley's home, There was, and still is, that marvelous window seat overlooking Mystic, and I sat in it, under the Ludwig tile roof in a thunderstorm, listening to the water course through the green copper gutters as I followed the tragic last trail of fever-ridden Carl Ackley vanishing into "the vertiginous African gloom."

During school term, we had Edmund Gosse's *Father and Son,* which, I had the word of an old schoolmate just a few months ago, is still "the dullest book ever written."

He and I used to read about jazz, Nat Hentoff and Barry Ulanov and George Simon, and babble by the hour about "overleafs," "cadenzas," "substitute chords," "modulations," and our heroes: Diz, Miles, Theolonius, et al.

Our football coach was also our junior English teacher, and he got mixed up often and would shout Shakespeare and T.S. Eliot on the field while demonstrating things like the Bowdoin Bear block in class. This was a maneuver in which you ran at your opponent and, at a discreet distance, dove forward into a somersault, then came up leaving your cleats whirling in your opponents' face. No one, not even the coach, tried it on the field, but it sure looked good in English class, the great man's massive body rotating through the chalky air, his legs flailing as silently as a flower opening, so that even when he landed again on his feet there was no more sound than if a petal had dropped:

> And I will cry with my loud lips and pub-a-lish
> Beaut-tee . . . which all our power shall never establish
> It is . . . so frail.

I went to college for some six or seven years and acquired, well, what I suppose is known as a healthy "perspective" on the merits of Kipling, Longfellow, and Robert Service.

Nevertheless, I soon found myself stationed on a lighthouse working for the Coast Guard. It was there that I met perhaps the greatest reader I've ever known.

Lighthouses, of course, are known to be places where people read. Literary journals are fond of asking hypothetical questions such as, "If you were sent to a lighthouse, what ten books would you take?"

One of my favorites at the time was John J. Floherty's *Sentries of the Sea:*

A long straight arm of stone stretches out from the coast of Delaware as a sort of peacemaker between the turbulent Atlantic and Delaware Bay . . . The protected zone is known as Harbor of Refuge from which the lighthouse on the end of the breakwater takes its name. Long considered one of the most exposed lighthouses on the Atlantic coast, Harbor of Refuge station has had a history in which death, destruction, and conflict with the sea occur with a startling frequency.

And was I not reading John J. Floherty but two and a half miles out in the Atlantic, climbing up an iron ladder with my ten favorites in a box on my shoulder?

"That don't look like the chow."

Above, where the voice came from, there was a big man dressed only in an inverted sailor's cap and boxing trunks. "I say, boy, that don't look like nuthin' useful you got in that box there."

Of course, I had brought the chow, and other useful things, like light bulbs. But all that had come up on another cargo sling.

So about the books, he had just been, well . . .

After all, he, who had grown up in the ghetto of South Philadelphia, had been a boiler stoker and fleet-level boxer in the navy, an infantryman in the army, and an (eventually de-aproned) Coast Guard cook. Now, after nine years on a lighthouse cooking in his own juices, this man—who I was to replace because he had been caught asleep—saw no reason to capitulate to some pale honky just out of boot camp. This was *his* harbor of refuge.

We had to have it out.

So, though usually one sleeps while the other watches, we stayed up together half the night pawing through my books, arguing whether my men Rilke, Valéry, and Mallarmé were better than his (all of whom seem to have had three robust names): John Greenleaf Whittier, William Cullen Bryant, and Alfred, Lord Tennyson.

> Sunset and evening star,
> And one clear call for me!

"Now, I'll bet you think that is too sentimental."

"Well, my grandfather did like Tennyson. He liked to chew on him."

"Chew on him? What kind o' grandfather you got, boy? I bet your grandfather'd be disappointed in you with these abstract Europeans."

"He would, but try this." I'd hand him a translation of Rilke's "The Panther."

He'd pace around the inside of the round tower reading, his eyes wide under the inverted dome of the yellowed sailor's hat, his boxer's muscles flexing as he pumped the book like a bicep builder.

Outside, through the deep reveal, the beacon hammered the sea.

> The easy motion of his supple stride,
> which turns about the very smallest circle,
> is like a dance of strength about a center
> in which a mighty will stands stupefied.

"Hey, boy, you saying I'm stupefied?"

"It's about a panther. A panther in the zoo. In the zoo in Paris."

"Paris, huh? We got a lens upstairs made by a Mr.—a miss-*sear*—Frey-nel."

"Finish the poem."

> Only sometimes when the pupil's film
> soundlessly opens . . . then one image fills
> and glides through the quiet tension of the limbs
> into the heart and expires.

"Well, maybe," he says.

"Maybe what?"

"Maybe this one's okay for the An-thol-ogy."

"What anthology?"

"*My* An-thol-ogy, boy. All these years out here, you think I have no . . . Anthology?"

Up aloft in the old watch-keeper's room, just below the lantern where M. Fresnel had his lens . . . there, where in days before him, the old keepers had kept an eye on the clock-drive and a nose on the whale oil . . . up there, in that cold attic-of-attics some sixty feet above the sea, this man had sat on and off for years, copying out the things he liked to read. Poems from library books and magazines, even one or two I had brought aboard that day (though, besides "The Panther," he never told me which).

Into bulging notebooks, he had copied out what he called "my personal anthology."

"Someday," he said, "when I retire from all this . . . sepulchral gloom of sisters and sullen noises in the mid-watch, I shall take these poems up to a man in Philadelphia I know and have them all printed in a book, in one copy, so that I shall have them with me always."

For the moment he stuffed them all in his sea bag, one of the old white ones, very salty, very old . . . "Because I was in before they changed the regulations, I get to employ this device."

In the morning, they came for him in an iron utility boat, and he climbed down the ladder with his old-style, rotten white sea bag, so old that when the engine man dropped it onto the deck, the cloth gave way and the "personal anthology" went fluttering off into the wind to the derisive cries of the engine man and the coxswain,—pages and pages of poetry scattered to the sea like a flock of maddened gulls.

The old lighthouse keeper shadow-boxed vainly after the poems and the sailors . . . and then he just stood there, hanging onto the great three-pillared towing bit behind the pair of diesel engines, and he got smaller and smaller and the boat itself diminished in the sharp opening V of its shoreward-moving wake.

And there was only the water all around me.

And inside the tower . . . a box of books.

PART TWO

High Summer

. . . unfettered leewardings.
— Hart Crane, *Voyages*

GETTING IT TOGETHER BY THE SEA

In Which Some Famous and Some Not So Famous Demonstrate that a Moment along the Sea Shore Does Wonders

I shall wear white flannel trousers, and walk upon the beach.
—T.S. Eliot, "The Love Song of J. Alfred Prufrock"

The waves broke on the shore.
—Virginia Woolf, *The Waves*

ONE EARLY AUTUMN afternoon at Montauk Point, laden with fishing gear, I staggered across hunks of the deteriorating sea wall beneath the lighthouse to discover a middle-aged man sitting in a lawn chair wedged into a broken part of the concrete. There had been over fifty people fishing directly beneath him and as many working over the rocks and rubble around the turn of the point.

Most of us had been up since before first light, wading into the sea to reach the bass we could only smell out beyond the breakers. Later, when the sun was up, we had struggled over boulders, wet clay, and exposed reinforcing rods to fish pools where the bass might sweep in to feed when—just for a moment—the smack of the sea would brim a hole.

We had employed open-faced spinning reels, bait-casting reels, poppers, swimmers, gaffs on telephone cords, collapsible-handled fishing nets, and chain fish stringers. It had been indeed a tremendous industry, and we had been, as we muttered to each other in passing, "producing meat."

And here in the midst of all this activity, or rather slightly above it, was this perfectly healthy man.

His hands rested on his ample stomach. Form beneath a floppy hat, his half-open eyes blinked seaward. There was a fishing pole near by, but it was not rigged. Furthermore, it was outmoded in design and even in its day suitable only for a tired pan fish that might be snoozing under a lily pad.

Reading my alarm, he said, "Just getting together with my thoughts."

I could only snort and wonder what possible thoughts such a man could have. That evening, in the high-intensity light at the fish-cleaning rack back of the motel, we were rhinestoned in shucked scales, embroidered in entrails, haloed in bass oil and mist, yet our talk was not of this gory triumph, but of the man who had been getting together with his thoughts. It seemed each of us, as we'd climbed on the broken wall, had encountered him, and each of us had had the same exasperated . . . thought.

That fall there was a television ad depicting a middle-aged man wandering down a beach much like the one around the corner at Montauk Point. The camera zoomed in only close enough for us to appreciate his board-room silver hair, knit shirt, and madras shorts. The usual lyrical music of the beer or deodorant pitch was missing. Just the sound of the sea. The camera pulled back to allow us the immensity of it all and a crawl line overtook the beach walker, announcing simply the name of the office machine company that had footed the bill. The implication was clear: men of power get their strength from the sea (and, of course one of the tips they presumably gather at the beach is precisely which office machine to buy)

There is also help from the classics. We have, as Pound reminds us, ". . . old Homer, blind as a bat / Ear, ear for the sea surge." Given that ear, it is natural that Homer have Agamemnon and his Greek allies holding crucial business meetings by the wine-dark sea. True, the visitors had just been pushed to the water's edge by the counter-attacking locals, but we get the feeling Homer would have had the visitors pick this spot even if they'd had the entire windy, ringing plain of Troy. Here "they purified themselves in the salt sea-water," and here, even when the rhetoric got out of hand, there were acoustical compensations, for "the meeting was moved / Like the rolling high waves of the broad Icarian sea." In the *Odyssey* Homer also uses the beach to get his hero turned around. Calypso looks for Odysseus and

Him pensive on the lonely beach she found.

Demosthenes, we are taught, introduced the first Dale Carnegie course by placing pebbles in his mouth and trading diction with the sea. I was always very impressed with the story until I got to Poros, a kind of Greek Block Island, where this elocution drill supposedly took place, and discovered that what our man was probably trying to out-enunciate as not the surge of Poseidon, but the braying of the donkeys in the lemon groves across on the Peloponnesus.

Shakespeare's Prospero has the reputation of being a mellow product of seaside meditation, given to "life is a dream' stuff, but underneath all the cloud-capped rhetoric he strikes me as yet a bit uptight, with a self-confessed "beating mind" that is set mainly on contriving to get back to the city. Philosophy aside, from a real estate man's point of view, the old fellow has gotten a little far away from our ideal of the lone one getting thoughts together by the sea. What with his household help Ariel and Caliban, to say nothing of his constantly chirping daughter, Miranda, he's hardly alone even before he receives his house guests. Another point against him is he lives too far from the beach, as his guests demonstrate when they have to wander from their "shipwrack" through woods and even a horse pond before they can find the damn cottage.

No, for good old Shakespearean seaside concentration I prefer the more acidic Timon (formerly) of Athens, a retired man of urban power, who:

> . . . hath made his everlasting mansion
> Upon the beached verge of the salt flood;
> Who once a day with his embossed froth
> The turbulent surge shall cover

Not only does Timon have genuine waterfront property, but he muses without servants or relatives, and moreover gets rid as soon as possible of his former business associates and would-be investors and other cottage crashers, pets and all.

> . . .Get thee away, and take
> Thy beagles with thee.

Of course Timon was a bit sick. Picking up this seaside health spa idea, Romantics often connected the beach with illness, either seeing it as a cure like poor coughing Keats considering a sea voyage, hoping for the restorative powers of the *moving waters at their priestlike task / Of pure ablution round earth's human shores,* or Shelley, who said that poets were the unacknowledged legislators of the world, and while getting his legislation together, washed up on the beach at Leghorn, Italy, dead. At the cremation on the sand, Shelley's associate, Lord Byron, got his thoughts together by strolling down the shore away from the fire and going for a swim, a bit of beach work that got him so badly sunburned that a few days later much of his skin peeled and it was hard to tell him from Shelley.

There is Wordsworth, granted basically a lake man, nevertheless standing on a cliff, cheering on old Triton blowing on his wreathed horn, but I find the best story about him thinking at the beach was the night he and Sam "Ancient Mariner" Coleridge were overheard strolling about on the sand muttering German transcendental aesthetics and were picked up for questioning by the authorities, who suspected them of plotting some sort of continental revolution, which of course they were, though in a way more lasting than any mere military beachhead.

In probably the most famous bit of nineteenth century beach-thinking, Matthew Arnold, who was a power as an inspector of schools, is famous for avoiding seduction by sidestepping into a meditation on "the Sea of Faith" at Dover Beach "Where the sea [English Channel] meets the moon-blanched land." There are complications when mixing genre, however, and lately Anthony Hecht, who claims to have known the girl involved, reports she resented being brought *all the way down from London, and then be[ing] addressed / As sort of a mournful cosmic last resort . . .*

Alfred Lord Tennyson reigned as Poet Laureate of England for what seemed the entire nineteenth century, and his most famous poems were influenced by the sea. One thinks of his "Ulysses" with its "thunder and the sunshine"

> . . . when
> Through scudding drifts the rainy Hyades
> Vexed the dim sea. . . .
> · · · · · · · · · · · · · · ·
>   . . . for my purpose holds
> To sail beyond the sunset, and the baths
> Of all the western stars, until I die.

More modest in terms of its navigational ambition is his "Crossing the Bar," written on a twenty-minute ferry ride from Lymington to Yarmouth. Though in this meditation there is, from a nautical viewpoint, much confusion about taking on a metaphysical Pilot outward bound, there is this marvelous watching of the waters. *But such a tide as moving seems asleep, / Too full for sound and foam . . .* Another time, on a cliff overlooking the sea, Tennyson noticed an eagle who *clasps the crag with crooked hands; / Close to the sun in lonely lands,* while *The wrinkled sea beneath him crawls.*

Most pure in its invocation of the lonely seaside meditation, however, is his *Break, break, break, / On thy cold gray stones, O Sea!* in which the forlorn state of the poet is contrasted with a fisherman's boy who plays with his sister and with a sailor lad who *sings in his boat on the bay!*

None of this maritime comradery is for our man as he watches the waves *Break, break, break, / At the foot of thy crags, O Sea!*

Lonely, sea-edging crags may have produced some immortal lines in the Poet Laureate, but his predilection for them caused his companions in the summer of 1860 great anxiety. Shortsighted as well as rhapsodic, Tennyson was known as a man who even when indoors occasionally tried to "go out by the chimney." The thought of him hovering at the verge of the cliffs of Cornwall was heart-stopping. Among the group with Tennyson that summer was the famous anthologist F.T. *Golden Treasury* Palgrave. Perhaps in order to insure that there would be sufficient Tennyson seaside material for his anthology, Palgrave assumed the role of chaperoning the Laureate amid the crags. He saw to it that Tennyson was never out of sight, or at least earshot, chasing him along from boulder to boulder. Each time Alfred had managed to achieve even a moment's state of proper poetic sea-haunted forlornness would come the frantic Palgravian cry, "Tennyson! Tennyson! Tennyson!" Eventually so shattering was this pursuit that Tennyson called his party together one night and told them that he was cutting his excursion short and going back to London. "There is no pleasure," he said, "for any of us in this."

More successful in insuring his seaside privacy was fin de siècle dandy Sir Max Beerbohm, who made no pretenses at all of getting wet and avoiding precipitous edges. Max began by braving the British seacoast, where he specialized in off-season browsing of the low-slung winter promenade:

Around me are the usual ornaments of sea-side lodgings. Through a little bay window I look out over the wide sea. I have looked, so, through many little bay windows. But, on my heart, I do not distinguish one from another; they are all as one for me, all symbolize home for me, quietude and home ... Yes! in whatever sea-side town I find myself I am filled with a quiet pride, a restfulness of possession. With the first breath of its wet salt, all the stains of the town are purged, the vapours blown quite away.

In summer Max preferred, in his youth, the French coast at Dieppe, where biographer David Cecil finds him "in high collar and boater jauntily on one side, and with his delicate hand clasped on the ivory knob of his walking stick, as he gazes idly at the sea glittering in the August sunshine." As for getting down on the sand into the water, Max found "bathing makes me liver-ish always: I sit watching other people bathing."

He found an ideal spot by the sea and retired to it for the last half of his long life, at Rapallo on the Mediterranean. There, high upon a hillside, but safely walled from Tennysonian vertigo upon his terrace, nattily attired in a white pajama suit, he wrote short, perfect essays or drew his famous caricatures or simply idled the day away, where portraitist Sir William Rothenstein remembered, "Max presumably goes to the terrace to work, but usually he does what I show him doing—[he] just contemplates." S. N. Behrman, from the American mill town of Worcester, Massachusetts, bought Rothenstein's pastel of this terrace scene and was so enchanted by the purity of this seaside vignette that he crossed the Atlantic, in true American fashion, to visit the original:

> In the years before I met the model for the relaxed figure leaning over the parapet, I often reflected that Max must occasionally have straightened up, crossed the terrace, and immured himself in that workroom. He must have sat at a desk and exhaled some writing. But the mere possibility of such exertion seems remote in Rothenstein's drawing. It is a study in contemplative—even sensuous—immobility. It conveys the spirit of a man who knows how precious the passing moment is, containing as it does, an expanse of sea and sun, of mountains in a blue haze, of villas purring at the water's edge— who cherishes too intensely this evanescence, this miracle of sight and sound, to replace it with the vulgar self-assertion of work.

Unfortunately when Behrman actually looked down from the same spot on the terrace, he saw between him and the water the main highway between Rome and Genoa, a highway tight with trucks grinding gears, and, worse, it was a road that Max confessed had once seen Mussolini himself parading at the edge of the sea.

Max's friend Swinburne was perhaps the most outrageous of all English writers when it came to the edge of the sea, filling his poems with so much foam that even his admirers were soon dancing on one leg, wringing the water out of their ears. His father was an admiral, and envisioned major voyaging for his son, but alas, even when adult, Algernon, if Ford Madox Ford is to be believed, mainly did his navigation in a bathtub, albeit fully clothed. Here, in one of his novels, is the kind of undertow Swinburne would have us sucked into:

> In thunder that drowned his voice, wind that blew over his balance, and snowstorms of the flying or falling foam that blinded his eyes and salted his face, the boy took his pleasure to his full; this travail and triumph of the married wind and sea filled him with a furious luxury of the senses that kindled all his nerves and exalted all his life. From these haunts he came back wet and rough, blown out of shape and beaten into color, his ears full of music and his eyes of dreams: all the sounds of the sea rang through him: he felt land sick when out of the sea's sight, and twice alive when hard by it.

The French seem to get their seaside loafing and working together a little better. Alphonse Daudet in "The Lighthouse of Les Sanhuinaires," one of his *Letters from My Windmill,* has the spirit perfectly:

> . . . It was to this island I used to go before I had my windmill, when I felt the need of fresh air and solitude.
> And what did I do there?
> What I do here [at the windmill], more or less. When the mistral or the tramontane did not blow too strongly, I used to settle down between two rocks near the water's edge, among the seagulls, the water ouzels, and the swallows, and there I would remain for almost the whole day in that soporific stupor, that languid sense of delight which comes from just looking at the sea. You must have experienced it, surely that wonderful rapture of the spirit? You cease to think, even to dream. Your innermost self escapes, flying, drifting. You become the seagull swooping, the frothing foam floating in the sun between two waves, the white smoke of the streamer far off on the horizon, that little red-sailed, coral-fishing boat, this pearly drop of water, this drifting wisp of mist . . .

And then Daudet hits on the essential paradox of getting your thoughts together by the sea, "you become everything but yourself."

As if putting into practice Daudet's analysis, French poet and mathematician Paul Valéry makes his cliff-top thought into what many believe to be one of the great poems of the twentieth century: "The Cemetery by the Sea." Looking on "the calm of gods the sea disposes," Valéry contrives to juggle Zeno's paradox, Minerva, marble, mortality, jib-sails, and even that most unpoetic hour, noon, in order to recreate "how peace is conceived in this pure air."

Sometimes Connecticut resident Robert Penn Warren forsakes hotdogs at Hammonasset to imagine Valéry on the Pointe du Cognet:

> His breath stops in his throat
> And he stands on the cliff, his white
> Panama hat in hand,
> For he is Monsieur le Poete.
> Paul Valéry is his name,
> On a promenade by the sea, so
> He sways high against the blue sky,
> While in the bright intricacies
> Of wind, his mind, like a leaf
> Turns. In the sun, it glitters.

The hat seems important to these French meditators of the littoral. Roger Martin Du Gard recalls André Gide:

> This afternoon he went to the shop and bought himself an indescribable linen hat; he now can't be separated from it. And he's begun to work; the translation of Act I of *Hamlet.* But from time to time he can't help making off

for the sea; and off he goes through the pine trees, with that hat on the back of his head and his arms full of books, notebooks, grammars, and dictionaries. Then he comes back, deep in thought, and at once begins writing again. As he splashes along the water's edge, he's been looking for the equivalent of some English phrase. And the amazing thing is—he's found it!

There is a similar, more ponderous story Victor Hugo tells about his own translating of Shakespeare to the sound of the sea hitting the stone of his island refuge in the English Channel.

Perhaps this kind of Valérian breathless sway among the bright intricacies was what the aging German youth I saw in Ireland had in mind. He was also a cliff-top man, standing on the undercut limestone rampart of Inishmore's Dun Aengus, the broken fort of the Firbolg aborigines. Half the original place has already fallen away in a phenomenon known as "the grand subsidence," and the rest is crumbling day by day. This nervous bit of geology did not bother our Teutonic metaphysician, who stood right at the edge. No linen hat in sight, his blond hair was streaming back in the breeze, his gaze epic on the horizon, so that he looked like a 1930 hood ornament. It was just as well he kept the cosmic focus, because up there, overhanging some three hundred feet above the Atlantic, you cannot actually see the waves smack the shore, and the sound of their doing so can merely be charged up to some Sturm und Drang effect rather than anything that might actually be going to drop you overboard.

That night, at the pub down the hill from Dun Aengus, I made the acquaintance of another German, and after discussing a Don Redman arrangement of a 1920 Louis Armstrong record for two hours, I asked him about the cliff-topper who was sitting not far away. "Is he a poet?" I said.

"Oh, no, that man is not a Dichter, but a Doktor." He began to laugh. "He is a Doktor!" This provided the jazz fan with several moments of mirth, for as he tried to make clear between hiccoughs, a Doktor was something you had to take seriously only when you were in Germany. In America, he said, we would probably call him a "professor," but it was not really the same thing.

"But what do you suppose the Doktor was thinking?" I asked. "Was he, seeing he was on holiday, in spite of being Herr Doktor, perhaps thinking poetical thoughts?"

"Not a chance. At best he was thinking Ur-thoughts."

"Ur?"

"These are the best thoughts a Doktor can think while actually on a cliff such as the one upon which you saw him."

Our American answer to this cliff-top, aboriginal mood I witnessed about twenty years ago at Gay Head on Martha's Vineyard.
The wind was still roaring in from the Devil's Bridge below, where
the crosscurrents were sending up fountains that rainbowed in the
strong sun. There were a half-dozen Gay Head Indian youth hanging
about, rather, I thought, like any other American teen-agers, until I
noticed that what they were leaning on was not a drugstore wall, but
the invisible, but no less solid thermal. At times, playing the wind like
a sailor milking a flaw, they seemed to be leaning out almost thirty
degrees.

This daring of the Gay Headers might put us in mind of the
famous "hard-boiled" school of by-the-sea thinkers, headed, of course,
by Raymond Chandler. In Chandler's first novel, *The Big Sleep*, detec-
tive Philip Marlowe reports:

I braked the car against the curb and switched the headlights off and sat
with my hands on the wheel. Under the thinning fog the surf curled and
creamed, almost without sound, like a thought trying to form itself on the
edge of consciousness.

The cognitive motive of this seaside meditation is immediately broken, however:

"Move closer," she said almost thickly.

More pure is a later adventure in *The Lady in the Lake* where Marlowe
tells us he left the lake to go down to the sea, where "I sat there in the
car a little while, thinking, looking out to sea and admiring the blue-
gray fall of the foothills towards the ocean. I was trying to make up
my mind . . ."

In *Farewell My Lovely*, he is still looking to the sea for answers,
though he is yet unable to get out of the car:

I got down to Montemar Vista as the light began to fade, but there was
still a fine sparkle of the water and the surf was breaking far out in long
smooth curves. A group of pelicans was flying bomber formation just under
the creaming lip of the waves. A lonely yacht was taking [tacking?] in toward
the yacht harbor at Bay City. Beyond it the huge emptiness of the Pacific was
purple-gray.

In fellow Californian thirties hard-boiler James M. Cain's *The Postman
Always Rings Twice*, the two main characters decide to do their final
thinking, or what passes for thinking with them, by the sea. They even
plan to get out of the car and into the actual water. The waitress says,
"We'll go way out, the way we did last time, and if you don't want me
to come back, you don't have to let me. Nobody'll ever know. It'll be

just one of those things that happens at the beach." When they really do go to the water, the drifter decides that "all the devilment, and meanness, and shiftlessness,and no-account stuff in my life had been pressed out and washed off, and I was all ready to start out with her again clean, and do like she said, have a new life."

Almost equally primitive, Walt Whitman was proud of getting his thoughts together at the beach, "where day and night I wend thy surf-beat shore / Imaging to my sense the varied strange suggestions."

Whitman's seaside style, however, seems to have been more of the Demosthenean school of projection rather than Odysseyian med-itation. He was fond of "declaiming" huge, manly hunks of culture back into the "husky-haughty lips" of the sou'west fetch:

... and down to Montauk—spent many an hour on Turtle hill by the old light-house, on the extreme point, looking out over the ceaseless roll of the Atlantic ... some years later ... I went every week in the mild seasons down to Coney island, at that time a long, bare unfrequented shore, which I had all to myself, and where I loved, after bathing, to race up and down the hard sand, and declaim Homer or Shakespeare to the surf and sea-gulls by the hour.

Thoreau, strolling Cape Cod's great beach, was no doubt quieter, but being a surveyor on vacation, he was not above turning his back on the intertidal zone to do things like borrowing the

plane and square, level and dividers, of a carpenter who was shingling a barn near by, and using one of the shingles made of a mast, contrived a rude sort of quadrant, with pins for sights and pivots, and got the angle of elevation of the Bank opposite the light-house and with a couple of codlines the length of its slope, and so measured its height on the shingle.

It's too bad that Eugene O'Neill couldn't have had Henry along with him on the Cape Cod beach to keep track of the erosion. The often confused playwright was fond of introducing the ocean as a kind of moral anchor to windward against his lifelong sea of domestic trou-bles, with the result that his house on Monomoy Point washed out into the literal Atlantic.

Safer was his estuarian childhood home on the banks of New London's Thames, which still stands. In it is a picture of O'Neill as a child perched up on a boulder looking out at the river mouth directly across from where I happen to work. The memories of these child-hood meditations saturate his finest, mature work, *Long Day's Journey into Night,* where the sea and the characters interpenetrate each other.

"Act Three. Scene . . . Dusk is gathering in the living room, an early dusk due to the fog which has rolled in from [Fishers Island]

Sound and is like a white curtain drawn outside the windows. From a lighthouse beyond the harbor's mouth, a foghorn is heard at regular intervals, moaning like a mournful whale in labor [probably the diaphone of Southwest Ledge], and from the harbor itself, intermittently, comes the warning ringing of bells on yachts at anchor." (Bells are no longer required to be rung in the "special anchorages," but there is the "intermittent" clang from various buoys on the surge usually present even in calms at the river mouth.)

Not only does the sea-borne fog move into the "Tyrone" (O'Neill) house, but O'Neill's alter ego Edmund Tyrone moves out into it:

(Staring before him) The fog was where I wanted to be. Halfway down the path you can't see this house . . . Everything looked and sounded unreal. Nothing was what it is. That's what I wanted—to be alone with myself in another world where truth is untrue and life can hide from itself. Out beyond the harbor, where the road runs along the beach, I even lost the feeling of being on land. The fog and the sea seemed part of each other. It was like walking on the bottom of the sea. As if I had drowned long ago. As if I was a ghost belonging to the fog, and the fog was the ghost of the sea. It felt damned peaceful . . .

Some seventy years later, with the O'Neill house a museum, that road that runs along the harbor where life could hide from itself is the subject of considerable neighborhood anxiety. So many alienated young men are congregating along the sea-wall at dusk that the property owners have put in well-publicized requests for additional police patrol.

A better man for sheer hanging in there and meditating on the beach was O'Neill's contemporary Henry Beston. Beston, a World War I sailor about to turn farmer, paused all one winter in a cottage at Nauset on the Cape and wrote *The Outermost House,* perhaps the best sustained record of beach-concentrated prose. Even later, in writing an herbal, Beston allowed the ocean to seep back through the garden wall. Brooding on the old medieval subject of cosmic harmony, he asks, "Was the sound but the unconfused and primal voice of the planet welling forever from its cores of stone, or did a sound of rivers and many oceans, of leaves and immeasurable rain mingle to make a mysterious harmony?"

Melville wrote the greatest of all sea novels a hundred miles inland, looking at a blue mountain when he wanted waves and the family cow when he needed a whale, but in the opening of that book he pays tribute to the "thousands upon thousands of mortal men fixed in ocean reveries. Some leaning against the spiles; some seated upon pier-heads; some looking over the bulwarks of ships from China; some high aloft in the rigging, as if striving to get a still better seaward peep."

Almost every ye Giftie Shoppee these days has a stack of "beach-comber manuals," to aid those of us who, following Thoreau's puritan streak, must have a solid "scientific" basis to our wanderings at the water's edge. One of the earliest of these in anything like the modern seaside poke-about spirit was by the English naturalist Philip Henry Gosse. Gosse combined scientific enquiry with a fundamentalist religion in a way which, until very recently in our nation, we would have to say was a quaintly Victorian manner. In addition to his manual, he produced in the grand amateur manner of the fin de siècle such volumes as *Evenings at the Microscope* and *Romance of Natural History,* in which he attempts "to present natural history in aesthetic fashion," his meditations ranging from life in dust at sea to sperm whales at night. So popular was Gosse's work that he soon discovered, much to his horror, that a generation of British beachcombers were frantically prying every sea shell from its rock in search of confirmation of cosmic thoughts.

A manual that retains the leisurely, meditative style of the last century, while still remaining useful upon North American beaches in its Dover reprint, is Augusta Foote Arnold's *The Sea-Beach at Ebb-Tide: A Guide to the Study of the Seaweeds and the Lower Animal Life Found Between Tide-Marks.* In addition to providing us with almost five hundred pages of facts, Ms. Arnold has the poet's ear:

... the beach is also a vast sarcophagus holding myriads of the dead. "If ghosts be ever laid, here lie ghosts of creatures innumerable, vexing the mind in the attempt to conceive them." And there are certain sands which may be said to sing their requiem, the so-called musical sands, like the "Singing Beach" at Manchester-by-the-Sea, which emit sounds when struck or otherwise disturbed. On some beaches these sounds resemble rumbling, on other hooting; sometimes they are bell-like and even rhythmical.

In contemporary terms we have the books of commercial collector Jack Rudloe, which include his manual, *The Erotic Ocean,* and Philip Kopper's *The Wild Edge: Life and Lore of the Great Atlantic Beaches.* The latter is not so much a manual as a companion which will pause to include a mediation on driftwood as well as information, or rather hatch the information out of the meditation. John M. Kingsbury's *Seaweeds of Cape Cod and the Island* contains a page essay on each type of seaweed found in New England. Soaking within the pungent wrack of each weed is some marvelous bit of ecological poetry uttered in a style later made famous by Lewis Thomas.

No naturalist's book on beaches, however, succeeds to my mind in the sustained synthesizing of the dreamer and the technician as well as Charles Ogburn, Jr.'s 1966 volume *The Winter Beach,* which is probably a better book to read in summer than in winter.

Laid out in the form of a tour from Maine to the Outer Banks, Ogburn's book begins:

Several years ago a picture of a deserted beach fixed itself in my mind. There was an expanse of sand, a half-buried candy wrapper that collected the drifting grains, a cottage boarded up against the weather and for all sound the crashing of the breakers. In my thoughts, the seas kept rolling in upon shores abandoned to the cold by the last vacationers and the vendors who ministered to them. I began to have the feeling that this was what lay ahead of me.

On the south shore of Long Island Ogburn discovers what is perhaps the most comforting of beach-thinking, "You can walk for hours on the beach with no sense of loneliness, as a dog may walk with its master, whose company is an end in itself."

A degenerate form of the Ogburn book is the jeep or pickup tour, usually commissioned to accompany a generous sheaf of glossy photographs. Such a book is *Cape May to Montauk,* where David Plowden's first-rate pictures are panted after by an obscure newspaperman with the unlikely name of Nelson P. Falorp. The fatuous jacket blurb assures us Falorp has as "one of his hobbies . . . chatting about the wind and weather with the older inhabitants of the shore communities from whom he has acquired considerable local ecological knowledge to supplement that which may ordinarily be found in books." Here is Falorp speeding along the narrow road between beach and bay, trying to take the curse off his locomotion by fantasizing he is in one of the old oystering catboats he has seen rotting in the weeds:

Out beyond the fish trap the cross seas on the bar are beginning to catch fire with the autumn afternoon sun. There was already a good deal of amber in them from the roiling sand. I set sail in my pickup down the beach road. It was no longer macadam shining with a thin layer of rain, but a channel quivering with a load of wind-blown water. To the right Shinnecock and Moriches bays had seeped past the outer guard of duck blinds, up through yellowing spartina grass and red pickleweed, past the wet blond phragmites and around the final sentry line of telephone poles, and as I headed west for Patchogue I imagined I was boom out in one of the grand thirty-five-foot catboats of the late famous Patchogue shipbuilder Samuel Wicks. Plumb bowed, we'd be, with a heart-shaped transom raked like the stern of pilot schooners. A gust came over the dunes, and I was glad Miriam Wicks had put four sets of reef points in the mainsail and that I had lashed my oyster tongs inside the cockpit.

Captain Cousteau, of course, is a good man to stick our noses in the water once in a while, but even the "raptures of the deep" are not

necessarily what we are after when we walk along the beach. I'm not
sure "the myriad creatures of the inter-tidal zone" are even always
what Captain Cousteau has in mind himself. I happened to fall in with
him one day along the water as he was walking back from a crowded
lecture. He had been temporarily abandoned by the several atten-
dants that had surrounded him ever since he'd landed on the green,
god-like in a helicopter, and there were just the two of us plodding
silently along in a raw wind. His people had walked on ahead to eat,
but he couldn't seem to track the restaurant, which was straight ahead.
Glancing nervously at the water, the famous navigator allowed himself to fade further and further downwind until he was soon headed
about for the dangerous lee of the parking lot, a fate from which I
was only awkwardly able to snatch him.

But manuals on beach erosion, sanderlings, and skate cases aside,
it is a mistake to think it required that a beach-thinker be concentrat-
ing on the beach itself. I have an uncle, a successful businessman, who
owned a boat that had under its previous captaincy sailed all the way
to the Dry Tortugas. My uncle used it to get his thoughts together by
merely chugging down the Connecticut River from Essex to Duck
Island Roads. There, protected by the breakwater' from the chop of
Long Island Sound, he would drop anchor and read his tax manual
for a few moments before letting his mind wander.

Nevertheless, it is difficult in America these days to imitate the
solitary Whitman or Thoreau or Valéry. Timon's acid curses would
probably merely draw a crowd of admiring punk-rockers. Browsing
on the winter brume of Beston and Ogburn may be helpful for seeing
below the flesh of summer to the deeper structure, but summer in
twentieth-century America is what we have. It is tempting to go the
way of Woody Allen, who tells Dick Cavett, "I can never understand
what all this going to the beach is all about. I prefer to stay home in
my apartment with the air conditioning."

Indeed, flying low over the beaches of Connecticut and Long Island one August Sunday, I wondered myself. As I looked down at the
wriggling tan mass at the water's edge, the scene looked like one of
those rubber polyp change mats by the cash registers of fly-blown
luncheonettes. But here were people at the edge of the sea, and, no
doubt, as they waved up at us, some were having thoughts, if not of
Zeno at noon, at least a moment aerial, some group *gopping* at tran-
scendence.

Such a sight might be more appropriate to India, and there are
moments when one wonders if there is a difference between the sight

from above Hammonasset and an overhead shot of the swarming
squalor of a Ganges ghat. Less cosmic profundity, I suppose, in our
case but at least over the Atlantic one has the illusion that the infinite
edge is insatiably sipping at all those pores and follicles, rinsing, dis-
persing all poisons into what St. John Perse calls "the golden salts of
the open sea."

In any case, it is not only not necessary to be thinking about the
sea, perhaps it is not necessary to really be alone. With a few camera
tricks the sea can still be hyped as a bottomless source of energy that
the Great Man in solitude has somehow received special permission
to tap.

There is an official White House photo of the bare-headed President Nixon gazing seaward, his windbreaker being mildly nuzzled by
the First Lady, her head wrapped in a kerchief. The idea seems to be
that the commander-in-chief, the former navy lieutenant, knows what
it really is like out there, while his wife can, in the face of all this
oceanic awe, merely be wistful. William Safire's comments are perhaps more helpful: "The President likes to be on the water and in the
water; fresh air and salt spray do something for him, and accessibility
to a beach (California, Florida, the Bahamas) has always been part of
his life."

Nor is this beach soul-searching confined to Republicans. The
staple of any Kennedy picture book is the moment when JFK com-
munes with athlete's foot along the Hyannis sands. Often this is accompanied with an off-camera caption, after the manner of the San-
dymount Strand sequences in the film made from James Joyce's *Ulysses*.
It is easy to make fun of such stuff, but let us remember the heroic
background:

Kennedy went down the beach a short distance from the men . . . [He] was
restless. He did not just want to sit in the shade all day.

This nervous day at the beach, of course, is from *P.T. 109* and the
sand is courtesy of Plum Pudding Island, where a breast-stroking
Kennedy had led his men after his vessel had been sunk by the Japanese. Later, President Kennedy preferred his sea musings to take place
aboard a yacht under sail, here, in J. Julius' Fanta's *Sailing with President Kennedy*, the old Coast Guard Academy yawl *Manitou:*

After lunch [Jim] Reed took the wheel, while Kennedy stretched out on deck
on a cushion near the forward mast. Smoking a bantam cigar, he enjoyed the
relaxing moments, seemingly in deep meditation.

Like the New London hero of Eugene O'Neill's *Long Day's Journey into Night*, however, the president found the bowsprit the place:

Another spot that became favorite for him was riding at the extreme bow. From this perch, sitting on the pulpit rail, he could view the length of the entire deck as he looked aft as well as a clean sweep of the sails winged outward; and from there, too, an upward glance took in the extreme height of the mast . . . There were times he meditated aboard the *Manitou,* as he was seen in deep thought, especially while relaxing on the fore deck. If his inescapable thoughts dealt with affairs of state, he never revealed what was on his mind as he gazed out to sea.

When toasting the Australian Cup challengers at Newport, the sea-gazer did reveal some of his inescapable thoughts:

I really don't know why it is that all of us are so committed to the sea, except I think it's because in addition to the fact that the sea changes, and the light changes, it's because we all come from the sea. And it is an interesting biological fact that all of us have in our veins the exact same percentage of salt in our blood that exists in the ocean; and therefore, we have salt in our blood, in our sweat, in our tears. We are tied to the ocean. And when we go back to the sea—whether it is to sail or watch it—we are going back from whence we came.

My favorite man-of-power-and-the-sea photo is not of a president, however. It is a black-and-white picture that appeared in LIFE in its first picture-mag incarnation, and I have not seen it in years, but what I remember is the eighty-year-old cellist, Pablo Casals. A man who confessed that "one of my greatest ambitions since childhood has been to live in a lighthouse," he is standing on the beach in Puerto Rico in a long bathing suit and shirt. Like the poet Paul Valèry, Casals wears a Panama hat. Over his head he holds an umbrella, not some modish Côte d'Azur striped job, but a bleak bumbershoot that would have done for J. Alfred Prufrock's creator in a drizzly London November on his way to the bank. The old cellist is looking out to sea or at least he is facing away from the land, and the caption says something like: "Whenever I am oppressed by the cares of the world, I go to the sea and it refreshes me."

I remember a man from my childhood, not a musician, but a man who it was said had made his money by developing the plastic liner to the inside of bottle caps. He lived between me and the beach when I was growing up, and when my companions and I would charge the alley to the sea, there in the late Augustian glitter would sit this elderly man awash upon an inner tube in the trough of the last wave. He was always rigged in shorts to his knee, a long-sleeved white shirt, and straw boater. This hat he had neatly vented by inserting grommets, round and brass hardware which, abob upon the wave, gave his head the look of carrying portholes.

It was true that beyond him sported more vigorous sights, the Lightning class coming home under spinnakers, the Block Island boat churning up Sound fully laden with waving passengers, and perhaps the Du Ponts' brass-funneled admiral's barge *Maid of Honor* making for Fishers Island, but on the old gentleman's nose were his steel-rimmed spectacles, through which he read the evening newspaper, and from the downwind side of his face, indeed like the smoke from a steamer, came the mild effusion of his cigar.

WAITING FOR
THE WHACK

We however pursued our navigation . . .
—Samuel Johnson to Mrs. Thrale, Oct. 23, 1773

O UT ON the front lawn of the place where I work is an area
scattered with fragments of pink Italian marble. If you look
closer you can see that it has been worked to make steps and
curbs and there are even the fragments of a giant urn that once stood
upon a pedestal. These are the pieces of a great formal garden that
occupied this space now taken up by World War II-era cinder block
buildings. For almost forty years they have lain beneath the sea at the
end of the lawn here at Avery Point in Groton, at the mouth of the
Thames River. In the last year or so divers from the National Guard
have been working out by retrieving these marble pieces and placing
them on the grass, presumably with the hope that one day at least
part of the garden may be restored.

How did the garden get into the sea? Our own Coast Guard bulldozed the horticultural works on the property of the late railroad
millionaire Morton Plant in order to make room for detecting systems
that were being designed to protect our coasts from the barbaric hordes.

When the sunken garden was rediscovered this year, many noted
the irony of our Coast Guard's anticipatory vandalism. In answer, the
officer who was in charge during the bulldozing said, "You have to
remember the atmosphere of the times. You have to have been there
when we really thought the Germans were going to show up on the
beach any day."

I was one of those who was there within sight of the Coast Guard's
garden at Avery Point in those days, and while I never thought that
an eight- or nine-year-old made much of a war correspondent, since
all the noise about shielding our young against the fallout from nuclear entertainment I have begun to wonder if maybe an eight-year-
old's perspective isn't worth something. If people are really concerned with what to say to young children about growing up in a
world that may suddenly end, perhaps an eight-year-old old from one

generation can talk to an eight-year-old from another. What I would
tell young children is something about what it was like to be their age
during the early part of World War II when we thought we were
going to lose, how it felt to be waiting for invasion along our coast.

When one thinks of bombing in a domestic way, one is very apt
to consider first the roof. The roof under which I lived in 1942 on
Groton Long Point, across the water from Avery Point, was made out
of pink slate. To me this was good because the beach below it was still
strewn with pink shards excellent for skipping across the sea. These
shards had been torn from the roof not by a bomb, but by an invasion
of a different sort four years earlier, the 1938 hurricane, more momentous scars from which lay all about the partially repaired white
house, built in the late 1920s.

There were boulders rolled up out of the sea that were too big to
return and so lay scattered ominously about the lawn. They annoyed
my grandfather, who wanted a well-trimmed landscape about him,
but he could do nothing about removing them. One of them, right
down to its maimed right fin and lichen eye, looked like a sullen white
whale breaching, an association my grandmother found especially
disturbing as she did not approve of men who were obsessed with
what she considered "lower forms."

The second floor of the house, where we slept, was supported by
big concrete posts, as it hung out over a wide veranda. The hurricane
seas had swarmed upon that veranda with such violence that they had
peeled off the top layer of cement, exposing the raw pebbles and
pockets of the concrete below, so that lying in bed at night and listening to the waves you remembered that the water could be up right
under you, eating the house.

When my grandmother complained about the raw porch, my
grandfather took her to the window. "You see those pieces of land
lying out there on the water? Any cement around here is going out to
those islands to make machine-gun nests and watch towers." To add
to this feeling of local disaster, there was the whispered news that the
previous owner of our house had hung himself in the linen closet.

The main attraction of the house, however, its pink roof, had an
added dimension, the implication of which we were only dimly aware
at the time: It was visible from five miles away over water.

In any case, we could not go out on the sea to appreciate our roof,
as my father, who would have taken us, was away in a place called
The Pacific. In his letters he said that he was using concrete to build

machine gun nests and watch towers. And so, some forty years later, exactly what made our roof famous finally came to me.

I chanced to meet a man who had spent the war years nearby as a torpedo bomber pilot based at Groton's Trumbull Airport. A large, hardy man in watch cap and down vest, he now drives a big truck, and boasts in flu season how he's never had a sick day in his life. "Sure, I remember the pink roof. We were supposed to develop our maximum effectiveness at fifty feet off the water, so we took off from Trumbull and used your house as a sight."

I would be out in the backyard, using the house as a shelter from the prevailing sou'wester coming in off the water. Unlike the Coast Guard at Avery Point, our garden was not an ornament to be tossed overboard at the first sign of the barbarians. It was what was known then as a "victory garden," and even my grandmother, a Victorian grande dame of the Formidable Class, was to be seen bending to the insolent needs of the cherry tomato and the more lugubrious demands of the eggplant. Just outside the garden was a good spot to toss a ball, and since my father was not there to throw it back, I would fire the ball straight up in the air as high as I could.

Up there unfortunately there often was something other than a ball. With a roar that would make me almost physically ill, the small torpedo bomber would come in off the sea over the roof. There were days when I did not dare go outside. We tried to get some sense at least of the hours the planes would come over, but they always seemed to take us by surprise, coming suddenly in off the sea with their noise behind them. "I'm going to call up the airport," said my grandmother.

"It's better that they are ours," my grandfather would say. "It could just as easily be Germans. You could look up there some day and it will be Germans."

I did not always have the nerve to look up, but one day I was tossing the ball as high as I could and there—the bottom of the plane just missed the chimney, just missed the ball—in the isinglass cockpit the pilot was looking down at me over his left shoulder, and I could see through his goggles the rolling whites of his eyes.

The sound of the engine, the wicked look of the pilot's eyes, made me run inside.

My grandfather looked up from one of the many newspapers he read. "They're still ours?"

I tried to remember the insignia, but all I could recall were the eyes through the goggles. "He looked Japanese," I said.

"No," said my grandfather. "He'd be German at this stage." And
he turned to the next item.

At night we had, of course, the blackout. With their husbands off
in the war, my mother and aunts would spend the day sewing thick,
black padded curtains which toward dusk they would pin together
over the cold glass that looked out upon the sea. Huddled inside, we
would sit in absolute silence around the black fireplace before which
my grandfather had placed his latest gadget, a small radio.

The lineup consisted of a grim parade of fifteen-minute newscasts commencing at 6:00 with the network that featured garbled "on
scene" reports from people like the cellophane-stricken Jack Begon
in Rome. Then there was Gabriel Heatter, Lowell Thomas, Fulton
Lewis, Jr., Drew Pearson. My grandfather displayed what seemed to
us an awesome midair ingenuity in jumping up to dial the radio from
station to station just in time to catch the next commentator.

Our job was to sit still and, as my grandfather said, "absorb the
news." In spite of the thick curtains, drafts assaulted us, seeking us
out through the wicker furniture as we sat with our heads in our hands,
elbows on knees, absorbing the doleful tone of Gabriel Heatter as the
talk slid imperceptibly from "40,000 killed on the Russian front" to
"buy Serutan, it will relieve you, friends, and remember . . . it's na-
tures . . . spelled backwards."

One day we managed to escape the house at this hour in the car
and were heading for Hartford, then close to a two-hour journey up
narrow, winding roads. The radio was on, of course, but as we began
up Fort Hill in Groton, Jack Begon was in worse shape than ever, so
my grandfather pulled into a stranger's driveway where the reception
was still at least marginal and we sat there absorbing Gabriel Heatter,
Lowell Thomas, Drew Pearson, and Fulton Lewis, Jr. while the people
in the house thrashed at their curtains, and my grandmother fumed,
"We could have been there by now!"

"Yes, we could have," said my grandfather, "assuming that there
would have been some place up there left standing."

Sometimes he would take me to the window at home and point
out to the sea and tell me about his father who had come from Ireland. "He had to leave home and when he got off the boat in New
York he had a dollar in his pocket and a plum."

A boat trip with a dollar in your pocket and a plum seemed like
a good deal to me, so my grandfather grew angry. "It won't be like
that this time," he muttered. "This time they'll laugh at your dollar

and take your plum. That is, if they don't shoot you first."

My grandmother had no stories she chose to tell about her side of the family having to start all over again, but my mother told one out of her hearing. Someone in the old country had to leave with just the clothes on his back and was writing a letter to let his wife know where he was going when there was a knock on the door, and he went out the window into the hedges. The letter somehow got to the wife, but all that it said was, "Gone to A——a," the handwriting between the two A's being accomplished in such haste as to leave the destination a mystery. Betting on America, the wife came to New York but never found the man. Years later it was discovered he had actually gone to Australia, but it was too late. The dark cloud of the husbandless woman wandering the land was already upon us.

After the nightly newscasts, upstairs, in order to read forbidden *Submariner* comics, I would use the red-shielded air raid warden flashlight my father had been issued before he joined the Seabees. Or more seriously, I'd study my book of military silhouettes. Everybody had silhouettes, "ours" and "theirs," and even my aunts learned to tell a Bell Airacobra from a Messerschmitt. We had air raid practices, too. Or later we found out they were practice, for they were not, as now, conducted in Saturday sunshine to the accompaniment of lawnmowers and chain saws. I can remember one night diving under the table in the breakfast nook with my mother. It was very quiet. I had brought the flashlight so we could study silhouettes in case something of doubtful shape flew over.

One night we listened to Winston Churchill. My mother was convinced he was going to be shot. "They'll do it during 'God Save the King,' " she said, and we listened to the ponderous tones of that anthem with a painful intensity even beyond that which we brought to bear on Gabriel Heatter. When all the snapping and popping seemed to have been no more than static, she revised her prediction. "They are going to shoot Winston Churchill during the 'Star-Spangled Banner.' " Eventually there was nothing to do but listen to Winston Churchill make his speech.

Snap, pop, went the assassin's static. "Mouwfph, bewaaaaaar, ow-ow-owaaaaa," plowed on the redoutable Winston Churchill. Then, in an alarming burst of clarity, right as if he were in the room with the wicker furniture and us, he said, ". . . and a great darkness shall fall over all the world . . . as we have come to know it."

When I asked what would actually happen if the Germans did land, my grandfather sent me to bed. Later my mother explained that the Germans would rape all the women and bayonet the men. The bayoneting I understood and hoped it would not hurt as much as the torpedo bomber engines did. As for the raping, she finally explained that it meant "forcing a girl to have a baby."

Why the Germans would want to do this, or how they would even have time, was beyond me, for it seemed like an awful lot of work. Like all boys then, I had studied strategy and tactics, and the fact that the Germans would pause over something with such little discernible military value did not strike me as encouraging. It seemed to be a further demonstration of the insane world they would impose.

I had already seen a movie in which they had lined up children in a doctor's office and injected them with disease, a scene which still colors my reactions to inoculations. In 1942 I had also watched the movie *Wake Island*. In this little drama, Brian Donlevy, who looked something like my father, and William Bendix, who looked something like my uncle, tried to defend a piece of sand surrounded by the ocean. In the final scene the Japanese flag came up out of the sea to overwhelm the men and we left the theater.

"Why do Germans and Japs want to force women to have babies?" I said.

"I think," said my grandfather, "that taking him to this movie was a mistake."

"This is not what the officers want," my mother agreed, "but what the men cooped up in the submarines will do."

And what did the officers want? "What Winston Churchill said." The enemy officers wanted it to be dark always.

"And now it's time to go to bed."

It was at night, when we were in bed, that four German spies were caught on the back side of Long Island. I dreamed of them often—their blackened faces, their dripping hands come out of the sea.

My dreams were of bayonetings and grotesque, balloon-fragile bodies being shaken and squeezed out of other bodies, and the sea coming up full of goggled men. Sometimes my father would be out in the garage. He would be working on a Sunday project, but he would be in his full dress navy uniform and uniformed Japanese would come down the driveway as if they were soliciting for church, but we knew better and yet could do nothing when they would open fire. After all, hadn't we sold our scrap iron to them?

The bullets were made of scrap, bright curly sharp things you could see coming at you, and they tore into your chest like a bad cough.

Each morning the sun did come up, however, and I would cough and look out through the black curtains to see if there were any Germans with bayonets on the beach.

The torpedo bomber pilot told me where our submarine nets actually were. One sequence was well inside South Dumpling, a drumlin always considered a cuddly island, atop which sat a cute, little mansard-roofed lighthouse. It was situated halfway between Groton Long Point and Avery Point.

That is, we were on the outside, beyond the pale.

Of course, the nets were changed every night. "First you got 'em zigging this way," he told me, "with every once in a while a zag that way. The next thing you zag 'em back the other way with an occasional zig or two, just to throw them off. We fly over in the morning to see what's in there and dump some cans on 'em. You know old Bacchi, the fisherman out of Noank? We used him, too. He was working outside the net and he let us know if he thought anything was going on. Got two or three that way in one net back of Fishers Island."

Does this check out with War Department records? I don't know. The point is, with only a bit more precision, it matches what we thought was happening.

"Be careful when you go down there." Even in daylight now the women came to part the blackout curtains only enough to fill the room with stabs of sea light. "Anything that washes up, you know, may be a mine or a booby trap."

So just to get into daylight I would tiptoe down the hurricane-wracked steps to the beach to see what part of the war had come ashore in the night. And there would be shattered packing cases with strange writing and odd bits that might have been clothing or leather. I did not pick these up or report back to the house about them, and no one from the house did more than peer over the crumbled sea wall. While they watched, and even when they didn't watch, I sidearmed the bits of pink roof off toward the warships always on the horizon. The record, I believe, was seventeen hops, a half-dozen fat skips with a whole bunch of little ones pipping at the end like machine-gun fire.

My grandmother feared I was losing my sanity. "He's obsessed," she'd hiss back of the blackout curtains. "Obsessed with stones."

The ships I was firing at were only off Avery Point, anchored in the waters where the great formal garden had been bulldozed, but some days you couldn't see them at all in the fog. Some days they seemed to be right in the living room, bristling with detail so that as my aunt went about the room with a rag she seemed to be dusting off

their turrets. Other days they hovered in the middle ground: sometimes gray, sometimes green. Were they "ours" or "theirs"? There
were days the atmosphere made them so oddly shaped they fit no
book's silhouette.

What they were, of course, were "ours." Aircraft carriers, the sharp
flight deck cutting the mist high up, planes landing and taking off like
gnats above dead fruit; heavy cruisers with vague piles of gear clus-
tered about the superstructure; destroyers, viewed head-on, always
looking painfully thin and often a bit wonk-eyed. There were submarines, sinister as sharks, and there were the heavy guns.

The guns were sometimes on the cruisers, sometimes on the end
of Fishers Island off the New London coast, out past Dumpling. The
ones on the island were 16-inchers, capable, it was said, of carrying
sixty miles, so that when they went off we could never be sure that
they were merely practicing. There seemed to be no one on local radio to explain what was happening out the window. There was, of
course, no television. After dark there was Gabriel Heatter going on
about the Russian front and constipation.

In any case, like the mere sound of the torpedo bombers, the
heavy guns rattled the windows and felt like someone had punched
you in the stomach. It was a noise you feared, and when I saw the
heavy cruisers on the horizon, I avoided the front of the house and
its raw concrete and was jumpy all day waiting for the whack.

When it would happen I never knew whether it was better in the
house where the windows rattled and the drawn curtains made it already dark, or outside in the daylight. If I went inside, my grandfather would look over his paper and say, "I suppose that's ours." And
I would suppose he was right.

But if I stayed outside in the sunshine I never knew.

TUG OF WAR WITH
THE SEA
Lobstering

I have a desire to instruct myself in the whole system of pastoral
life, but I know not whether I shall be able to perfect the idea.

—Samuel Johnson to Mrs. Thrale, Sept. 30, 1773

FOURTH OF JULY was good for a performance from my eighty-year-old neighbor Tony, the recently retired lobsterman. A couple of days before, I'd smell his Parodi drift by, cutting the scent of his garden and even altering the odor of low tide at the end of the street. He'd be up on his back porch, which overlooked my yard like a balcony in an opera house. It was a good place to rest the walking stick he'd cut from a branch and peer down between his carpet slippers to supervise my attempts to repair my lobster pots.

"Hey, you got them so they come up in the yard?"

"What?"

"You got the lobster so she swim up into your yard?"

"These are pots I've taken off the boat to repair."

"You must have some new, special-kind lobster . . . she swim up into your yard."

"I've got to overhaul this gear." I'd gesture at the various cracked laths, loose bricks, torn nets that made up the traps. Minor repairs could be made aboard the old 26-foot Noank lobster boat itself, but some mornings I'd be out alone or it would be too rough to do any carpentry and I'd have to bring the damaged gear home.

"Fourth of July pretty soon, you know."

"Yes," I'd say, "summer people."

"Never mind summer people. First catch the lobsters. Fourth of July they run like the crazy man." He'd jab south with his stick. "Then come the summer people."

"OK, first the lobsters run, then the summer people."

"Don't laugh. I sell three hundred dollar one day—right here off this porch."

There would be the sound of Parodi juice hitting the chrysanthemums.

"Well, we've been having some rough weather," I'd say.

Another juicy comment from above.

"Lately," I'd say, and brandish the hammer. "Lately something has been affecting—"

"You got to make the gear right the first time." He'd hold the ragged cigar out from his lips, regarding it as if it were the kind of cigar you'd buy if you'd just sold three hundred 1950 dollars of lobster off the back porch. "Then you all set for the Fourth of July."

Being all set requires, as Tony well knew, a good deal more than throwing over a few dozen weighted boxes and hauling them up the next day. Though Connecticut lobsters are as good as the more famous Maine product, inshore fishermen in Nutmeg ports like Stonington, Mystic, Noank, New London, and Niantic have seldom since World War II been able to make a full-time living at lobstering and must work a shift in a submarine factory or a high school if they have a family to support.

The economics of the business are tough: lobster prices are high, but so is the cost of marine equipment. The biologists and the fishermen debate why the crop varies. The main problem remains: the sea. Tony's stick and slippers, for instance, were testimony to fifty years being "all the time damp" handling the gear. Some of his more dramatic moments involved full immersion.

A rolling deck made slimy by kelp mixed with brine from lobster bait and the algae sloughed off pot warps does not make for the best of footing, especially when you must reach out to grab a waterlogged pot aboard. Often the boat is in gear to keep it headed into the sea or merely maintain the location of a fruitful trap.

On such an occasion, Tony found himself overboard and saw his boat moving away. He was just able to grab the side of the hull, but, burdened with boots and rubber apron, was not able to haul himself aboard as the boat dragged him through the water. He began to wonder if he could hold on until the gasoline ran out, but recalled he'd just filled the tank the previous evening. If he let go of the boat to shed his clothes, he'd never catch up to her again. As it was, it was hard enough merely to hang onto the low, wet rail. But, ah, just the other side of the rail was his gaff, a long pole with a hook on the end that he used to snag the pot buoys. With a final effort, he was able to thrash one arm up far enough over the edge of the boat to finger, then clasp, the gaff.

Back down in the water he held on with one hand and reached up with the gaff toward the crude control panel that was fastened loosely to the engine box. Poking about blind, he felt what he hoped was a mass of wiring. Convinced that he was as close as he could get, he took what in most boats would be a gamble and let go the rail, holding onto the gaff with both hands. If he had the wrong wires, say the running lights, they would come loose and the boat would simply keep on her course while he watched from astern waving the useless gaff.

Fortunately his rig was simple, if illegal. He had no running lights or any other frivolous wires, so that as he sagged back on the gaff what pulled free was the connection to the engine coil, and the boat coasted into a drifting pattern. It allowed him to shuck his boots and apron and board her at leisure.

Working his line of pots in strong winds, Tony might be blown back on one of his own buoys or perhaps that of a competitor who had set his gear in the same hot spot. If he did not know the buoy was under the boat, he might have the engine engaged and the propeller would suck up the line. In such cases the propeller could cut the line, and the pot would be lost or the line might spin around the propeller shaft until the wrapping shut the engine down.

Before the advent of styrofoam, in the era of the heavy wooden buoys, the shaft might whip ten waterlogged pounds of cedar buoy right up through the planking. One of Tony's competitors had sunk that way. In any case, once the propeller was fouled, there was only one thing to do: turn the engine off and go overboard pirate-fashion, with a knife between the teeth, to saw the line, turn by turn. In summer this was difficult enough with the barnacled boat bottom banging the head and the whole works moving toward the rocks, but lobstering goes on late in the year and once, faced with losing the boat, Tony had gone overboard on Christmas Eve.

What with rocks and competitors, one did not have to go overboard to have problems. Lobsters lurk in the very grounds that boatmen are advised to steer clear of. Rocks and turbulent water provide the creatures with the right combination of refuge and action. To fish hard, one must go into these waters, putting the boat in jeopardy daily. Not only is the lobsterman trying to maneuver the boat among the rocks, but if, like Tony, he works alone, he must handle the fishing gear at the same time.

That's why a lobsterman spends much of his time making sure all his gear is sound, and on board and where he can find it but not trip over it. He thinks a lot about weather. Even after his retirement, Tony would be up on his balcony sniffing the east for signs of the wind that brings fog.

All these preparations would seem to make lobstering an assembly-line procedure as the buoy is sighted, approached, gaffed, and hauled, and the pot brought aboard, opened, cleaned, baited, and reset. Problems occur, however, at any stage.

In strong seas or fog the buoy often cannot be sighted. Even on calm, clear days following heavy weather, the vertical pot warp may have been kelped under by horizontally moving bands of heavy sea-weed ripped from the bottom by the storm. Occasionally these buoys twist themselves free after a few days of tidal movements; sometimes they shake free months later; often they are buried forever.

Often it is one of these low-lying buoys that ends up in the pro-peller. A pot might roll along the bottom and wind up its warp, or canter into a hole too deep for the line. A buoy could be cut off not only by an entangled competitor but an enraged yachtsman or a sport fisherman who has trolled a bass line across the warp. Gear may be simply, without any excuse at all, stolen or vandalized. The pots alone now cost around fifteen dollars each, not including the line and buoy.

Once alongside the buoy, the lobsterman still has to snag it. If the line is kelped down, there may not be much of a target. With one hand, he must make last-minute adjustments to the boat while the other hand is doing the gaffing. The event is more like polo than golf, with the added risk that the ball may not only not come up for you, but pull you off your horse should you not rein in your transportation in time.

Once it was snagged, Tony would then set the line into the snatch block, an open-faced pulley on the end of the davit, a small crane that has been swung outboard. As long as the pots are in the water they are not usually heavy unless kelped down, but once they break the surface they weigh enough to sprain a man's back if he is not careful, especially in a confused sea.

In Tony's day the snatch block and davit were the only mechani-cal help the small, inshore lobsterman got, his arms providing the full motive power. "You pull thirty pots, you glad to go home whether you catch anything or not." Now most lobstermen have a mechanical hauler, and with much faster boats pull three times as many pots, which they must do, of course, to pay for the fancy gear and all the fuel.

These haulers may reduce heart attacks and back spasms, but they can cause their own problems. A friend of mind got a riding turn on his winch and before he knew it the hauler had pulled not the pot to the surface but the boat toward the pot, which remained wedged underwater between two boulders. The boat didn't sink, but it did swamp. The season was late, and when he was found he was unconscious from the cold water. Another time a local man was thrown to the deck by his hauler and lay there pinned until his brother on another boat nearby noticed the first boat circling out of control.

Once up, the pot, if it is still in good shape, is not actually taken inside the rail, but kept on a widening in the edge of the boat, known sometimes as the culling board. Here the pot is opened. To guests along for the ride (a practice, incidentally, frowned on by the licensing agency), this is the Christmas-morning moment, though the experienced lobsterman usually knows even before he opens the door pretty much what sort of goodies await.

And what is in there?

There are, to begin with, two chambers in each trap. The "front parlor" is rigged with a tight, conical net known as a funnel, presented wide end out to entice the lobster up the primrose path. Having crept into the parlor, he is encouraged by the middle arch from which dangles the bait. He takes this in his claws and, like a cafeteria customer with his tray, passes on straight ahead through a looser net that flops down behind him in a manner to discourage the reverse passage.

The back room or "kitchen" has no way out except an inch and a half space down by the floor for undersize lobsters and other undesirables to escape. There are, nevertheless, all manner of flora and fauna besides full-sized lobsters that may remain. It is necessary to go into the trap with one's hand and pick out what is worth keeping.

Poet John Malcolm Brinnin, who has watched the sorting process off Stonington, finds the lobsterman much like the artist who, "patient, throws out almost everything."

The lobsterman begins his rejection with the seaweed. The weed not only wraps the pots, it is often stuffed down in the parlor, and here, hidden in floral confusion, may be some beasties as well.

Most animals found in a pot, though quick of claw and bizarre of antennae, will not be lobsters. Crabs as well as lobsters are attracted to the bait, and in fact will often eat the menu clean before the lobsters get a chance to be seduced.

Besides crabs one may find blackfish, an ugly but tasty fish that pursues not the bait, but the lobsters themselves, their small but sharp teeth equipped for battle with shellfish. We once found a smooth shark jammed in a pot. Like the blackfish, it had been in pursuit of the trapped lobsters. It was a half foot or so longer than the trap, but unlike the blackfish, it was not easy to transmit into a marketable commodity. Furthermore, in its fierce entry and subsequent writhing, it had confounded parlor and kitchen so profoundly as to ruin the trap.

The most voracious visitor connected with my lobstering, however, appeared as a result of what would appear a mild enough creature: the spiral-shelled channel whelk. There were conditions under which these creatures would creep up the funnel and fall into the parlor by the twos and threes. Many made it into the kitchen. Like most lobstermen then, we had been just firing them overboard, but one evening, back at the dock, I looked up to see an old fellow standing above me.

He kept glancing over his shoulder to the shore, where a large woman seemed to be waiting for him in a car that needed a paint job. The paint on the car was not rusty; it was worn off, burnished one felt by years of massage. He spoke in an accent I could not identify and I had some difficulty understanding what he wanted. It finally occurred to me he was not interested in discussing Polish-American dance music for Golden Agers but wanted these big snail-like creatures. I told him we often did find them and he said he'd appreciate all the whelk we could get. Just call him up and he'd be glad to come over any time we had any and pay us what would now be a dollar apiece. We shook hands. He waved to the woman, who waved back, a big, fleshy arm in the dusk, and deeper in the car the hint of more ample, pale flesh.

There was a stretch of days when at the end of the string we might have a bushel. True to their word, every time we called, our couple arrived: himself lean, unsmiling yet eager, dangling his exhausted bucket; she on land, in the old car ensconced, voluptuous in twilit upholstery, waving her fleshy arm, smiling. One night I got up enough nerve to ask what he did with the whelk. For the first time he smiled. I think his answer was "sauce." Someone else told me whelk were a "notorious Mid-European aphrodisiac." That night, as the old man lugged his overflowing bucket back to the car, I shouted to her a more than usually cheery greeting. I could have sworn she winked.

Whelk, weed, crabs, sharks . . . What then is left after all this throwing out?

Lobsters, one hopes. Lively ones. Green of course. The red only happens when they are cooked, though if you look carefully at them crawling across the deck, you can pick out orange and blue mixed into the camouflage of the shell. It is a bit unnerving, however, to stare down a lobster, for their eyes are on stalks that seem to rise up at you, along with an assemblage of feelers, mouth parts, legs, swimmerets, and other aggressively fragile gear that is somehow more terrifying than the more famous, but well-defined, claws. Fortunately on the deck they are slow and usually opt for a corner to back down and sulk.

All this dancing about with the beastie is of no worth if the lobster is not of legal size or if she is carrying eggs under the tail. The length is measured with a brass gauge set one end in the eye socket. (The eye, on that weird stalk, moves obligingly out of the way.) If the lobster is legal, the other end of the gauge falls short of the carapace, or big back segment of shell ahead of the tail.

Lobstermen like Tony learn to size up a lobster quickly and, without fooling much with the gauge, return the shorts, in the words of the regulations, "to the waters from whence they came." Ashore, an experienced handler like Noank's Orion Ford can cull lobsters by weight into appropriate tanks as fast as the eye can follow him. Aboard, marginals sometimes require a little more time, difficult to give them on a diving deck, especially as the smaller lobsters are quicker, and their claws seem to articulate much further back of their heads, which is, of course, the direction from whence you'd best approach them.

Still, lobstermen are seldom bitten by their catch. The rubber bands are, after all, put there by the lobsterman, but not for him. The bands are used merely to keep the creatures from chewing each other up, should the fisherman be lucky enough to get more than one. To aid the process, there are banding tools now available. They work like reverse pliers, stretching rather than compressing the elastic so that it fits over the claw. The only danger comes when a handler's thumb slides up a claw and into one of the spines. This not only hurts right then and there, but can cause poisoning, the effects of which might linger for days, sapping strength like a low-grade fever.

Lobsters with eggs under their tails are tempting to keep because they are usually bigger than anything you've caught all day. Some lobstermen therefore brush away the eggs or blast them off with their wash-down pumps. Such a practice, of course, is not only highly illegal, but ecological suicide. Nevertheless, this and other grim maneuvers do take place under the pressure of making a living.

Occasionally when the pot is lifted, its door is already opened, a sure sign that the lobsterman has received what is known euphemistically in the trade as "help." Some of the helpers are rival lobstermen; probably the majority are restless teenagers or ignorant "yachtsmen." In any case they have not built the pot, baited it, or set it. Nor do these helpers even bother to close the door after helping themselves, so that if any lobsters do come into the trap after the theft, the rightful fisherman does not even get these.

There are various tricks used to foil thieves, from trick locks to submerged buoys. The law is fairly strong and specific. Thou shall not tamper with thy neighbor's gear. There are not only fines for each offense (which could mean each lobster taken or pot opened), but the violator may have his license suspended. Catching someone with the goods, all lawyer style, however, is tricky. Usually there are witnesses or at least rumors, or that failing, reputations.

Since most cases are handled in the ancient vigilante manner, it is not good to get a reputation for pulling other people's lobster pots. A boat unguarded at its mooring at night is, after all, a very vulnerable thing. A skin diver working at night, the newest villain, may find that his sport is darker, lonelier than he ever imagined.

Sometimes these reprisals turn into "lobster wars," especially if territory is at issue as well as a cleaned-out pot here and there. Unlike licensed oyster beds, the lobster territory within the state is all open. Only the gear is private. Nevertheless there are not an unlimited number of good spots, especially in summer, and there are no rules as to density. Add to this the problem the Connecticut fishermen face on the lobster-rich eastern end of Long Island Sound where New York and Rhode Island boundaries pinch into Fishers Island Sound, a problem exacerbated by the fact that at the height of the tourist season, just after the Fourth of July, the lobsters tend to run out to the deeper New York waters where it is cooler.

Under such circumstances it is tempting for Connecticut men to, in Tony's phrase, "jump the fence." During the Depression, when he was trying to support a large family and an invalid wife, he did set gear in the good, cool waters of New York. This should have been a matter between him and the New York State game warden, but Tony suspected a certain Fishers Island lobsterman of merely taking over Tony's work as a contribution to his own cause, hauling the Noank man's gear right along with his. To discourage this cooperative venture, Tony put some of his wife's sewing needles in the pot warp where he knew he could find them and his unwanted partner probably could not. "One day I see him up in Mystic where he come to sell his catch, and he got the bandages on both his hands all wound up. Just like the big mittens on in July. 'Hey,' I say, 'you got the blizzard falling on you?' He just shake his fist, all bandaged up."

The next day, however, Tony found that not only had his pots been opened; they had been removed entirely. He waited to hear from the game warden. When he didn't, convinced that the bandaged fellow was his man, Tony went up to the farm supply back in the apple orchards above Mystic and got a big scythe blade. In his cellar, where he made his lobster pots in winter, he whet his new possession until it was like a razor. Then he drilled a hole in each end of the blade, to which he attached two trolling lines.

The following morning at dawn, out of Fishers Island Sound, a little shy of the glacial erratics known as The Clumps, just as his rival was approaching the string set west to east, Tony came towing serenely up the line east to west. The scythe blade was behind him some thirty yards, down maybe six feet. The sea was smooth and pink. Suddenly the surface was broken by small eruptions: *Pop-pop-pop*. Forty years later his eyes still lit up with the festival of all those buoys broaching free from any further obligation to mark his rival's pots.

Once the pot is cleared it must be inspected for damage. If the pot can go back over it still must be baited. Just what to use depends upon what is available as much as one's philosophy upon the ideal bait. Commercially produced artificial products wax and wane. Down in Noank at Ford's Live Lobsters, where toward dusk the fishermen sit out on old automobile seats, there are discussions of what bait is running, who's catching it, and what it's going to cost.

Lately there have even been miniature versions of sports page talk in which so-and-so has landed a "contract" with a certain fish market by which he receives what is left after the fillets are taken off the fish in swap for selling the place all his lobsters. Many lobstermen these days drag for their own bait, which allows the conversation to expand into the realm of the otter trawl door, the gallows frame, cod ends, dauber buoys, whip lines, and a whole area of winching beyond the straight lobsterman's dreams. As the daylight thins, there are apt to be yarns about pots baited merely with bricks soaked in kerosene, or some other outlandish methods. The last story of the evening, which usually arrives with the first armada of mosquitoes, but in any case signals the session's end, is the tale about the pot that fished better with no bait at all.

All the cheery bait talk aside, what usually happens is a solitary, muttering man sticks his hand in a plastic bucket so ugly that not even a gas station rest room would have it. It is at such moments that the lobsterman stands aside from Sunday flukers and even the foot-oozing clammer. Whether our man keeps his eyes open or not is up to him, but what he must pull out are some trash fish he's strung the afternoon before: alewife, skate, menhade, small flats.

Perhaps he's spent some good money for a big sack of salt and layered it through his barrel of fish at some time in their history, in which case they are now, in the summer sun, merely awful.

If the lobsterman has not salted his dead fish they are probably alive with maggots. As I said, there is no law about whether he must cast his own eye on this scene. There are enough dead ones looking up at him, and as for the maggot himself, he goes it blind. Though there are, of course, a number of nice juice-proof gloves on the market, the bait string must still be passed around a nail on the middle arch of the pot, and to do this you've pretty much either got to look it or feel it home. In any case, as Hamlet says, you will nose it. After a while you may get used to working the bait, but notice how often lobster men order seafood.

It is time to shut the pot door, making sure to fasten the two wooden latches. When you like the look of where the boat has meanwhile gotten to, make sure the line is not tangled, especially around your own foot, and with a thought for whoever has been old Tony in your education, throw the whole business back overboard, keeping the wheel clear from the line as you move away.

But beware.

It is this last phase of the process that is so often witnessed from the shore or a passing yacht. To the observer this seemingly cavalier gestures does not have the look of a man husbanding his work so much as walking out on it and slamming the door on the way to, if not the South Seas, at least the neighborhood tavern. For all the unseen preparation, the sleep- robbing calculation often involved, this brine-haloed fling is an act that seems but to court pillage, or at least investigation, and I have seldom been on a yacht when someone, often the owner, has not suggested we "stop and take a look." While I stand there aghast at this suggestion, the yachtsman invariably says, "What the hell, if we pull it up, haven't we done as much work as he has?"

THE FINE ART OF HANGING OUT THE LAUNDRY

O Epic-Famed, god-haunted Central Sea,
Heave careless of the deep wrong done to thee
When from Torino's track I saw thy face first flash on
    flash on me.
. . . .

And there across waved fishwives' high-hung smocks,
Chrome kerchiefs, scarlet hose, darned underfrocks;
Often since when my dreams of thee, O Queen, that
    frippery mocks . . .

—Thomas Hardy, "Genoa and the Mediterranean"

W HEN APPRAISING a mortgage," my grandfather loved to say, "we always knock down 20 percent right off for laundry flying in the backyard."

Maybe it should be understood that he had left high school to work supporting his brothers and sisters as a carpenter while his father, a wheelwright from Ireland, wandered across the United States building water towers for the railroad. It was then perhaps natural that when my grandfather-the-carpenter later went into partnership with a WASP Hartford banker, he should develop a fondness for formulae which disposed of such reminders of shanty life as overalls a-flutter in the alley. That a line of laundry had no structural bearing, that it could even easily be cured by a machine worth far less than 20 percent of a tenement's value, made no difference.

"Went down to Garden Street today to look at that property for the bank: bloomers and blankets sailing in the breeze."

Sailing in the breeze? Sounded good to me.

Years later, when drifting down a stream in Rhode Island on a raw spring afternoon, I came upon just such a sailing of laundry, through which the sun was setting. The line was rigged high from the third story of an unpainted frame tenement and carried across the cold pink sky to a blasted oak whose only function, now that it was limbless, seemed to be to support this flamboyant display. Below, urchins played in the mud, hard at it to maintain the need for future laundering, and I could not help but wonder what that home would have been without that fine armada sporting above.

For is there not another life we may achieve through airing our wash, a dancing if damp doppelganger, a life-in-laundry that, with proper rigging, can transcend the sandal that so offended my grandfather on Garden Street and Thomas Hardy in Genoa, March 1887? Didn't Robert Frost say "You may string words together without a sentence-sound to string them on just as you may tie clothes together by the sleeves and stretch them without a clothes line between two trees, but—it is bad for the clothes . . . ," a statement that implies that the presence of a clothes line would make the whole thing poetic?

Tony, the old fisherman who lived behind me, wore a mackinaw of pistachio-green-and-black squares. His cap matched and he clamped a cigar made, it seemed, from roofing paper. When he was too old to lobster, he used to hobble to the town dock every sunrise, his feet in split slippers to ease the rheumatism. If you looked east, then toward the harbor, you would see just the crooked silhouette that the rising sun made of him and his stick. The cigar would then be added as another appendage, followed by the emerging texture of the black-and-green square of matching cap and coat.

One day he did not come up from the harbor. His daughter called down into my yard from their back porch. The old man's joints had finally frozen from all the years in and near the sea. He could not even manage the slow walk to the dock with his stick. This man who had in his youth sailed to Crete and Capri on square-riggers, who had been on a yardarm coming into Venice in 1900, this man who had for forty years run a string of lobster pots across Fishers Island Sound and chased deer through the channels with his sharpie, this man lay paralyzed by pain upon a first-floor couch.

That afternoon, however, I glanced up from my gardening and there above me, dancing off his porch, was my mentor. His cap thrown back in delight, his sleeves in the full tarantella, his legs capering upon the wind, the old sailor squeezed and twittered in song. It was only when I saw that his partner was his daughter securing the laundry rig that the illusion ceased.

"My God," I said, "I thought it was him up there complete."

"It's him, all right," she said. "All but the cigar."

What is more redolent of the glory of a long voyage at sea than to come into a harbor with one's baggywrinkle and lazy jacks augmented by spinnakering pantaloons, great gollywobblers of blouses? A gallows frame of glory! What capes one has rounded! What squalls endured! Every laundry bag a flag locker of triumphs!

There was a yawl near us once in a Connecticut River backwater. Every day there was bedding hung out to dry. Drenched in morning sunlight the man would sit in his cockpit sipping juices, stroking his mustache, while his shapely woman draped every available rail with sheets. "She's . . . Swiss," he'd explain and wink lewdly.

Not all maritime displays of laundry are handsome, or at least handsomely received. There was a fellow who had great contempt for the noveau riche and so to escape them bought a yacht. This boat, unfortunately, was the very sort of vessel the people he was seeking to evade would buy. Made of "modern materials," its color scheme was influenced by the tints of Secaucus tank farms. It was its shape, however, that was its most characteristic quality. Blunt of purpose, like its owner, it shouldered flat waters into waves, stacking them sullenly ahead, so that in five minutes it had run up a whole afternoon of head-seas against which to butt.

Why had he bought such a boat? He had money. Had he then no friends to warn him? He had, but they were simply not those from whom it was customary for him to take advice.

There was one grace note to the design, a tiny mast, like the phallus of a fat man after a cold shower, and from it depended a string upon which hung our man's laundry.

Into one of the more exclusive Connecticut ports he motored. All about him lay a large pleasure fleet and, toward the sún, one of the most prestigious yacht clubs on the coast. A landmark dazzling in late light, the shiplap building was ornamented by a spacious veranda, its bulwarks the epitome of neat canvas and rope work. The lawn ran crisply to the catwalk, where the dinghy float was rich with the varnished and well-bumpered. The launch that serviced the club moorings was itself a gorgeous craft of mahogany and brass, its smooth inboard engine run by a man immaculate in pressed khaki and club cap. There was also, of course, another club on the other side of the harbor, where the late afternoon sun was cruel to its porchless new plywood and plate glass. The spindly pier crept forth from a mud hole, where tethered was an outboard-driven launch that looked like a sink-lining with an egg-beater attached. Our voyager glanced at it with a shudder, for wasn't there something familiar in the design of its pushy bow?

But such shuddering was momentary. His eye was on the sundazzled yacht club, and he thought of how impressive his entrance into port would seem from that famous veranda. True, his cruise had not been one of the momentous journeys in history, but it had been

one long enough to produce laundry, and his boat was decked out as
if he were in a regatta.

With his wife on the boat hook, they managed to spear a mooring
can on the first pass, and without dropping it once, they succeeded in
lashing it to their stout bow. There it was, a dripping trophy, complete
with the initials of his chosen club. Killing his engine, he faced the
veranda, and, as he had money, put his galvanized fog horn to his lips
and blew. Trumpeters from Roland to Armstrong would have welcomed the adoration on his wife's face.

But ashore, there were no stirrings on the neatly canvassed veranda. There was no movement on the green lawn. The dinghy float
remained a rich display of varnish and bumper, the launch and its
attendant a monument of well-rubbed mahogany.

He blew again, three distinct bleats, the horn tilted, as in an artil-
lery problem, for full trajectory toward the veranda.

The sound echoed off the canvas and shiplap.

All remained as it had before, a dazzle, a celestial city.

He pursed his lips and wondered, since he had money, if he were
giving the proper call. The thought crossed his mind that his wife
should duck below to fetch one of the several manuals he carried on
yacht etiquette.

While he was so considering there was the whine of an outboard.
It came from behind him, and there was the sound of its blunt bow
shouldering the flat harbor so that he knew without looking just what
boat it was, for didn't his own bow push waves in just that way? On
and on came the excruciatingly familiar sound. It grew and grew,
competing with the gentle flap of the laundry overhead, until there
was only the sound of the launch.

There was the unbumpered smack as it hit and our man's knees
buckled slightly, the laundry kissing him as he almost gave. But he
held onto his horn. His wife was tapping him on the arm . . . There
was a man's voice behind him in a harsh accent. The voice said they
were ready, they were glad, they were willing . . .

But our voyager was not. He had his stance; he had his horn, and
by God, he had his . . . club.

Haloed by laundry, he blew his three toots, pausing in between
each trio to allow for just the right grouping.

There are some displays of laundry that I think even my grandfather and Thomas Hardy would mortgage at full value. There is
Odysseus, himself a piece of badly laundered goods, all matted and
brine shotten from his most recent wreck. On the shore, however, he

spies the king's daughter and her maidens, who have been taking armloads of clothing to the mouth of a clear stream. There they trod the garments, frothing the fresh water into a millrace with their lovely white legs. And when the clothes have had "all blemish rinsed away," the girls "spread them, piece by piece, along the beach / whose pebbles had been laundered by the sea."

James Joyce in the "Anna Livia Plurabelle" section of *Finnegans Wake*, however, illustrates the difficulties of letting a literary man hang out the wash. While there are any number of overtones, Joyce's lyrically gossiping women have been literally washing all day in the "hitherandthithering waters" of the Liffey River above Dublin. The day is fading and "it's churning chill." The Poolberg flasher (an aid to navigation) is "beyant," and there is a fireboat out in the bay. Close by, "dark hawks" listen as bats "flitter" and "bawk."

Nevertheless, this mocker of Celtic twilight finds the hour propitious for drying laundry! "Wring out the clothes! Wring in the dew! . . . Will we spread them here now? Aye, we will. Flip! Spread on your bank and I'll spread mine on mine. Flep! It's what I'm doing. Spread! It's what I'm doing . . ." At least somebody is onto the practical problem and says, "Der went is rising. I'll lay a few stones on the hostel sheets." One woman who apparently is a-dreaming is admonished, "Throw the cobwebs from your eyes, and spread your wash proper." The hope is that "the strollers will pass it by," a safe bet given the "greasy" and "suety" nature of much of the laundry even after Liffeyizing. Yet one must surely wonder about the drying qualities "beside the rivering waters of . . . Night!"

No less artistic, but far more practical, was the riparian laundering which took place regularly along the upper Mystic River. Or I assume it was regular, though I only observed it once. Surely it was not a matter improvised for the occasion of my passing. Perhaps water travel puts one in a more sympathetic mind for the observation of wind-blown cloth.

In any case, we were gliding under the porch of a long, white house when we looked up and saw a man begin to take in his laundry. Gray-haired, with immaculate mustache, he drew upon the halyard hitched to the far porch post, plucked the pins, and folded the laundry with breathtaking precision, one function flowing so smoothly into the next that by the time each item fell into the basket on the rail, it was as neatly composed as if it had reposed years in the linen closet of the Ritz. There was nothing for the three of us in the boat to do but applaud. For the first time the man on the balcony took notice of the riff-raff in the ditch below. He bowed stiffly, pivoted, and, with the basket under his arm, vanished behind the swish of the screen door.

Technique, of course, is a great thing to make sure your laundry levitates, and we not only have Robert Frost's word for it, but the Coast Guard, which had no less than three paragraphs in the *Manual* when I was but a lad in dirty chambray. There among such items as "overtaking a rum-runner," "speaking over sound-powered phones," "symptoms of and immediate treatment of shock" and "handling of frapping lines while lowering lifeboats at sea," we find:

Clothes should be secured on the clothes line by stops made fast to the eyelet holes in each piece of clothing. These stops may be bought from the supply officer. If two lines are used, all blue clothes must be on one line and all whites on the other. If one line only is used, all whites will be together above and the blues below. Clothes should be stopped on with corners lapping over so they cannot slip down and leave "holidays" (vacant spaces) along the line . . .

Unfortunately, on the lighthouse where I was stationed during most of my hitch we not only had no frapping lines for lowering our small boat, but no supply officer to sell us stops by means of which we might have controlled our holidays. The machine we used to froth our water was wheelable and lived for the most part in the pantry among canned peaches, onions, fids, and spare beacon bulbs that were the size of grinder loaves and often on mid-watch mistaken for such by the boatswain mate. In use, the laundry frother was hitched to the long brass spigot on the sink, belching its gray waters forth into the dirty dishes, there to swirl and gurgle in parody of the winter sea that awaited at the bottom of the pipe seventy feet below. A wringer, such as is now found only in crude expressions referring to female anger, hovered above the drum to aid in drying wash.

However, it remained for us to carry our sopping clothes forth onto the blustery gallery in order to complete the drying. There above the confluence of the Delaware and the Atlantic might one string his dripping trophies. A cloth sack of wooden clothespins was in the pantry. Of course the boatswain mate did not deign to use them, and the engine man had his own oily recesses below in which to dangle his private dampness. On this rock pile two and a half miles offshore, it remained for me to appreciate the sheer nostalgia of this item, so redolent of back yards, green cut lawns, and trees.

Since the current ran so hard past our place, no one was encouraged to tie up. This left our dock lines free for more significant use, so I took one, and knotting an end to a man rope which hung from an upper gallery as a fire escape, I secured the other end to the lower gallery rail. Then carefully I gave each trouser and shirt the recommended "slight hand-stretching to remove wrinkles." Plucking a wooden pin from the sack which I held in my teeth, I fastened the clothes to the line. The soft southwesterly lifted the blue clothes against the two blue backgrounds of sea and sky.

There was, of course, other work to do, and while I went aloft to wash the lantern windows, I dreamed of my blue clothes drying below. Tankers bound out for Venezuela held down the far horizon. Gulls took their whiteness straight up overhead until their cries were lost in the general brightness. I breathed deeply in the sway and knew that somewhere far beneath my feet every fiber of my denim would be breathing the same clear world.

Unfortunately, when I went below a few hours later, the improvised line was all that was breathing. The blue sea was still there and so too the blue sky, but the blue clothes had simply, like the gulls, vanished into the background. What was this, I wondered, some sort of lighthouse optical phenomenon, some sort of counterpart to what Arctic explorers experience with too much white-on-white? Was this a blue-out?

I reached for the line. There really were no clothes there. If it were not for a few guilty clothespins rolling in the gutter of the gallery, I should have thought I'd never indulged in a laundry orgy at all, or, having done so, I must have become so intoxicated on cleanliness as to have run to the rail with my armload—and in full enthusiasm heaved everything into the mother-blueing sea.

To steady myself I grabbed the rail in both hands. Yes, down there three stories below on the riprap lay a crumpled body or two. Slowly I backed down the necessary ladders, inched across the concrete base, dropped onto the guano-covered rocks. A couple of trousers and a shirt, all well soaked in seagull excrement. The rest gone down-tide to the great rinsing waters of the Atlantic.

Coast Guard on shore duty may also have problems hanging out the wash, even as commander of the base. Captain Richard Goode reports that when he was head of the yard at Curtis Bay, Maryland, he had no dryer. Hung out in the Chesapeake breeze, his wash was constantly under attack from the sandblasting work being done on the weather cutters in for repairs. "That grit was everywhere," he said in a recent interview. One must commiserate even with captains:

> When seeming safe ashore
> I lug about
> harbored
> in my deepest parts

the residue
of North Atlantic keels,
stout bottoms
that themselves have kissed
the ice floes' bluest hour
or done duty
to Sargasso's
darkest
eels.

Techniques do indeed abound even in such a seemingly simple field. Naturally there are controversies, heresies, and all the usual paraphernalia of any cult. There are the plastic-pin people versus the wooden-pin purists. The latter have even developed a schismatic publication broken off from the orthodox *Outdoor Laundry*. At the moment *Wooden Pin Magazine* is perhaps better illustrated than it is written, their pens too impetuously deployed in attempting to purge what they consider to be "the spring-hinged heresy" in behalf of the traditional mandrake model. The T-shirts offered with a two-years subscription, however, are a real inducement, as they not only display the slogan "Wood for Wet Wash" but contain a kangaroo-style pouch to hold the pins. There are, of course, the trolley-bag adherents to consider, as well as the bull-wheel advocates (versus the double block and fall folk), the users of wire cable (plastic sheathed), the employers of synthetic lines in variegated hues, the traditional cotton rope people, the galvanized iron yardarm gang versus the cedar crucifix school, the indoor-outdoor folding bunch (a shifty lot), and the merry carrousel clique.

The galvanized yardarm and the carrousel are especially susceptible to maritime exploitation. The former makes, when removed from the laundry yard and hammered into the ooze, an excellent boat trolley stanchion, while the carrousel, when left right where it is, serves as a first-rate rack for painting lobster-pot buoys.

There is another variation on clothes pole use, though clearly we are here in the realm of outright laundry-line abuse. An elderly friend of mine was apt to take a few drops down at the local. In this matter he was not, of course, unique. What set him off was that he owned one of the few garages in the village. Not that he drove, thank God. Rather the purpose of the garage was to provide a stable mooring for the far end of the laundry line.

The function of the laundry line itself was to provide a kind of navigational mark much wider than might be the back stoop itself, and, much as swordfishermen coming from Block Island in fog might run north until their lead hit bottom at a certain fathom curve, turn left, and come in on this curve, our man "came in on the laundry line."

Alas, the clothes line as rhumb line would always alert the wife, for the pulleys at the far end never quite received the lubrication that the navigator did.

His solution was simply to cut the offending wheels out of the system. Having stripped the endless rope of these traitorous devices, he secured what was now the bitter end with the knot he considered to be most proper.

It may well have been the proper knot from his point of view, but from the wife's there was now no decent rig at all. Whereas before she could stand on her porch and haul in her work (and at night her husband), now there was the full sweep of the back yard, a muddy waste over which floundered damp items beyond recall.

And so the line came down entirely, giving way to the folding indoor-outdoor rack which, being a strictly day beacon, left the navigator with no choice but to keep his evenings soberly at home.

My own favorite outdoor laundry gimmick is the forked stick, which I first saw on Cuttyhunk, where its presence seemed to loom as one of the tiny island's larger cultural objects. Seen apart from its laundry line, such a piece lying against a weathered shed, or, even more provocatively, merely tossed on the ground, might set off a whole day of speculation among visitors. Was it an aboriginal eeling fork perhaps cleverly adapted by Yankee fishermen to indigenous use? If it were just a little better crafted, it might have ended up in a museum of Ancient Folk Utensils. Surely antique dealers would soon be knocking them out in the back room. Indeed the sticks looks like a slingshot for very tall, but precise, people. And as for eeling forks, there are several early Baltic Sea models which do not seem to surpass it in sharpness of tine.

Only when one has a sagging laundry line, his sheets sweeping the spring mud, does the beautiful simplicity of this device come home. That the damn thing always falls when your back is turned, that your kids employ its shattered remains as a slingshot for very short people or a variation on the Baltic Sea eel fork, does not deter you from looking for it long hours in the bushes or from, having found it, spending more time in the shop lovingly taping and winding it back together. It is truly one of the great anonymous creations of civilization and its simplicity, even its failings, are at the heart of what outdoor laundry-hanging is all about.

Some say that to hang out the laundry is like having children, that is to say, one does but give hostages to fortune. But who is to say that a white sheet decorated by songbirds who have been eating blackberries is not just the kind of serendipity that tie-dyers are rewarded for? Frost says, "Accidents happen to everyone. It is the artist who knows when to keep the accident." As for the bugs in my bed, I would certainly prefer a robust, bark-munching earwig, its antennae all atwiddle from a vibrant day in the great outdoors, to some low-rigged cockroach cringing from drain-creeping, its lips battened on the underdrippings of set tubs.

There are, naturally, dangers in hanging out one's wash beside bugs, birds, the risk of scandal, the damage to mortgages, the offense to turn-of-the-century British poets, and the loss to oceans.

Some of these problems are beyond mere questions of technique and might be considered under the realm of politics, that is if we consider the military as an extension of statesmanship. When Falstaff was recruiting his army he found that he had but "a shirt and a half in all" his company. Lacking either General Washington's or Sergeant Bilko's talent for requisition, the famous fat one nevertheless found a sufficient quartermaster's expedient in sending his future cannon fodder through Saint Albans and Daventry, where he knew they'd "find linen enough on every hedge." It is, of course, part of Shakespeare's humanity that we do not actually have the scene where the rag-tag soldiers are slaughtered by Hotspur's men, or, what would have been even worse, the wrath of the housewives of Saint Albans and Daventry upon discovering the loss of their laundry.

In more modern warfare the hanging out of laundry was thought to be at least as crucial. In the mid-1940s in Groton, Connecticut, the rumor went round that Japanese spies were up in the hills by the submarine base. They were not watching the submarines themselves, but peering at the women in curlers who worked the laundry lines behind the great rows of temporary married housing. In those days submarines spent a fair amount of time on top of the water and in refueling ports, so the men were responsive to the climate where they sailed as well as the ports from which they departed. Their uniforms would change accordingly. The notion was if a Japanese agent spied through his glass summer whites flying in winter, he presumably would conclude a cruise to warmer zones was in the offing. *Ah . . . , transfer of North Atlantic submarine to South Pacific.*

Nor with the advent of nuclear weapons has this particular danger to the hung-forth linen subsided. In our village have lived a succession of navy officers whose duty while on tour here is to oversee our submarine forces. Some years ago the wife of one of these men, a woman both stout of heart and ample of physique, was called upon, like all her predecessors, to stand for hours in reception lines. At squadron functions, such events as keel-layings, launchings, commissionings, de-commissionings, changes-in-command, retirements, and awards for Sailor-of-the-Month, she outdid all previous wives.

To help her maintain what she referred to as her "military brace," she had, however, a secret weapon. And secret it might have remained had it not been for the outdoor laundry line, and a modern-day Falstaff. The device she employed in this nuclear age was, however, a traditional item, for which the whalers of Mystic had once provided a key, stabilizing member.

If I do not name this garment outright it is only out of deference to the lady's style, for when the garment was missing from her outdoor line, she too refused to name it. The investigating officer came to the house; she opened the front door only far enough to slip him a picture of the absent garment which she had clipped from the Sears catalogue. Or at least so she told me herself after a meeting of the village property-owner's association, called especially to deal with The Rising Wave of Village Crime.

"And if it isn't bad enough they've taken to pilfering my laundry," she said, "the other day when I came home it was clear that someone had been using my shower."

Ordinarily I probably wouldn't have thought much of the matter, but it so happened that a friend of mine had told me a week before that one of the old fishermen, a rugged cuss, now dead, who in his day could do the deep-water trips with the best, had been uncharacteristically capering about the town pump in women's clothes.

It so happened I knew this fellow, saw him, in fact, most every day. After all, we both lurked in the same part of the village under the hill. Usually we talked about the old days down there, how the deep-sea men used to come into the dock to use the town pump which then was "full of good, dark water." Lately he had been concerned about the pump, and we'd lament the present day, what with the pier fallen in and the pump broken and no fresh water public enough so a man could take a shower or at least slosh a bucket to his head.

It was no problem, then, to track him down in the shed of a mutual friend. You could hear them in there most every day, a group of fishermen drinking beer, swapping yarns, and making bluefish jigs.

There was a kettle of simmering lead on a hot plate and the smell of the heated metal was stronger than the beer and tobacco. In spite of our mutual under-the-hill connection, I found "capering in women's clothes" not an easy subject to introduce in a conversation mainly about tile fishing on the Georges Banks.

Fortunately, enough beer was being consumed so that it was necessary to go back of the shed from time to time. Even at the risk of being misunderstood in the Comfort Station manner, I followed the fellow out back and let it be known that up on the hill product X had been reported missing, while down by the pump, well, frankly, product X had been spotted cavorting. The old fisherman looked at me with sheepish eye.

"It's only a matter of time, Cap," I said, "before On-the-hill comes to Under-the hill."

There was a slight shift in his jaw and his battered hand clenched and unclenched.

"All she wants is restitution," I said. "And you know, it really is a matter of maintaining our Posture of Defense."

He snorted and we went back inside, drank some more beer, and poured the lead into molds.

Damned if the next day the commander's wife didn't call me up to inform me that my committee on the Crime Wave could relax, for the backbone, as it were, of our military posture had been mysteriously but effectively restored. She also promised not to be tempting any more of our citizens by flaunting such matters of vital defense in the future.

"Well, you know," I said, "my grandfather always used to say when he appraised mortgages that when you hang out the laundry it cost—"

"I know. I know, but to hell with the mortgage. What I miss is the way when the southwest wind blows, it creates a sea surge right through my . . . well, you just can't get the same effect with a dryer."

PART THREE

Fall

But though its flatness is itself maplike, it was difficult to gain a vantage place from which to view it. They took every opportunity they could then to climb the many towers or coastal dunes for this purpose.

—Svetlana Alpers, "The Mapping Impulse in Dutch Art,"
The Art of Description

THE MAN WHO BOUGHT McGUGAN'S

Here are the foods of the old ceremony. . .

—Catullus, CI (translated by Robert Fitzgerald)

Part One: The Encounter

IT WAS a cool day in mid-fall. I had come to McGugan's old boat-yard on the Mystic River to check the bilge in my fishing boat. He was there ahead of me, looking at the For Sale sign on the big shed where the McGugans used to have their workshop.

They had moved their Dock & Dredge company downriver to slicker quarters and now there were only a dozen slips, inhabited mostly by houseboats and older wooden craft. By the shelter entrance to the building lay the rusty mud scoup discarded from the modernized dredging operation, and it was by this ancient, outworn device he stood.

His gaze, however, was not upon the mud, but aloft where leaned against the second story, a sequence of wooden arches that one of my neighbors had placed there ready for use as gallows frame for his winter cover.

"Going to buy the place, eh?" I was only half joking for he looked something like the wonderful old fellow who had recently bought a lighthouse in the area and spent a fortune on renovating it with black walnut tavern rooms, Japanese gardens and aeolian temples where once had stood the fog apparatus.

He mumbled something and inched to his right, his back still to me as he examined the building, his gray hair shaking slightly from left to right, right to left. To aid in the precision of his survey, he shifted some of the winter cover frames.

I noticed he was in a kind of improvised diver's wet suit and, as if to demonstrate he was not merely aping fashion, he was actually dripping.

Although it was the middle of October, the water was still warm.

The only unusual thing about a swim would be the location. Scuba divers, employed by one of the nearby boat yards, occasionally struggled with bent propellers or a foul bottom, but no one plunged into that section of the river between the two bridges for pleasure. There had been, in fact, a death that summer when a man had fallen overboard. The search had lasted three days, with the police boat trolling back and forth into the blue-flicked gloom of night, so that the people who lived along the waterfront now seemed to look at the river a little differently.

I asked him if he'd been swimming.

He said something that might have been technical. Clearly his survey of the building could at the moment brook no merely social noises. I thought of other prospective buyers since McGugan had put the yard on the market a few years ago. This one, it seemed, had merely gone a step further by inspecting the piers underwater.

I went around the shed and down the last pier to pump out my boat, and I thought, odd as this fellow is, he's really not out of keeping with some of the people who had looked seriously at the property. Sure, there had been orthodox agency men in three-piece suits detonating polaroids, snapping measuring tapes, and, as my rent represented part of the equity, eagerly shaking my hand. There had even been agency women bristling in tweed business suits who also worked polaroids and tapes and shook hands. Their conclusions were that the "property would require someone possessing vision."

Visionary indeed seemed the circumnavigator who'd stopped off five years before and was "looking for a more permanent venue." His safari shorts and bare feet in that yard infamous for rusty nails and splinters had been no more ludicrous than the present man's diving suit. Nor had his British accent been any easier to untangle than the present man's mumble. "What this place needs is someone who will set up a proper ship chandlery." He had a clipboard and, like a doctor writing a prescription, dashed off the items this emporium would carry.

Later he did become involved in such a place on another continent and has sent me a list much like the one he suggested for McGugan's: "bronze and lignum vite snatch blocks, baggywrinkle, marlin, pelican hooks, charts, nautical instruments, relevant publications, notices to mariners, cordage, winches, foul-weather gear, rigging services, fancy knots and rope work, hand-carved name boards, trailboards, figureheads, tonnage boards and crests." As he intended at McGugan's, he offers "instruction in sail, seamanship, navigation, and yacht delivery anywhere in the world." At McGugan's, he promised to restore the old railway to haul "real" vessels. "And you, sir," he concluded, "shall have an honored place there among us."

No less dramatic had been a friend of mine who had recently bought a dragger and was going back in the business his father and he and his brother had practiced for years. He had taken early retirement from a local factory for health reasons and he wanted to make sure he could give his boys what he knew about the old family ways. If nothing else, fishing in the fresh air would save him from the factory, where he himself'd spent too many years. "I want to rip out all these 'finger piers.' " He'd pronounced the word 'finger' as if it represented the most puerile level of maritime interface. "Rip out all these . . . finger piers. Put in a steel bulkhead so some fishing boats can get alongside here. Raft em out if needs be, raft 'em out halfway across the friggin channel. Hell, Mystic and Noank are supposed to be *fishing* ports, right? What you got now? No place to get a fishing boat in here, not a real one anyway. These guys in the red pants are driving us all out of the harbor."

Equally mysterious as the present prospect was the darkly clad man who one day cornered one of the houseboat dwellers and, in between knowing nods at various items about the yard, rendered sotto voce references to elaborately contrived plans he had for seemingly every object in the yard. Unlike the circumnavigator or the draggerman, however, he seemed offended that the property was on the water at all and promised to blacktop, condo, and signage all before him. All we had to do was "just wait and see everything drop [wink] into place."

I myself was involved in a scheme. There was a local real estate man who had friends in one of the slips. He and I had met by chance on a train to New York and had conspired like generals all the way from the Connecticut River to the Turtle Bay, cooking up the most marvelous of marine condo delights.

Now we had a man so serious he dove to personally inspect underpinnings. While I pumped my boat I thought of what I would have to tell this fellow about McGugan's.

He would need to understand that it was a region of old wooden boats and wet dogs and rats and cats who ignored the rats to prowl beneath the long shed where once Sam McGugan had fed them from a trap door in the middle of the machine shop. In the alley by the shop the old road between Boston and New York came over the final hill down to the river and the ferry landing. It was just a humped crust of a trail now, covered with leaves in autumn, dusted with snow in winter when you could best imagine the coach canting down the hill at twilight.

The ferryman's house, which had also served as a tavern, still stood, its gambrel roof tottering precariously above the unpargeted brick, its double crusader door sold off at auction and replaced by a slab of delaminating indoor plywood.

I would tell him how at the ferry crossing one autumn twilight I was bailing a rowboat when a breeze ran up the back of my neck. It was a great blue heron, and it came in creaking, slate blue on dusk, to land a boat length away. We faced each other like that as the light went out of the alley and the chill came up from the river. When he left, the great frangible wings labored just above and slightly outboard of my work. There was a sloop at the next pier and once free of the sheds, the bird found itself drifting among the wire rigging. I braced for the expensive crash. But somehow the bird got going again, altered course, and slipped loose out over the river, where it turned and creaked upstream, low and at last solid in its prehistoric pose.

There were the people, too: Pepe, the lobsterman who told tales of his New Bedford swordfishing days on the great bowsprits made from telephone poles, when they'd search the sea so hard in summer brightness of the telltale fins that at night they had to put sections of potatoes on their eyes to draw out the fire.

There was the sailboat couple that had arrived by way of Canada having weathered a storm in the cavernous St. Lawrence, when they sat for forty-eight hours hip deep in their cockpit, their anchor clinging to the top of a tiny underwater hill.

There was Gunner, last of the submarine cannoneers. He often stayed on a tired old cruiser that had a lurid past. The former owner had been a bank robber who refused to share and had done in his two companions up-river, where he buried them. Police bulldozed an acre's worth of topsoil off to find them one winter dusk a year later, but had not yet located the $350 thousand. When he first bought the boat, Gunner had gone forth each day among his bilges to seek his fortune. Later, he contented himself with titivating his cabin top. "Ah, what would I have done with all that money, anyway," he'd say. "There'd be blood on it. This way, what I got is really mine."

There were the McGugans themselves. In the 1940's when I was growing up at Groton Long Point, they had been figures of fascination. The harbor was like a theater, and while, of course, I had heros who were ball players, in those days before television, it was the Brothers McGugan who put on the most compelling show.

There had been a bad winter. At low tide ice had grabbed the pilings and held on as the tide rose. My father, the harbor master, was much alarmed, but helpless. A few such cycles and the piers were so jacked up in crazy angles that the result resembled an explosion in a pagoda factory. What could possibly ever put everything back to rights?

When the ice went out, in chugged the two McGugans in their chubby wooden work boat *San-Joy.*

She had a fat, mustached bow and the brothers moved in and out of the pilothouse and back and forth from the derrick. In spite of the shockingly good acoustics of the harbor, I never heard them shout. Everything was done in a gentle dance and most graceful was Sam, a man whose proportions in those days matched the *San-Joy* herself. With a tap-tap here and a tug and pluck there, they restored order to the harbor in time for summer.

George, who was skipper of *San-Joy,* (and father of Sandy and Joy), always had a story about the yard. "There's an inside door we have—beveled glass. Got it from the ship-breakers when they were doing in the paddlewheeler *City of Worcester.* My father grabbed it, not to be goddamn 'historical,' but because we needed a door and he was there working on the waterfront when they were set to throw that one out.

On the second floor is the bar from a place in New London. They threw that out one day with my father. This whole neighborhood was very rough. There was a boiler factory here and they say a woman couldn't walk down here without being raped."

George's favorite story, however, was about the combination dredge and pile driver *Captain Frank.* "I wanted to name the boat after my wife Gwen, but she'd none of it. 'I don't want,' she'd say, 'someone to come by and announce I just saw *Gwen* up on the ways getting her bottom scraped.'

"Well, so then here we were with a hell of a good rig all made up and ready to go and no name. Sandy, though only a kid in high school, he'd done the machinery out of old parts here and there. Sam and I'd cut an old barge in two and put some more middle in for all the new gear. Fortunately, there was Captain Frank himself standing by.

"Captain Frank was quite the fellow on boats in his day, but now was retired. He used to wander down to the yard because his wife didn't like baseball on the radio. We put the proposition to him about naming the dredge after him and he wasn't too sure. Maybe he was used to those fancier boats. We pointed out that in fancier places he wasn't allowed to listen to the game, so he saw the light. Besides, he knew a good rig when he saw one.

"I spent what I know now was the happiest summer of my life on that rig . . . off in a backwater, all by myself, moving just a little bit each hour, from dawn to dusk, just digging in the mud and making lots of money."

Sam lived upstairs and when I had been a little kid he used to holler down at me not to throw stones in the water. Later we got to be good friends and we both hollered at little kids not to throw stones in the water. I always thought Sam, as a dredger, felt he spent most of his life pulling stuff out of the water and hated to see it all just go back in like that.

An important device in maintaining the balance between land and water was the trap door in the shed. It seemed to me to be a way Sam sought to control the relationship of water to land. When in the course of every few years the river managed to seep up into the building, it was up to the trap door to hurry out the falling tide. Even in years when there were no great storms, Sam would stroll over to the trap and peer down from time to time. I thought he was doing this to check the tide, some sort of survey on making sure the right amount of water was over the right amount of mud. I believed if anyone could do anything about this sort of thing it would be Sam. But one day he admitted it was only for cats he was looking. He fed them at low tide through the door. "It's good to know," he said, "when you lift up that thing, there's friends below."

When Sam was in the hospital, I went over to see him. The woman at the desk said, "Mr. Go-loo-gun, he done gone." And I said, "Oh, good. I'll catch him back at the yard." She just looked at me. 'Well, then," I said, "if he's not back at the yard, where has he gone?"

"Mr. Go-loo-gun, he just up and done gone . . . dead."

But I hadn't been so far wrong about his going back to the yard.

"He wanted to have his ashes scattered in the river," George said one evening. "Figured he'd go down river about as far as Noank, then turn around and come back up past here to Old Mystic before he'd turn around again. That was about as far as he wanted to travel.

"After the funeral, though, I couldn't bring myself to go to the you-know, the . . . parlor . . . to pick up that, what-do-they-call-it: 'urn.' Finally my daughter-in-law come down here and said she'd go with me, so we brought it back here and I just set it down on the table saw inside the double floor. In the old days, you know, that's where the horses went out. That whole floor in there is reinforced to bear the weight of the wagons piled up with the boney fish nets." He stopped and I figured he was thinking about the days when the horses pulled the wagons full of boney fish nets, days before even he and Sam had bought the place.

"But that way, what with the ashes on the saw just inside the door, I saw it every day first thing when I opened up. This, what they call an 'urn', I believe, it got on my nerves, so one day I come down here, opened up the door and there it was on the table saw, this 'urn,' just a tin box really with a coat of silver on it, so I grabbed it and carried it out right out there opened it up and shook it out on the water. You know, it was all supposed to be just ashes in there. But . . . there was bones. There was some good sized big pieces of bone. They made a pretty good splash, too. I mean I didn't mind the ashes so much. The ashes I kind of expected."

To get his mind off the bony business, but not appear to be switching the subject with too much abruptness, I asked him about where in the river this ceremony had taken place.

"Right about there," he said, "right about where your boat is now we moved it."

One evening George showed me Sam's room upstairs: a corner of the old net loft partitioned off with plywood from the surge of rope and chain, huge double blocks, shackles and thimbles. There was the bar that had been thrown out with McGugan, an elegant mahogany affair half buried in come-a-longs, snatch blocks and pelican hooks. In Sam's room itself were a simple bed and a bureau and an open-faced closet. On the bureau was his old lunch box from grade school, a strong iron box it was, too, with no cartoons. There was no mirror, but a note pinned on the wall from a woman who wanted him to join her in Florida.

"Would he have gone?" I asked.

"He thought of it," said George, "but . . ." His gesture trailed off toward the back of the loft where the twilight was dying among the gear.

When I pumped the boat after that, I thought of Sam going back and forth on the tide. I stopped tossing over bottle caps, even hesitated to sweep paint chips out the freeing port. What would happen to Sam when the new owner took over?

He was still there when I finished pumping. The gallows frame for the winter cover was really annoying him, so that for a moment I thought, no, he's not going to buy the place. What he doesn't like is the composition, as effected by this temporary gear. He's one of the *plein air* artists who every week in summer set up their easel here.

What with all the "restoration" and cute condos going up in the area, except for McGugan's there was hardly a legit ragged shingle left to get a pallet knife into.

Watching him scan the structure, however, I soon thought that rather than merely trying to reproduce the place, he was really figuring out how to modify it in some grand way. And there was that dripping diver's suit, a style that even no plein air man would be so literal as to employ.

"This place goes way back, you know," I said. "They had a machine shop in there. All kinds of inventions and modifications for dredging apparatus. Three generations. Before that another outfit made seine nets for menhaden, or boneyfish as some call 'em. Many generations of that."

He looked back over his shoulder and mumbled something technical. It seemed to concern structure.

"Well, the floor is reinforced," I said. "In the days of the net making, they used to drive a team of horses and a wagon in there. Those menhaden nets were huge, you know. One would fill up a whole wagon so it looked like a load of coal."

He cocked his head as if to hear the rumble of the wagon coming in over the double wooden floor, the echo of the hooves and felloes over water.

"Of course," I said, "because of the old ferry right-of-way, there is some tedious hassle over the mere stone that marks the south boundary."

He brushed the objection aside. Here was a man clearly poured from the same mold as the fellow who had recently bought of the lighthouse and sparing no expense, defying the sea itself, had managed to turn it into his play thing.

"I guess," I said, "that things like that only matter if you're into heavy financing needs."

Facing me, as over a tennis net, he served a pair of terms that seemed to smack of Wall Street. I managed to race to the end line and bloop a few back.

"Of course," I said, "the real thing here is the way that old New York–Boston coach road comes down the hill there by the ferryman's house. Could you believe this was once right on the main route between two of our greatest cities?"

He actually took the time to look across the road at the ferryman's house with its sagging brick foundation and its boarded-up windows.

"Prime condo country, eh?" I watched him.

He frowned.

"But," I said, "that is really another parcel over there. Another parcel, from the real estate point of view, that is, of course."

He winked, made a smile, a little wet grin.

Good, I thought, if the landlord is still one of the gods, and the gods yet come disguised and dripping, then I have at least treated him with respect.

I have demonstrated that I am aware that my concerns are bound by the real world of finance, yet I have also given him something of the true nature of the place, something of vision to carry into the new dispensation. Perhaps, I thought, he is indeed our man of vision, a man who will maintain the best of the past with enough of the new to survive.

But I did want to hang around just a little longer . . . to make sure. I knew I would not quite confess that I couldn't sleep nights with my refuge continually threatened, but, I thought . . . I might suggest that some sort of deal should be made at once. He should secure the place before it went the way of the other old boat yards. As I watched him, however, his mouth hung open again and the eyes leapt back to the top of the building.

"Well," I said, "good luck, sir."

His hand reached up. It was not the gesture of a man about to engage in negotiations of any kind. This hand clawed the sky.

I backed off. Indeed, why should he bother with me or my sentimental palaver? Here was a rough diamond who put his trust in no hired divers or steeplejacks. Hadn't he already just plunged to the depths to inspect the watery foundation? Now, to complete the survey of his kingdom, he would scramble somehow to the topmost battlements.

Or perhaps arrange to pull them down to him, rafters, ridgepole and gutters.

Part Two: To the Bridge

There seemed to be nothing left to do with the new owner except irritate him with my history lesson. And afterall, what was I worried about? Didn't we have the Historical Society with powers "on the books" a good deal more effective than mere poetry? Why, poor George had already had to go to no less than three hearings just to move a door to the dockside shower three feet up-river. Of course what resulted was historic indeed: a 1960 tract house style door over which he hung a naked bulb that seemed Depression Hotel Corridor. Around the wound the shingles dangled, tar-paper (Early Tobacco Road) a-flutter.

I decided to take a therapeutic walk uptown, sticking as close to the river as possible.

As a tentative goal, I had the bascule draw bridge. There always seems to be some sort of show there. A great mass of weights and gears with various shacks stuck about in its structure like boxes in an Elizabethan playhouse, it could literally upset the very middle of the town, throwing its lamp and walks high into the air in a drunken parody so convincing it called into question all the lintels and sophettes of Main Street. Even in repose, when the pigeons gawk among the struts and the cars hum ominously over the snow grate, there is all that potential.

With the counter weights in sight, I made my way along the river. There were already signs around the old brick trolley powerhouse announcing that the apartments inside were ready for occupancy. Rumor had it they were renting at a rate per month that would get you, only a few seasons ago, a decent place for a year. At least the new owners here had left a walkway that connected with the boat yard. You could also still walk the Mystic Art Gallery waterfront. I crossed the big parking lot back of the stores, where there used to be a spar pool, and in later days a shack for shipping fish to New York. I had bought my first lobster boat there. It was now all condominiums. There was, however, still one relect of the past, the de-commissioned wooden, work trolley that served some elderly gentlemen as a ham radio shack. Standing near it was the official village eccentric.

He had long, gray hair and a thick body encased in leather. Rumor had it this fellow actually lived in New York City but returned to town from time to time to sleep under the bridge. The path took me close to him. He did not need the bridge just yet. He knew where it was. It would be there. Right now he seemed entirely occupied, despite the chill in the air, with controlling a flight of river midges that apparently danced before his ravaged face.

More personable was old Ralph, who was coming toward me down the alley that lead from the bridge and Main Street. Behind him was the restaurant over which peered the masts of three big, new schooners that had been built expressly for the tourist trade.

Two were locals, but the other was a strange three-master.

If the passage of time were going to make off with the waterfront from here to McGugan's, then at least one could take advantage of the new things each day brought, and Ralph certainly always managed to pick up the latest along the river. I knew he would have the story of the third schooner. Perhaps it was not merely a tourist boat, but some vessel with a tale of long voyaging to tell.

Of course he wasn't going to begin with the most sensational item. He was more of an artist than that. The first part of what he knew today had to do with the series of slipping brown sacks he was hugging. He usually stopped and revealed what sort of errand he was running and we would joke about our hats.

Sometimes he would get serious and tell me about the different houses he had once lived in, describing them in great detail until I acknowledged I knew them, too. He had ended up, however, in a single room in a place that did not satisfy him, and although he was the last man in the world to complain, he knit his brows and his speech fell into a near-mutter when he told of the succession of loud, drunken, and doped-up young men who now occupied the rooms all about him. He was grateful, however, for even this, because it was the last place anywhere near the river where he could afford to live now.

It was for this reason I did not quite trust myself to tell him about the man who bought McGugan's.

That left us with Today's Hat. Today's Hat filled him with cheer. It was a baseball model with a three-digit number on it. "It's a submarine hat," he said and chuckled. "I found it in the river." He adjusted his slipping sacks under one arm. "These belong to the schooner over there. The one you can see with the three masts."

"Good," I said. "I knew I could count on you to keep me up to date."

"They're just in from Den—"

"Denmark?"

"Yes, Denmark."

We stepped back and looked up at the roof over which were the heavily rigged masts from Denmark.

"And I got to get," said Ralph, "donuts for the bridge tender."

"You're a busy man," I said.

He still had some news about the hat, however. Maybe it was going to be more important than a three-master just in from Denmark. He pointed to the three golden digits. "They have a number for each submarine and this is the number."

"Good for you," I said. "In the river it was, eh?"

"Sure," he said and popped my shoulder. "Right in the river."

The river, for some reason, was always a great joke between us.

"Right at the edge, you and me know. Where the stuff comes ashore. The stuff caught in that . . ." He made his finger vortex.

"Back eddy."

"Yeah, back eddy."

"Back eddies can be weird," I said.

His eyes narrowed. "Say . . ." He stepped forward and shifted his sacks under his other arm. "You know that kid on that submarine?"

I told him I knew lots of young men on submarines.

"The one who . . . who . . ." He put his finger to his cap, almost touched it.

"No," I said, "I didn't know that kid."

"He . . . he . . ." Again the finger at the brain. "Right when he was on duty, too. He fell . . . into the river."

"I didn't know him."

"You don't think maybe . . . this . . ." He almost touched the cap. "They got numbers, each has."

"Wrong river," I said.

"Wrong river?" He looked around bewildered. There were the masts above the restaurant. There was the bridge with its great counterweights poised over the narrow street.

"Submarines use the next river over," I said, "the Thames. You can't get a submarine up this river, Ralph. Hell, you know that."

"No, not a submarine, but maybe . . . maybe . . ." His fingers fluttered near the bill.

"And not a hat, either," I said. "I mean sure a hat could float up this river but—" I reached in my pocket.

"Look, I'll tell you what I'll do. I know guys in the submarines. I'll write down the number of your hat and ask them if it was the same number as the one on which the kid shot himself while standing watch. Then I'll get right back to you, OK?" I wrote the number down, batted him on the bill with the envelope and we parted.

As usual, after talking with Ralph I felt a little better. After all, the point wasn't so much if the old buildings stayed as long as the old people could still hang around. And here, today, its top masts competing with the counterweights on the bridge, was this magnificent schooner. Two young, strapping Danes stood on the pier, their backs to me, facing their vessel. The three-masted schooner seemed to be one of the Baltic lumber carriers one saw occasionally in the New World, complete with the forward port in the hull for stowing the longer timbers. In fact, the diesel from one that had brought some refugees from the Iron Curtain in the fifties was the one that lay half-shrouded under a tarp at McGugan's.

Up on deck was a girl in ski sweater. She was no bunny wrapped in fluff. Her sweater was a serious, sea-going piece of gear. Densely knit, the white had worn gray with rubbing up against the rigging.

Even the reindeer seemed working hard pulling their load. Her face was beautiful, if somewhat worn. She was working on the ratlines just above the men, her fingers skillfully mousing the lower rung.

Behind me, noontime diners looked out from the restaurant. On tables as yet unfilled were napkin tepees, inverted water glasses, and brass nautical lamps.

There was a sudden tumult of water.

It was like simultaneous bilge pumps ricocheting aqueous echoes between the pier and lumber schooner hull. At McGugan's, when bilge pumps lit off, we often joked about someone's taking a leak. Now I marveled at the fullness of what I assumed was the bailing of this transatlantic bilge.

What I had in mind was some sort of international joke about long voyages, and so boldly advanced, to encounter the two Norsemen pissing, great thunderous arcs.

Ya-ya.

Talking to the girl right above them as she worked on the rigging.

Ya-ya.

Since I was there, and Ralph had not adequately prepared me, I asked them whither were they bound.

"We go to Bermuda tomorrow, maybe couple days."

I looked up at the girl.

"That's right," she said, "Bermuda, we go on the water."

Their bubbles, however, went on the tide up-river vanishing beneath the bridge.

The pier inclined sharply up from the water to meet the sidewalk that ran out onto the span. I was excited to be stepping out onto that balcony with its views up to the square riggers and Lantern Hill. As I was about to step off the end onto Main Street, a stranger in a porkpie hat and corduroy car coat with up-arched fur collar backed around from the street onto the pier planking. It was as if he'd just been spotted out there selling filthy postcards and was easing himself into an alley. He even had a briefcase. "Phew," he said. "It's not what you think."

I was simply going to ignore him and walk around onto the street. "Not out there," he said.

"Whats amatter?" It didn't seem possible that what he would be afraid of should be anything I needed to fear. "Is there really a problem up there?"

"Oh, boy." He tucked his briefcase under his chin in order to rub his hands. "Oh, boy." He grabbed the briefcase in both hands and eased up against the brick wall. There were tears in his eyes. He blinked and seemed to relax a little. "A sunny lee."

There was indeed a chill draft coming down from the bridge. It was as if all the weights, struts, and gears had conspired to manufacture this teary wind.

"Yes, sir, nothing like a sunny lee."

He stood there basking a moment in his porkpie and car coat and briefcase. "Those urinating Danes," he said. "They didn't seem to mind the cold. Of course, they weren't up here now, were they."

"Oh, then you saw them," I said. "I couldn't believe that, right in the middle of town, in the middle of the day. And no one even seemed to notice."

"Well," said the man, "frankly, I thought they have managed to convert this up-tight Yankee tourist harbor into something really rather . . . Scandinavian. A kind of open, rude health."

"Rude, all right."

"Rude health. It's not the same thing. We need it. A tonic to the sick American soul always hovering about over its possessions." He held out his briefcase. "Hey, I'm no different. I need it, too."

"Well, the weather's been strange today," I said. "No one seems to know what time of year it is." I looked down at the water. The rude bubbles were just passing under the bridge.

Ralph came past with a different bag under his arm. "I hope, these are the right kind of donuts for the bridge."

"Listen, Ralph," I said "Did you see that, back there? I mean, those Danes of yours." I pointed to the bubbles.

"Hey, them fellows had a long voyage."

From up on the hill came the carillon from the Baptist church. The tune seemed to be "I am One with Jesus." Even though the music was on tape, it began to warm me.

"Well," I said, "I've got to go up there anyway." On the street itself it wasn't as bad as right there at the top of the pier where the wind funneled.

I found shelter up along the store fronts. In the windows in all sizes were carvings of eccentric old men in foul-weather gear. Some were helpfully labeled "Old Salt."

It was quite warm in the thrift shop where I tried on a tweed topcoat. The label said "Made In America, The American Way with Wool." Nevertheless, despite my patriotism it was clearly too small. I tried it in various combinations of under-sheddings and buttonings. Each time the mirror revealed, however, the same buffoon, a rather rumpled man who looked like he might try to con somebody into believing he was going to buy McGugan's.

"Is there anything I can . . . help you with?"

The woman's voice shocked me back into reality.

"This is too small, isn't it?" I said.

"It is," she said.

Already I could hear the police sirens. There were at least two cars outside.

"And it's the only one you have?"

"It is."

Part Three: The Jump

On the street it was crowded. Not only were there the usual pedestrians, but the shopkeepers themselves had bailed out and were swarming along the sidewalks on both sides. The bridge was the center of attention and crowded out beneath its dramatic struts and pigeons, everyone was so agitated it was difficult to tell if they thought they were in a box at the opera, or on the stage itself.

There was another siren and a blue-lit ambulance marked "Rescue Squad" bounced over the bridge towing a tin boat also marked "Rescue Squad."

Ah, I thought, it must have been that fellow in the porkpie hat. He certainly seemed the type, a man carrying around with him literally a case of mental disorders.

Like a lucky ticket holder, I found a place at the bridge rail facing up river.

"Apparently he jumped from right here." Next to me was the man in the porkpie hat. The way he kept shifting his briefcase about on the bridge rail, I expected him to spring it open and yet display his wares.

"Well, well," I said, "what can we say about those 'rude-health' Danes of yours, eh? They sure know how to use the local waters."

The porkpie man jerked a thumb over his shoulder. There, high and dry on the bridge a few feet behind us were the two Danes and their girl. They seemed much more interested in the pigeons that were just resettling in the struts after being disturbed by the passing siren.

"So," I said, "I guess we can cross 'rude health' off our list."

In fact there was nothing in the river, not even bubbles.

"So who was it?" I said. "Who was actually at the heart of all this?"

The man on the other side of me still had on a bib with a cheerful red lobster on it. "I was sitting there eating my lunch," he explained.

"Several of us, in fact, were sitting there eating lunch." He blotted his lips. We were under one of the machinery shacks, out of the sun, but not out of the wind, and I still had the uneasy feeling that the jumper was someone I knew.

"Where is he now?" I said.

There was the smell of the river and the cooking from the restaurant, some of which still seemed to cling to the man in the lobster bib. "Tide," he said, "tide took him."

The only traffic on the river I saw was the museum's work garvey *Maynard Bray,* low of freeboard, heavily mustached, its big brine cask admidships. Named after a much-admired marine Jack-of-all-trades, she was employed about the yard up there in a variety of tasks, including hosing down the old vessels when their hulls began to dry out in summer. At the up-river edge of the automobile agency, she did seem a little below her usual territory.

Somebody asked again who the jumper had been.

"That guy you see just wandering around."

"Oh, yeah," I said. "The guy who just wanders purposely around. I saw him down by the old work trolley. He was back there acting oddly."

"Well, this guy was odd all right."

"Odd, yes, but clearly he wasn't heading up this way. He seemed to have found himself a column of sunshine with midges in it."

"No, no," said the porkpie man. "I knew that guy. It wasn't him. This was the real old guy you see who hangs around the waterfront and acts busy." He leaned closer to me. "Frankly, I think he's your number one time killer, if you know what I mean."

"Old Ralph," I said. "Jesus, that submariner suicide hat . . ."

"Yeah, the old busy-body guy," said Porkpie.

"But he was carrying donuts to the bridge tender."

"They must have been the wrong kind of donuts," said Porkpie and slapped his briefcase.

"And what," I said, "you got the right kind in there?"

"What I'm concerned with," said Porkpie, "is precisely how they're going to get that rescue boat down to him."

"That museum boat's already got him." The man in the bib wiped his hands and waddled away.

Indeed *Maynard Bray* was pushing toward the shore just above the automobile agency, its mustache bumper shoving up white water like an old sot blubbering his beer.

On the way across the bridge I saw Ralph. He was not only not in the river; he could care less about what was. He was struggling with the bridge tender's doorknob and in his off hand was the donut bag.

"Oh, good," I said. "It's not you after all."

Confused, he looked into the donut bag.

I slapped him on the arm and ran on.

I was happy for Ralph, but ashamed I had doubted him.

My guilt fed my stride as I trotted through the used car lot. The dock there, usually crowded with flounder fishermen that time of year, was abandoned. There was a knot of people where the end of the car lot slipped into the river.

Priests and ministers.

The garvey was nudged up onto a little piece of mud left between piers. In the middle of the boat was the great brine cask, and apparently huddled up in a blanket, alive, but badly stricken, shrunken, was the victim. The two men and the woman who had run the garvey were still aboard. They alternately touched the blanket and attended to the housekeeping in the boat. There seemed to be a lot of it, lines that needed coiling, gear adjusted.

They were not the only ones who seemed at a loss as to what to do next. There was the man who had jumped. But he certainly wasn't jumping now. So who was he to justify this tremendous focus?

Really a rather small man, and there he just sat in an ugly blanket in a small square boat, merely being alive, as was, of course, everyone else who was looking at him. If his act had been a demonstration up at the museum, some sort of whale-boat or dead-horse ceremony, it would have been over and the public invited to move on to the square sail furling or the sea shantyman.

The police did have their standard program to run through. What were their options? Should they treat it as a lark and let him go? Should they arrest him for breach of the peace in violating the posted ordinance that specifies "no swimming from bridge"? Should they examine him further for medical problems? Should they treat him as an attempted suicide, a mental case in need of "observation"?

"Hey, I offered to throw him a line as he swam by." The man was standing nearby in a fishing vest. In fact, he still held his pole, a rather nice, light spinning rig. "The guys sez he was doing fine. What's the problem?" The fisherman, for lack of a more official audience made his case to some of us bystanders. "I mean maybe he stayed in a little too long, but if he'd have wanted to drown, he could have. If he wanted to come ashore sooner he could have. Way I figure it, he did just about what he wanted to."

"You mean," said a guy next to him, "they should just give him some coffee and let him go?"

"Hey, what's the crime?"

"Well, there's always the bridge."

"Yeah, the bridge."

"You ain't supposed to jump from it. It's like an ordinance."

"Hey, they ought to give the old guy a medal."

"Yeah, but there were diners and everything watching. You know, people who paid a lot for a noon meal."

"Let them contribute to the medal."

I walked over closer to the rescue boat. There huddled by the big brine cask was indeed this person. Folded away in the cowl of the blanket somewhere would have to be his own actual face, and, of course, he was going to have to turn out to be somebody.

On shore, above the boat, one policeman was saying to the other, "Depression."

"Yes," said the other. "We've had reports from the landlord but could do nothing up until now."

"They're saying he was just on a lark," said the first cop.

"Pretty old for a lark," said the other cop. "Pretty grim looking for a lark."

"Well, the lark's over now," said the first cop.

"I saw him earlier." My voice.

The first policeman looked at me. Up and down.

"It was at McGugan's," I said.

"Where?"

"McGugan's, an area boatyard." I pointed across and down the river.

The policeman followed my indication about as far as the bridge. "When was this?"

"About an hour and a half ago. He'd been swimming then. Down there. At McGugan's. I thought he was inspecting the piers."

"He jumped off the bridge. The evidence is conclusive."

"Sure," I said, "but before that, before he offended the ordinance and the diners, he was in and out of the river. A regular harbor seal."

"Somebody shot the last harbor seal we had up here at this bridge," said the policeman. "Put a hole right through him with a .38."

I looked at the blanket again. It did not seem to have a hole in it.

"Where is this you saw him?" said the policeman.

"McGugan's." I pointed. "I keep a boat there."

"Is he from McGugan's, too?"

"I thought he was going to buy the place."

"He was on a lark."

"It was the middle of the morning."

"Was he incoherent at McGugan's?"

I started to think of all the people I'd known through the years at McGugan's and tried to apply the standard of coherence to them. "Like I said, I thought he was going to buy the place."

The other policeman walked over to me. "Do you know this individual?" It was clearly time we got down to the present tense. It was time we confronted things face to face. Not everyone in the crowd had been selected for this purpose, and ordinarily this policeman would certainly not have selected me, but since I had thrust myself forward in this matter, it was going to be, at least for the moment, me.

He pointed behind him, trusting the individual not to have leapt in the meantime from the garvey.

The first policeman gave me my intro. "He says he met the individual in mid-morning at a bar called McGugan's and the fellow was claiming to have bought the place."

"Not a bar," I said. "A boatyard." I tried pointing toward McGugan's again, but the bridge still loomed in the way.

"But he did make these claims of grandiose nature?"

"It was me who interpreted them that way. I mean the remarks seemed to be about making some sort of purchase. That didn't strike me at the time as grandiose."

"A man like that . . ." the cop almost gave me a chance to look. "Claiming to have bought a boat yard, at today's prices?"

"He'd been in the water," I said, "and was wandering around moving the gallows frames—"

"Gallows frames?"

"Well, winter . . . covers . . . "I tried to make some with my hands. "Rain and sleet, covers for boats, the frames . . ."

"You say he was trying to hang himself?"

"No, he was trying to study the upper superstructure of the building. He was, for Christsakes, like an engineer. People use engineers around the waterfront all the time because of the filled land and the practical need to—"

"Probably looking for a perch from which . . ." The second policeman turned from me and dropped his voice down his colleague's collar.

"Ok," said the first policeman turning back to me. "Is . . . this . . . the man?"

He beckoned me and I stepped forward, now irrevocably separated from the crowd. They led me off toward the water like a condemned man. At the edge we halted. The three crew members in the boat paused in their bailing and fiddling. I searched their faces for someone I knew.

"Turn the individual around."

I almost cooperated by pivoting, but of course it was not me they meant.

The fellow who'd been running the garvey's outboard tapped the blanket and pointed. The cowled figure turned and looked up at me. Out from the hood spilled that gray hair. Stabbed those blue eyes. But now his look contained the knowledge that, like St. Brendon ensconced in his curragh upon the back of the great fish, *he knew what kind of island it was, but he did not want to tell them, lest they be terrified.*

His eye met mine for a moment, then fell, sheepish, and the blanket twitched back over the face. *Brothers, are you surprised what this island has done?*

"Well?" said the first policeman. "Is that the individual you saw at . . ?"

"McGugan's. Yes," I said. "That's him."

The first policeman turned to the second. "That does it. Norwich. Observation." Then he turned to me. "Thank you. You've been a big help."

I must have looked bewildered because the other cop said, "Hey, at today's prices, it's hard to get good psychiatric help."

They left me there on the edge of the mud. I walked back through the crowd. In the used-car lot the flounder fisherman was already at it again with his worms. He was informing his companion about famous larks. Up on the bridge new people were being entertained by some of the witnesses. The iron walk echoed under feet hitting the knobbed surface, and the drafts between the struts were unmitigated by views of ships. Down in the street the storekeepers were already back at work. The Danes had departed, even as had their bubbles, though their ship remained, actually a rather homely affair, needing paint. When I got to McGugan's there was the mud plow and the For Sale signs and even the gallows frames awaiting winter.

HITTING BOTTOM
A Mystic River Clam Dip

But as the mariners that sound
And show their lead upon the ground,
They bring up flow'rs so to be seen,
And prove they've at the bottom been.

—Andrew Marvell, "Upon Appleton House"

A small Noank oyster steamer sometimes does towing.

—*U.S. Coast Pilot,* 1892

ALL ABOUT US at the Mystic Seaport were the famous maritime relics of the nineteenth-century fisheries. The air was already scoured of its morning mist, and the coffee from the gallery overpowered the oil from the big Caterpillar diesel that lurked far below us in the old wooden boat's belly. Built in 1917 of long-leaf yellow pine and held together by wooden pegs, the Dolan Brothers' *Robert M. Utz* (rhymes with mutts) was nevertheless not, like her temporary neighbors, a museum piece, but a working commercial craft. From her asphalt, bridge-tile deck to the hexagonal porcelain knob on the inside of her varnished pilothouse, she was, however, a joyous combination of utility and elegance.

The pilothouse was warmed by a small gas unit that we moved past carefully as we looked down over the big varnished wheel to the deck. There under the mast and boom two young men dressed in yellow overalls were heaving the mooring hawsers.

"That's it, Dave." As if savoring the workmanship of his window, Captain Bob Bishop lowered the curve-topped, double-hunt sash and put his head out under the awning. He filled the opening, a big man in a blue-ribbed sweater and khakis, his hair cut short. "Just give her a flip."

There were four of us come to make a shellfish survey of the town's waters, and we tried to fade into the tongue-and-groove shea-thing as far as our bulky clothes would let us in order that the captain have all the pilothouse he needed. At the moment he was trying to back the 55-foot boat out between a schooner, a pilot cutter, and a tiny steam launch whose striped canopy fluttered in the north wind.

It was as if we were riding in a howdah high atop an elephant presently engaged in tiptoeing backwards out of a church pew.

There were, of course, several technical aids. The pilothouse, in fact, seemed full of them. Not that *Robert M. Utz* was decorated after the manner of modern jet cockpits luminous with color-coordinated plastic clusters. Rather she had stashed about her furniture various bronze levers and copper pipes, brass-knobbed toggle switches, and brass gauges. There were even two pull ropes running through lignum vitae and bronze sheave blocks overhead as if to summon servants in distant corridors. As survey pilot, I was trying to figure out just which one of these devices I'd suggest yanking when the anxious face of one of the young crew members appeared on the gallery outside. Clearly some disaster was about to occur. It was merely a question of which priceless historic relic we had in our propeller. The captain leaned through the window and exchanged words with his man. Then he turned to us, adjusted his glasses, and said, "Do you want cream in your coffee or sugar, or perhaps . . . both?"

We glided down through the sleeping town of Mystic, jacking the bascule bridge in a detonation of alarm bells and pigeons. Dave appeared at the door juggling the coffee. Captain Bob grabbed the porcelain knob and let him in. It was in big ceramic mugs like you used to get in truck stops. We passed around the hot mugs while a distant radio voice said something about bluefish.

In the crisp air out on Fishers Island Sound, it was a day when lighthouses aspire to be rockets and islands become flying wings. The magic was enhanced by Captain Bob's performance as he danced back among us to pull his strings.

Captain Bob had his head out the window and had shifted the big wheel to port. We all tiptoed up behind him and looked down on the deck. Hung from the boom was the dredge itself, a big iron cage with teeth on the bottom and a six-inch-diameter black hose uncoiling away aft along the deck out of sight. There was a rumble deep in the boat and the iron cage began to swing out over the water. Captain Bob waved his arm. "Let out a little more on that, will you, Dave?" The crewman who had brought us coffee paid out a few feet from the heavy nylon line that acted as a *vang* to control the boom.

"How's that, Cap?" said Dave.

"A hair more."

When it was right, he gave a thumbs up and Dave tied off the vang.

Captain Bob danced back through us and began working his levers and pull cords again.

"Jesus Cripes!" There was a hissing back of Eddy Edwards. He was eighty-one, but spent more actual time on the water than anyone on the Shellfish Commission. Now he was jumping up and down batting at his drenched pants. "It's a good thing I got on hip boots."

Captain Bob reached behind him and pulled the off switch. "Sorry, it's not supposed to do that," he said. "Bit of a backup in the hydraulics."

Eddy Edwards pulled his yachting cap down until it almost met his goat's beard. The hat looked as if he'd used it to wipe spark plugs in the collection of outboards he had back of his house. "It's all right, Cap. Usually I get wet sooner or later anyway."

I tried to keep my eye on the sonar. We were on a range in the Mystic River that biologist Susan Preston and I'd worked out the weekend before in her pulling boat. We'd rowed along the edge of the channel, venturing up into the flats looking for a six-foot shelf. The charts are not much help in such areas, sprinkling a few numbers to account for a whole cove. The idea is "stay the hell out, friend." Yet it is just such waters that are most apt to be rich in clams.

Since the 1950s these waters have been judged by the state laboratory to be polluted. However, with the proper supervision and licensing, people may depurate, that is, move clams out of closed waters into designated open areas where the shellfish clean themselves in about two weeks.

Practically speaking, the only people who are going to do this moving in any numbers are, of course, the commercial shellfishermen with hydraulic dredges. Since clam beds are not leased after the manner of oyster grounds, however, the clams are in public waters. In order to work, then, the commercial fisherman strikes a bargain with the town shellfish commission. He usually pays a license fee, which is at least a hundred dollars, then pays the town an additional amount based on a percentage of the haul. He may also give the town back a percentage of clams, which the town then puts on its own depuration grounds so that when these clams pass the state test the area may be opened up for recreational use by any citizen with a clam rake, a peach basket in an inner tube, and a pair of old sneakers.

What with growing population and dwindling food resources, both the state and the commercial clammers see depuration involving these closed zones to be a significant area of future harvesting. To prepare for this program, town shellfish commissions all along the Connecticut shore are setting up shellfish management plans based on surveys using a variety of rigs from scratch rakes by local commission members in shoal water to big commercial gear like the *Utz*.

Near where we were working in the Mystic River flats there had once been enough shellfish to get one mud pie dignified with the name "Clam Island." Mystic had even been saved by the clam bar there. In the War of 1812 Admiral Hardy of Trafalgar fame had dispatched three fire barges up-river to burn the town. They had run aground on the clams, where they were rendered helpless by grapeshot gathered from the junk lying about in the local boat yards.

Even modern sonars, however, can be misleading in navigating such tight spots. In our preliminary exploration the week before, Susan and I recalled Hardy in one of his more successful essays when, directly under the Danish batteries, he had personally sounded the harbor at Copenhagen for Nelson, employing a long pole. Working with an hour left of rising tide, we had discovered about a half mile of water that carried the seven feet of depth that would be required by *Utz*. This muddy underwater shelf stretched inshore toward the West Mystic flats about seventy-five yards toward a collection of glacial erratics, upon which usually perched cormorants drying their wings.

Nosing up into that area now aboard the huge *Utz*, I wondered if that preliminary survey would hold up. It was one thing to go paddling about with a lovely lady of a Sunday afternoon in a low-slung rowboat. It was quite another to bring to bear on the same scene a half-dozen men and tons of expensive machinery.

"Plenty of water," said Captain Bob, "though not all of it's spread the same thickness, I imagine."

Even with the tin awning outside there was a dazzle in the forward end of the pilothouse that made it hard to find the two little red sonar blips, let alone gauge the space between them that indicated the depth of the water. "She reads a little long," he said. "That is, there's not quite as much water under us as you see there."

In no time, however, we were onto the inboard edge of the range, which was between the Mystic Baptist Church steeple and a black can at the dog-leg off Sixpenny Island down-river. I cleared my throat; Captain Bob spun the wheel and went into his act. With a sigh and a grunt the *Utz* responded. We began to creep in a counterclockwise circle.

The hydraulics made the otherwise silent pilothouse sound like a night in the respirator ward. Captain Bob reached over onto the compass and took his coffee cup. Eddy Edwards coughed and began to tell a long story about Santa Claus and a ruptured elf.

"I certainly hope there's at least a sign," said Andy German. As chairman of the Groton Shellfish Commission, he held the clipboard. He also had a pencil. He poked his mustache with his pencil and consulted the clipboard. "It would be a heck of a thing to bring all this gear to bear on just a lot of mud."

"Oh, you're going to find something, I'm sure. I mean unless our pilot here runs us aground and we have to spend all day in one place." We looked around to see who the joker was. It was Tim Vissel, the regional marine extension specialist from the Connecticut Marine Advisory Service at Avery Point.

When he'd first come aboard I hadn't recognized him because of the watch cap low over his eyes. We had worked together in the summer in shallow-water operations dressed in straw hats, bathing suits, and sneakers. Now, in addition to the watch cap, he had rigged up with a large yellow foul-weather jacket that met his knee boots and his beard was sharpened after the manner of French duelists. It was a formidable set of gear, and since the survey had been his idea I wondered what sort of sloshing lay ahead.

There was a salvo from the switches back of Eddy Edwards, but this time no local attack. Captain Bob danced over to me and, reaching around my back, produced another noise. The *Utz* lurched to port and everyone splashed coffee over each other.

"Is everything all right?" said Chairman German.

I looked at the sonar. The blips were still banging each other.

"We have to keep circling," said Captain Bob, "or we have problems with the hose . . . Yup. Wrapped it right around the wheel like a wet towel. Rubber's steel-reinforced in that hose. Had to cut it off with a hacksaw. Was winter. Had to be towed in. And hey, you can do it any day, again." He lowered the side window and poked his head out like a locomotive engineer.

"It would be a lot easier, I bet, if you could set up ranges," said Chairman German. "Just run straight down them like an oyster dredge or an otter trawl dragger."

"Sure, but you can't," said Captain Bob. "That's why you have to stay awake and keep turning to port. Keep that fantail away from the hose. Sometimes you turn too tight . . . like we're almost doing now because this spot's so narrow. We'll be just screwing it into the bottom. End up anchoring ourself right here." He was dashing about working the controls and already the cage had broken water, the hydraulic jets shooting. "Or you kink the hose, flip the dredge."

The boom swung in and the boat came upright as the cage hovered over the culling table on the foredeck. Captain Bob went back of Eddy Edwards and let loose enough hissing to drown a nest of cobras

while way down on the deck the jets sobbed shut. Dave and his partner guided the cage inboard to just above the culling table, then yanked
open the toothy mouth. Out fell some glop and we all leaned forward.
"Well, said Captain Bob. "At least a sign."

"A sign of what?" I said.

"A sign of life," he said, and there was Dave holding up a big
chowder clam in each hand, while his partner had three or four littlenecks spilling off his sleeves.

A half-dozen clams, of course, do not a harvest make. Captain
Bob explained that he could get up to five bushels a tow. A tow takes
some fifteen minutes, in contrast, say, to an inshore otter trawl going
for flounder and lobster bait along a range, when the rig will stay
down closer to an hour. To break even, a boat like *Utz* needs a hundred
bushel a day of the large chowder or quahogs. Worth three times as
much are the smaller cherrystones, and the littlenecks are about six
times the chowders.

We eased down the West Mystic range to the black can at the
Sixpenny Island dog-leg, finding minimal signs. "I suspect this means
there's good stuff up in the flats," said Captain Bob, "but you'll need
a shallow rig."

There used to be an old circus performer who owned a boat yard
in Mystic. His background as a high-wire man had served him well
when it came to rigging the whaleship *Charles W. Morgan* and lesser
craft. Moreover, the tricks he'd picked up from the clowns had bought
him many a drink in the bars. One of his favorite moves was to pull
hard-boiled eggs out of the ears, pants, and noses of gap-mouthed
boatmen. So too Captain Bob seemed to be pulling things out of our
most intimate zones. No one was safe in any corner of the large pilothouse. You'd be lounging up against the door on the port side when
he'd reach past your pants pocket and *pffft,* pull out a switch to the air
piston for the power take-off, and first thing you'd know there'd be a
rumbling deep within the bowels of the boat while out on the deck six
hundred pounds of dredge would swing overboard. Or you'd be socked
way back by the bunk and he'd step over to reach into what seemed
to be your vest pocket and *spttttttf,* out would pour great jets of water
onto the foredeck. Stand by the front window and out of your ear
would come a cord that dumped a hundred spider crabs onto the
deck.

We ate lunch on the red-and-white-checked tablecloth in the gal-
ley below and aft of the pilothouse, augmenting what we had brown-
bagged with ship's coffee. The crew's bunks were set into the port side

at floor level between a stainless-steel sink and a brown oil-cooking stove, upon which sat an enamel saucepan and an enamel coffeepot. The stove looked as if some violent meals had been vulcanized there, upon or near. Forward, through a small passageway hung with wrenches and mallets, throbbed the Caterpillar that turned the propeller and the donkey engine that drove the winches, which themselves groaned away up through an even smaller passage under the working deck.

Overhead ran a maze of lines, which I realized with a shock were part of the puppetry from above, ancient-looking ropes that emerged in unexpected places to vanish as suddenly, but all obviously carrying anything but whimsical burdens.

After lunch, we passed up the crowded anchorages on either side of Noank, where there were few actual boats now, but a virtual carpet of mooring buoys. Instead, we steamed to the next big cove, which was the first area of state-certified clean waters we'd surveyed. Here the Commission's problem was not depuration, but finding a way to move clams in twenty feet of water in to where the Old Sneakers & Inner Tube Brigade could scratch out some chowder-makings. The idea was that if deepwater rigs such as *Utz* could be licensed to dredge these beds, they would in turn be required to turn over a certain percentage of clams that could then be moved into the town's shallow, clean waters, such as the Poquonnock River, where the quagogs have thinned out. First, of course, the Commission would have to see if there were deepwater beds rich enough to pay a large rig to come in.

Working now in fifteen to twenty feet of water, we relaxed a little and Tim Vissel and Captain Bob began to swap theory. Captain Bob seemed to talk more like a farmer than your usual draggerman or sport fisherman. "It's important to cultivate these areas or everything just gets buried and dies."

Tim Vissel agreed. "You should see some of the oyster creeks down Madison way. They just heap up with oysters until the beds are six feet deep and stretch maybe a mile. The oysters begin to poke up above the water at low tide. Being craggy masses, the beds not only catch but hold bits of earth. It doesn't take long for the shells to accrue a mess of dirt and pretty soon you have grass growing. You come back in a few years and you can't even find the creek anymore. At that point you almost feel you might as well start listening to people who want to build a shopping mall there.

"A few years ago we had the oyster set of the century and no one was prepared for it. Everybody had given up ahead of time. No one understood depuration or the need to keep harvesting an area. They either thought, 'It's too late—everything's gone forever,' or they thought, 'Leave the beds alone. The Indians lived off shellfish and never employed any of this aquaculture stuff. Let nature take its course.' Why, I just mentioned the word aquaculture at a town meeting and was booed. Another time I was standing on a pier talking to a clammer when I let the word slip from my lips and he picked me right up and held me over the water. It was a colder day than this, too."

"The ideal conditions are very delicate," said Captain Bob. "If the waters are too stagnant, like say the upper Mystic River, then the silt settles in and everybody smothers. If it's too open, on the other hand, say like maybe we'll find off Bluff Point, everybody just rolls away in the surf. Or maybe the bottom gets beaten too hard, like it may be off Groton Long Point, and nobody can get through the crust."

The "nobody" applies equally to the shellfish and the dredge. "If the clams can get in there somehow, it's hard to get the dredge down into that layer. But even if we don't find something after an hour breaking crust, the area will profit from the work. Sometimes, if we see a sign through the crust, maybe we stop to spend an hour . . . just going slow and trying to settle the teeth in. We let the dredge teeth dig in places like that before we let them have the water. If you sock the jets in too soon, you'll just float the teeth right up off the hard bottom. Heck, if we had time we'd just go crust-busting all day to open up an area for the clams to settle. Especially in early spring we have to break the edge. A piece of ground open to a long fetch will crust over during the hard winter seas. Come spring, it's like dragging a rake down the highway."

He looked aft over the glinting water and we saw, for an instant, the concrete. "Sometimes there's so much vegetable growth down there we tow with the gates open all day just to clear out the kelp and grass."

Captain Bob began mumbling something about "seeking a soft edge." he wanted a range for a line in outer Palmer Cove, where a faint line on the chart indicated a change in bottom. We helped him by matching up the end of a road on Groton Long Point with the chart.

"They're not everywhere, you know," said Captain Bob. "So you see a line like this on the chart where's there's a change in depth, or just as good sometimes, a change in bottom type like from hard to soft, and you get on that range with the depth machine. You don't just go down that range; you crisscross the line because sometimes that line, well, it's just a matter of a strip a foot or two wide, a little ridge, a vein, and you could never find it coming in end-on . . .

"But you don't need a big area, if they're there. Two hundred bushels a day can come out of a spot you can just hardly turn around in. On the other hand, there's something about a bottom where there may be a sign like we found up-river, and you set your gear and hours later all you have is the handful that sucked you in."

"Do you get them all?" I said. "That used to be the rap on hydraulic rigs: they clean you out forever."

"Not this type of rig. After all we want to come back. The Dolans been in business since before the thirties. As for the rig, the seeds slip through the rake. The bigger ones, after a while they know we're here and go down. Like I said, they're not dumb. They hide. Then they don't seem to be there anymore, but if you come back in a month, there's more than ever. They not only hide, they get up and move . . . Oh, not like scallops, say, but they do move.

"At Clinton, Cedar Island . . . six or seven years ago we put down over three hundred bushels. Actually I think it was closer to four hundred bushels . . . And the next time we looked they were all gone. Every last one of them. They hadn't died and they hadn't been harvested. They'd just upped and moved. We found them later a good deal further out off the bar.

"Sure, there's breakage, and that is waste. A diver told me that for every broken shell on the culling table, there were up to twelve broken shells below. But the hose like we got here is kinder than just a straight rake. Even with a hand rake, you bust 'em.

"Long Island Oyster Farm has divers who ride the dredge and report exactly what's happening down there. Sometimes you can predict by looking at seed oysters that ordinarily get washed out the teeth before you even bring the muck aboard, so I save a bit of the bottom I didn't wash out with the hose and dump it on the table and go down to see what's going to be coming up in a few years. Two or three years you got a bed of clams, littlenecks. Five or six years you got chowders.

"Some shell is thirty years old. Bloom Brothers of New Haven, they had a boat off New Jersey found a shell that scientists estimated was two thousand years old.

"Besides clams, the dredge brings up, in springtime, a few sleepy sand dabs. Once in a great while we get a lobster, but we like too stay away from the sort of cover they like. Plenty of crabs, spiders by the dredgeload in some places, a few rock crabs. Old bottles. Some things really can clog you up in the harbors: rotted-off pilings, bicycles, baby carriages, and shopping carts. Off Stratford Point we got the tip of a light plane wing. I called the divers and they came out and found the rest of the plane and two bodies. I didn't hang around. The nicest thing besides clams I ever found was up the Thames by the navy base, a silver teaspoon that by the engraving was off an old steam-powered battleship. I forget her name and I gave the spoon away.

"Other times you bring up sour bottom, a yellow, hard-wash bottom, and you know it's going to be no good if you stay there all day."

From time to time he lowered the window to punctuate his theory with more urgent matters. "Hey, Dave, wanna bang those teeth a little." Or, "Hey, Dave, let's knock them teeth out." Dave would perform the required dentistry with a sledgehammer kept by the mast for this purpose. "You've got to keep adjusting," Captain Bob would say. "The bottom is a funny thing."

It was getting along in the afternoon and I asked him who did his cooking. He shook his head and laughed. "I guess I do. I have one of them start it off, but when it gets serious, usually I have to get into it . . . There's no point in having one of them spend two hours and having the meal get smaller and smaller . . . all dried out before it's even served. So I cook it myself."

"How do you recruit your crews?"

"Somebody they suggest when they're quitting. Usually they last about a year. One day they come around with a friend and say, 'Try this guy, Captain Bob—he'll be OK.' Funny thing is they've always been right. At least the last ten years or so we been doing it this way."

"And after that, do you ever see them again?"

He looked ahead for a while, then reached over the wheel to the big compass upon which sat his latest cup of coffee. "No," he said. "Most of the time when they leave I never see them again."

Bob Bishop himself has a family back in New Haven. He started off shellfishing in a Guilford creek with an eighteen-foot New Haven sharpie, the traditional flat-bottomed Connecticut sailing oyster boat, which is much like the more famous Chesapeake waterman's craft. His had no mast, however, being propelled by an outboard. "One winter I lost her to the ice up the creek. Either that or someone stole her. All I know is come spring, she was gone."

Later he worked as a party boat fisherman taking small groups out for bass and bluefish. At one time he skippered for the Ram Island Company, owned by the famous Molloy family of Harrison's Landing above the Coast Guard Academy. He's worked twenty years with the hydraulic suction dredge method, the last ten aboard *Utz*.

Usually he's able to get home each night from whatever Connecticut port he's working, not in the *Utz*, which gives him only six knots per hour, but by car. That is, unless he has to stay aboard to protect the boat. Long Island ports are more remote, so he and his crew stay aboard, coming home only on the weekends. I asked him if any of his own family would be going into the business. He laughed and shrugged.

Robert M. Utz, named after her builder, an oysterman who is still living, on Long Island, has been in business as oyster dredge and clammer since she was built at Tottenville in the glory days of Staten Island shellfishing. Although designed on graceful sailboat lines, she had always been motor-driven, her original engine being one of the famous Cooper-Bessemers. Rebuilt in the 1950s when Frank and Joe Dolan of Guilford owned her, the trunnel (or treenail—that is, wooden peg) fastenings are still good. The boat is worked all year round except when the ice is too thick. Icebound in port, there's always plenty to do, and Captain Bob gets paid for "painting and fixing up." Big maintenance jobs come at haul-out time. In fact *Utz* had just come to us after her yearly stay on the marine railway, when her red bottom, gray topsides, and white pilothouse and trim had received a coat of paint. As for matters beyond the cosmetic, the only replacement was one plank back by the stern.

Once, when the dredge was aboard, Captain Bob grabbed a crescent wrench and flung himself out the pilothouse door and down off the gallery with the recklessness of John Wilkes Booth bailing out of Lincoln's box at the Ford Theater. On the way down he'd shouted, "You steer! You know where you are."

We were in a tight circle to port and so we left the wheel alone, and the old *Utz* kept going round and round while Captain Bob attacked the cage with the help of the crew. The circle moved on the tide, however, and when a lobster pot buoy threatened to become entangled in our propeller, one of us grabbed the wheel and wiggled the old *Utz* around the menace. This was so much fun we took turns driving around trying to keep free from other buoys.

With Captain Bob back at the helm, we worked the Groton Long Point beach, Mumford Cove mouth, and some deep water off the state park at Bluff Point, taking a bite here and there when we figured there was "a chance for a sign." The wind was strong, but offshore, allowing us to get in close to beaches that would, in the prevailing southwesterlies of summer, prove dangerous or at least inconvenient lee shores. "You get even a little swell sometimes and the dredge will just bounce along the bottom."

As Captain Bob had predicted, the Groton Long Point beach proved too hard, nor was there much of a sign off Mumford Cove, itself one of the traditional shallow-water grounds and where, except for some sea clams on one edge, we had found an alarming mortality where only two years before Tim had, in an extensive scientific survey, found the area packed. "It is true that the town has a sewer outfall at the top of the cove," Tim said, "but the clams died off mainly from overcrowding. They should have been depurated."

We got into a fruitful vein, however, off Bluff Point and in one dredge heaped the big culling table.

"OK, this is more like it."

We all looked at each other as if to say, "Now that we know how to do it, this is simple. What an easy, pleasant way to make a living. Just dip and take."

Down went the dredge. We were all out on the gallery now except for Eddy who was making festival down on the deck among the boys, and Tim who was also down there making use of his foul-weather gear to slosh through various kinds of marine residue. The crew culled chowders and littlenecks into wire baskets. Eddy opened up a littleneck and, tilting his beard toward the sun, commenced slurping. He smacked his lips. "Hey, am I ever so happy I told them people not to put that sewer outfall off here."

The sun was warm on my back. The sea was flat. The lighthouses and the islands were still taking off. Why didn't everybody do this for a living?

Up came the dredge, dripping just as before. Dave yanked the release and down poured a clatter of stuff just like before. Round objects the same size. Just as many as before. At least as many. Dave and his partner dug in.

"Hey, stones," said his partner. "They're all stones."

And they were. All those round, hard things that looked just like clams. Every last one of them. It was as if for our arrogance what was indeed a load of quahogs had been, by a kind of Rumpelstiltzkinian incantation, turned into stones. We even looked at the baskets where the last load had been culled to make sure they hadn't been transformed.

They hadn't, and we made several other passes with the dredge that were in Captain Bob's estimation "worthwhile." But there was always at the back of our mind now the load of stones.

The winter sun was low and we were glad for the heater in the pilothouse as we put the west behind us and headed home. Down on the deck Eddy stuck it out with Dave, helping him put the clams in burlap bags.

"Hey, Cap." At the door was the crew who had discovered the stones, a long, lean young man with a tangle of black hair over his face. He held the enamel pot from the fierce stove below. He held it out as if he were passing the hat, and in his eyes there was all the sundown sadness of a young man away from home looking for his supper. "I mean what do you want me to do with these onions?"

Captain Bob left me the wheel and went to the door. After some sotto voce instructions he patted the young man on the shoulder, and I realized that in the whole day we had worked together I had not heard hear him yell or even swear. The only time he had raised his voice was when one of the crew down on the deck had cupped his ear to signify he did not hear the instructions through the wind. Now the young man looked into the pot as if maybe the onions, like the quahogs, might have turned into stones. Not entirely satisfied this was not the case, he clapped the lid home and faded into the darkening air.

At out berth up-river we off-loaded the burlap sacks of clean clams. The ones we'd taken from the polluted waters we had already returned to polluted waters. Eddy Edwards backed his pickup down to the pier and the crew used his handcart to load the truck.

The next day he and a couple of stout companions loaded the sacks into one of his tin boats and set off down the Poquonnock River out under the railroad bridge, down through the cut where stand the ruins of the old trolley bridge, and into the wider spread of the river. Drifting with their gunnels almost awash, they opened the sacks and sowed the quahogs into the shallow waters, so that the townspeople in years to come might at leisure dig their dinner from the primal ooze.

THE SCATTERING
OF BELLE

Without planning and organization, most jobs could not be
done at all, and a progressive technique of work or play would be
inconceivable.

—George Soule, *Planning: U.S.A.*

Though earth hath engrossed the name, yet water hath proved
the smartest grave.

—Sir Thomas Browne, *Hydriotaphia*

T HE KETCH RIG held the bow of the old Norwegian lifeboat
solemnly into the gray seas. The captain gave the helm to his
wife and plunged below, his beard jutting a hole in the gloom
for him to follow. She tossed her hair off her cheek, but the ends were
knocked back by the hood, so she had to take one hand from the
wheel to make the adjustment to her tousled coiffure.

"I handled the watch coming up from Cape Town," she said in
her South African accent, "I bloody well ought to be able to take one
here in piddling old Fishers Island Sound."

The red nun, known as Intrepid Rock, however, jumped and
gagged. The nearest land was only a half-mile away, and it was covered with suburban cottages, but it was this very promontory that was
contributing to the sea's discomfort. The bleakness was increased when
you saw that most of the buildings were boarded up for the season.

"Bloody American waters," said the captain's wife. "And this an
ocean-going craft."

She bit her lip and scowled. A wave hit the bow and the spray
flew over the rest of the party, who were sitting on hatches or up
against edges, huddled in the wind like so many sea birds. From under their up-turned collars, out from under their down-jammed hats
and drawstringed hoods, they searched each other for news.

"Wind's against the tide," said old Ed. "I broke a forestay here
once on my little Herreschoff sloop." He had water running off his
nose which was made more noticeable by his face being framed by a
hood. In his lap a silver can gleamed in the dull light.

"I'm glad the children are below," said a woman huddled next to Ed.

"Why, you think they're too young to see a funeral?"

"I was thinking more of what represented sound seamanship." She pushed her glasses back up her nose, though they were covered with salt. "As for the funeral, as you call it, I hardly think that the scattering of ashes of an elderly person they hardly knew will make any impression on them at all." Nevertheless, she indulged in a glance at the silver can in Ed's weathered hands. "In fact," she went on, "when I just checked them a moment ago, they were all quite content with their comics and soda pop."

"I wish we'd been able to get organized a little earlier," said another hooded face. "As it is, how many hours of daylight do we have left?"

"If you call this daylight," said the woman in glasses.

"Wind against the tide," croaked Ed. He had cranked his stiff arms out so that the can was well away from his body.

I worked the valves of the cornet soundlessly, blowing into the horn to warm the pipes.

The captain emerged from the cabin with a blue turtleneck on, stretching his bearded chin, plucking at the cloth with a long finger.

"There." He fingered the collar. "I felt the bloody thing was only at the edge of a proper ecclesiastical furl."

"You look marvelous, luv," said his wife and she shoved a damp curl back under her hood.

"And how about this?" The captain commenced a buoyant gesture that looked like his old rum-bottle flourish, but which halfway through must have struck him as blasphemous because he fluttered off into something more "ecclesiastical." At the end of a now limp hand hung a slim volume the shade of his sweater. "Ah, *those in peril . . .*" he muttered.

"What's that, luv?" said his wife. "I'm doing my bloody best."

"*Those in peril on the sea,* luv. Old hymn, traditional." He tried a bolder shake on the binding. "In any case, luv, I was addressing the ship's bugle."

"Good heavens, luv, you're not going to sing it, are you?"

"I was going," he said, "to recite it. Traditionally."

"Fine," I said. "There is a tune to it, but I'm not sure I'll be able to move my valves much longer in this cold. How about something I can do open horn like 'Taps'?"

"Perfect," he said.

" 'Taps'?" croaked Ed. "What the deuce is this: a friggin' military funeral?"

"You were the one who asked me to play, Ed."

"I did?"

"Damn it, yes. You called me up, then later stopped me in the street, said you knew I played."

"I thought we were talking about Noank sloops."

"That, too," I said, "so if you don't like 'Taps,' I'll try using the valves on "Rock of Ages," or "The Old Rugged Cross" . . . "I Walked in the Garden Alone". . .?"

Increasingly sour airs ruffled the threads of Ed's magnificent white eyebrows. The silver can clattered about in his hands.

"What a Friend We Have in Jesus," I said, just to warm him. "How Great Thou Art."

"All right, all right." He huddled way down in his hood but could not put his hands over his ears. "Jesus, 'Taps'!" Something flew from his face.

The captain looked on the deck at Ed's feet, as if he thought some permanent part of the old man had broken loose, but it had only been the word *taps* that Ed had expectorated like beer foam.

"At least," said Ed, " 'Taps' . . . is wordless and it's short, isn't it? That's not the one that goes on and on and on, is it?"

" 'Tattoo' goes on a bit," I said, "and 'Evening Colors' may be sustained in order to compensate for any trouble aloft in the lowering."

"Lowering?" Ed craned about and hunched as if expecting a boom or a sail or maybe the entire sky.

"Flag," I said. "Once on a warm, buggy Virginia evening when the flag halyard—"

" 'Taps' doesn't have any words, does it?" With the wind at his eyebrows it was hard for me to see if he were stringing me out again. After all, he was sitting there with her ashes in his hands.

They had not been lovers, though apparently at one point she'd tried to make it that way. Back in the thirties, he had driven up to the New London police station in his Rolls Royce, two big brass headlights stuck on the fenders, and requested a place to sleep for the night. The police offered their pool table, which he accepted. The point of this story to her was how cheap he was.

According to him, it had been more complicated. He had been traveling from the Caribbean to Canada. She, as had many of his friends along the route, had invited him to stop the night. He was exhausted

and went right to sleep in her back room, but was awakened by conversation between women at the front door. While he had been asleep,
she'd unpacked all his vests and hung them about the room so that
they were perched on lamps, chairs, even curtain rods, hung, as he
put it, "like so many breeding fruit bats." When all was ready, she
phoned a neighbor woman over for tea and was in the process of
coyly denying her entrance when Ed awoke. "In the bad light, damned
if I didn't think she'd raised a flock of actual fruit bats. I'd had enough
of them where I'd just come from, so I took off out the back window
myself, and of course I didn't have any money to pay for a hotel because I'd taken my wallet out to sleep."

    " 'All's asleep, go to sleep,' " he now sang. "Aren't those the words
to 'Taps'?" This time the foam from his juicy enunciation hung from
his lips. "Taps."

    "In any case," I laughed, "I'm sure not going to sing it with the
horn sticking out of my face."

    "Rudy Vallee did it," said Ed. "I thought you might ask us to *all
join in.*" He wiped his mouth from the sheer tastelessness of such a
meal. "I thought you might ask us to *all join in.*"

    "Well, all I know," said the captain's wife, "is that I am to steer."

    "After the ceremony," said the captain, "that is, with your kind
permission, Ed, in the dinghy, some of these good people"—he indicated the slickered sea birds huddled in their hoods—"they were to
assist in the taking of coal from the abandoned lighthouse."

    "Coal?" Ed looked at the can in his hand.

    "The stove that you're paying us with for this trip," said the cap-
tain's wife. It might not have come out of her quite so bleakly but the
head seas were yet nasty off the promontory and she had the kicking
spokes in her hands.

    "Your, ah, stove," said the captain, "which we understand, mind
you, is only to be ours for the winter, and in your kind harbor, that
stove might run quite efficiently, our horn-playing friend assures us . . ."

    It made me nervous to have been the middleman. I wiggled the
valves.

    "He assures us the stove shall run quite efficiently," continued
the captain, "on some coal abandoned . . . ah, properly abandoned on
that . . . abandoned lighthouse up ahead."

    Ed looked at me.

    "North Dumpling Light," I said.

    Ed moistened his lips.

    "North Dumpling Light," I said again and by way of advancing
the argument pointed my horn. "An abandoned small mound of pea

coal, ah, abandoned halfway up on the left side of the path to the house." I kept my arm out with the horn pointing, but Ed would have none of it. "Pile's about the size of a pitcher's mound, Ed. Major league."

"I didn't suppose," he said at last, "that Just Adventuring Around would pay for itself."

The captain's wife raised her eyebrow on that one.

"North Dumpling Light," I said.

"Belle always liked that lighthouse." He stared at the urn.

It was strange to think that such a large woman with such a large life could have been squeezed into that small can.

I had last seen her the previous winter when I accidently came across her one dark afternoon while looking at a house that was for sale. The heat had been off in the front part of the building and the walls were running with moisture. The only comfort lay in a rectangle of light toward the back of the ramshackle house, but the woman who owned the place kept trying to avoid that area. Finally, I insisted, and when the door was opened, there, gaily lit, ensconced upon her plush Victorian couch in the only heated room, was Belle.

She and the couch took up most of the room that was left over from piles and boxes of books. Her white hair swept down over her shoulders. I had only seen it up in a bun. She was dressed in a low-cut dress I'd never seen and over the décolletage was spread lacework that looked disturbingly like the antimacassars on the back and arms of her furniture. As the room was very hot, she kept fanning herself with a slim volume of what turned out to be *The Harp-Weaver* by Edna St. Vincent Millay. Did she always dress like that when she was home alone, or had she heard us out there in the hollow dampness of the other apartment and prepared for our inevitable visit?

Of course I did know she lived back there. I just hadn't realized it was the same house, for her apartment lay hard by the hedgy side lane heading up from the cove. Ed and I would be lurching by from bass fishing just after dusk, and I'd rap on the vertical sheathing, "Belle Morton, your time has come!" "Don't do that," he'd say, "she'll ask us in to talk about Sinclair Lewis or South America." So we never went in and I had to be content to meet her in other people's houses.

There she would fill the stoutest chair in the room, making it into a kind of throne, and regale us with her days when Sinclair Lewis and Theodore Dreiser would come calling and get drunk and fall down "behind the hedge murmuring stanzas." Or celebrating with Archie Binns the day *Lightship* came out. Consoling publisher Curtis Hitchcock's widow the day he dropped dead on the street right after signing the contract for Malcolm Lowry's *Under the Volcano*. Or the night

Rockwell Kent, spouting "free love," just back from that "dreadful *Direction* voyage," tried to "board her at Ausable Falls." Or was it just back from Resurrection Bay, the boarding at Arlington, Vermont? These were the things she had yet to work out. It was known she was down on her luck and would take baby-sitting jobs, but whenever any-one called she was always unavailable, working she was, on her "auto-bee-og-raphy."

But there she was for us, giving a rare "at-home," and once we were in, to the great scandal of the landlady, Belle would not permit us to depart.

And did she have tales to ruin a house sale! Ghosts, she heard. Old Captain So-and-so, deacon of the Noank Baptist Church back in the old days when it was dry. "So he had to keep his liquor in the cellar, go down for it, don't you know, in the middle of the night, and I still hear him going down there . . . [dramatic pause] . . . rustling around and then . . . he comes up, his step lighter on the tread."

That was her way with a phrase, "his step lighter on the tread." "Very literary," Ed would mutter. One day I went to visit him and he was typing with irate-citizen fury. "Letter to the editor, again, Ed? *New Republic* or I.F. Stone?"

"No," he muttered, "a list of Belle's lies."

"You mean it isn't true about Rockwell Kent just back from that awful *Direction* voyage?"

"Oh, she did know him. We all did. And he did talk a lot of free love crap at one point, and I was there, but he certainly did not try to 'board her.' And, yes, she did know all those Sinclair Lewis people. What I don't like is she thinks she knows . . . all about me. I've got so far . . . thirty-two of these. Thirty-two lies about me she tells all about town."

And old Captain So-and-so, the ghost in the cellarage, how had he married? Why going around Cape Horn, of course. Just before dusk he noticed a sail behind him. A great storm that night. "More than Egyptian darkness," and a terrible beating they took, but sur-vived for the next day when they saw something white, something white wafting aft upon a barren Patagonian rock. Not a sail, mind you, but where the sail had been last seen. He hoves-to and dispatches a yawl boat. (Belle, besides being literary, always prided herself on getting in the nautical terms.) On the rock was a young woman, a young, beautiful woman, waving her dress. Her ship had sunk during the storm. Sole survivor. She had been on her way to San Francisco to marry her fiancé. It was her wedding dress she waved to save her life. Naturally the Noank captain married her instead.

The landlady was not amused by all this local romance, and pity for her agitation finally won out with us over sympathy for Belle. Outside, in the damp again, the landlady whispered, "Of course . . . if you do buy the house, that old woman will have to go."

We did not buy the house. Someone else did and Belle went, and her new apartment was in another town and had treacherous stairs. They found all the books by other people, but none by her, and now her narratives were compressed into this small can.

And Ed had it all in his hands. "She thought it was 'cute,' " he said. "The lighthouse."

Spray, just a few drops, swayed from his lip. In his hood he knew he too would have looked cute to Belle, but his eyes let us know he was just putting up with things like hoods and lighthouses because of the occasion.

"Usually," he said, "she didn't like cute things, didn't make the usual judgment. But this lighthouse was apparently all right that way." He sat there being all right that way.

"Well, 'Taps' it is, then," said the captain. He took the moment to correct his wife, slightly touching the spoke, not, of course, with his actual hand, but the hymn book, just the corner of it. Indeed we had fallen off, burying the lee rail in an alarming amount of dirty white water.

"We have seas like this all the time," said the woman with the glasses. "Out in Martha's Vineyard."

"Well, you know how men are about their precious boats," said the captain's wife, and she flicked the slowly descending hymnal away from her spokes.

"Belle always said that men in this village were about boats the way gauchos were about their horses when she was in Argentina," said Ed. "That was the best she could put it, she said. Admitting even that much, she said, took her thousands of miles of travel and a revolution. She always had to have a revolution when she traveled. I worked in the Caribbean twenty years and never got to have one. She'd just traipse through . . ." He blotted his mouth. "Just traipse through and according to her, she'll leave a whole swath of smoking firing squads behind her."

"I don't understand," said the woman with glasses. "You mean she was herself a revolutionary?"

Ed's free hand washed the idea of Belle's being a revolutionary from the conveniently low sky.

"Well," said the woman with glasses, "Belle to me was a whole revolution herself. I like that gaucho analogy. I like that one just fine."

"Was that the one where she claimed she was invited to watch the execution?" I said. "The revolution where they gave her the flag with the firing squad's bullet holes through it?"

"Yes, Belle went to some actual revolutions. You did that in those days. You went to them. Her husband was a journalist. She claimed her husband burnt it one night in a fit of jealous rage."

"Burnt the flag with the bullet holes you mean?" said the woman with glasses. "Merely because he was in a jealous rage over the revolution?"

"Well, over the man in the revolution, one of them. They did have men in the revolutions in those days and people often fell in love with them, as she said. She was in Bolivia, I believe, and that much was true."

"That was after the Argentine?" I felt I owed it, in lieu of a eulogy, to at least track Belle's activities carefully.

"No," said Ed. "I think that was after Mexico." A smack of spray flew aft, nicking selected passengers.

"Well, if you ask me," said the woman with the glasses, "this whole outing is just another example of how everything around here has to be sea-going macho. Why the hell do we have to . . . plow on so goddamn far out? For that matter, wouldn't the town dock have been good enough?"

"I'm afraid it was my fault, dearie," said the captain's wife. "I want to be warm this winter, if you don't mind."

"Yes, the coal," I said, "halfway up the lighthouse path on the left."

"Besides," said the captain, "isn't there something in the funerary regulations about performing a minimum distance offshore?"

"I heard there's somebody's ashes right now," said Ed, and he checked those in his lap, "somebody's ashes right now 'reposing' in the closet of one of our local clergymen for over a year now because he can't get out to sea far enough to satisfy the Department of Army Engineers."

"I don't believe it's the Department of Engineers," I said. "More likely something like a state graves committee."

"Well, he doesn't have a boat big enough to make it."

"Exactly why we are fortunate," I said, "to have this vessel here and its crew. Especially this time of year."

"I don't see anything fortunate at all about today," said the woman with glasses. "I think the whole thing should have been postponed to a more reasonable sea condition."

"It's almost always rough this time of year," I said. "Besides it had to be a day when everyone could make it." I indicated a quiet man sitting well forward, who fluttered an acknowledgment.

He had arrived at the last minute, in somber street clothes, midst muddled introductions. It was unclear if he were clergy, relation, executor, or possibly a representative of the state graves committee. Someone had given him a sou'wester jacket and though it was woefully short, he had donned it, his arms poking out so that it looked as if he had rolled up his sleeves in anticipation of some sort of gory employment.

"Yes," said the captain, and his eye shot out to the mysterious man, "we are all well apprised of the ceremonial nature of this journey."

"Well," said his wife, "I know it's not just ducking out to the dump, luv."

Wincing, the captain looked at Ed to see how he'd taken that.

Sensing he was on stage, Ed licked his lips. "The first time I ever heard that word was from Belle in 1927."

"A 1927 . . . dump?" The captain was still trying to deal with things head-on.

"She'd just come back from Argentina. Actually, I think she rather liked that 'macho' stuff. She was, you know, a bit 'macho' herself. They were in those days."

"A regular Tugboat Annie," said the woman with the glasses.

"Well, no," I said, "not exactly, would you say, Ed?"

"Her favorite story was about Ewell Thomas and that little fantail launch of his, or was it the converted catboat?"

"A Noank sloop converted to launch service," I said. "*White Cap,* she's up-country now drying out, going all to hell while somebody waits to take her lines off."

"She went along nicely through the harbor at about ten knots without making a ripple," said Ed. "Fine lines underneath her." He looked at me again to confirm this craft.

"Up on shore now with her transom hanging out."

"Sea-going macho stuff again," said the woman with the glasses. "What the hell's this transom hanging out stuff got to do with Belle?"

"That's where she got the idea," said Ed. He held up the can, less as a visual aid than as if he were raffling it off.

"Oh, Gawd," said the woman with the glasses. "Put that down,

Ed, before you spill it all over the place."

"There was a hurricane I believe coming up," said Ed.

"All the more reason," said the woman. "I knew today was ugly."

"In the story it was a hurricane," I said. "This isn't even the right time of year for a hurricane."

"Ewell Thomas was going around the harbor checking all his moorings," said Ed. "At least he was in Belle's favorite story."

"Because of this weather?" said the woman.

"The story, the story," I said. "Ed is telling a story. Belle's story, her favorite."

". . . in the fantail launch." He looked at me.

I waved him on.

"A man standing on the shore. In a homburg and dark topcoat, I believe. Had a can in his hand." Ed raffled it off again. The woman pulled it back down. "Shouted to Ewell from the shore, 'Come get me.' Ewell came, but told him he was in a hurry, storm was coming and so on. The man insisted, big song and dance about his wife's last wish"—

"And that was?" said the woman. "The wife's last wish was . . .?"

". . . was to be scattered . . ." He looked at the can.

"In that particular harbor," I added. "And he had to go back that day way inland for some reason."

"It was her favorite story," said Ed. He sat there with it all in his lap.

"I hate to say this," said the woman, "but it doesn't sound to me like you've finished this damn saga."

"He hasn't," I said.

Ed looked up. "It's where she got the idea."

"Yes," I said, "so Ewell says:'OK, get in the boat, but I warn you I gotta go fast as we can because of the storm.' Not much dignity, coattails flying, knees braced against the cockpit combing, man holding homburg one hand, scattering with the other, Ewell shouting . . ."

"When the storm was over, Mrs. Ewell . . ." Ed looked around. "Everybody here know Mrs. Ewell?"

"I think we are getting very near where we should, ah, make our move," said the captain.

"Listen, luv," said his wife. "Ed's not through with the eulogy yet."

"Sorry," said the captain and corrected the wheel this time with his whole hand.

"Mrs. Ewell," I said. "What did she say, Ed?"

"Not everyone here knows Mrs. Ewell."

"No one here knows Mrs. Ewell," I said. "Many people here don't even know Belle."

"Oh," said Ed, and he sat there staring down at the can in his fingers.

"For Godsakes, Ed," I said, "finish the story before we all run up on the lighthouse."

"I thought someone was making a eulogy over Belle."

"You were," I said, "or as close as we're likely to get to one. Now, Mrs. Ewell was washing out her house after the hurricane. It had been a real disaster. Carol or one of those in the 1950s. Anyway, the harbor water had been almost waist high in Ewell's house and there was a mark to show in the kitchen, silt . . . flood crap and . . ." I turned it back to Ed.

"Maybe I should stand up," said Ed, and he compromised by waving the can aloft.

"Ed," said the woman with glasses, "For Godsakes, do everything from as low a position as possible."

"All right." He took a breath as if he were going to blow up a balloon: "Mrs. Ewell, she sez, 'Eeee-welll . . .' " Ed looked around to see if he had offended anyone by the realism of his imitation of Mrs. Ewell's Yankee accent. Stone faces greeted him. He tried it again, but didn't back down one decibel on the twang. " 'Eeee-well . . . do you think . . . that woman's in he-ah?"

No one knew whether to laugh or not. Some of them perhaps had not heard all of it, or had forgotten just who "that woman" was supposed to be. One of the headsails tried to cue us by chattering, but the captain's wife sensed her error and eased helm enough to silence the sail. The bow wave soused and rattled aft.

"We had a story," said the woman in glasses, "a story just like that out on the Vineyard. Except it was all done from an airplane."

Everybody seemed too relieved to be on to the next business at hand to be annoyed.

"If that's all there's to be," said Ed, "I'll throw this over now."

The woman in glasses merely covered his hands with hers. The captain cleared his throat. "We should perhaps proceed as planned." He waved the hymnal and nodded to me.

"What's in that dark blue book?" said Ed. "The words to 'Taps'?"

I wiggled my valves. They had gotten very sticky during all the business about the dead woman's ashes in Ewell's kitchen.

The captain pointed to the leeward rail, then seemed to gesture for his wife to spin the wheel so the boat would head up into the wind and flatten out the angle of the deck.

"Shall I bring the CAN?" Ed held it aloft in one hand again, but this time had developed a maraca-shaker's mode. "Shall I bring the CAN?"

I wriggled my valves, then remembered that bugle calls required no manipulations, that, in fact, that was why the captain and I had chosen one. Nevertheless, there were my fingers and there were the valves and there too were the gray seas, and the gray seas kept my fingers running on the keys.

What I was afraid of, however, was not so much falling overboard as making a mess of the music. When in the Coast Guard, I had blown my reveille debut so off key as to constitute a Chinese fire drill. In an indirect way that had led to my being assigned to a lighthouse for duty, and damned if there wasn't another one dead ahead now.

To avoid making that mistake again I tried to remember what actual mechanical error I had committed and concluded that in the Coast Guard my mouthpiece had slipped at the last instant. At such moments my lips always seemed either too moist or too dry. I wished that like Bix and Louie, I had roughed the machined surface of my mouthpiece to prevent skids.

While I was going through all this, the captain had succeeded in arriving at the lee rail with Ed, the hymn book, and the urn. The wife, however, had not kept the bow into the wind. She had eased off, apparently at the captain's behest. He'd evidently come to sense that putting the ship in irons with some four sails luffing would create too undignified a clatter.

With the boat heeled now, however, the boom was periodically dipping to obscure Ed and the captain from me as I stood aft, one arm around the mizzen rigging, the other on the cornet. I could hear some torn speech, saw the captain touch Ed lightly on the arm. It was not a seaman's clutch in the pitch of the ship, but the hand of a publican as he leans across the bar in mid-yarn to wink you home to the punchline.

My own hand was not that delicate. I found it white-knuckled and fastened to the mizzenmast, just above and aft of the captain's wife at the wheel. It was this very mast, or rather its direct predecessor, that had, I recalled, at least according to the captain's adventure series film, carried away as they fought a gale off Sydney.

Nevertheless, I continued to find it a useful object in the world, this mast, for despite the captain's bedside manner, I felt myself but one step from a dance that would have had my embouchure on no other mouthpiece than the large, gray kiss of the aft-running sea.

> Eternal Father, strong to save,
> Whose arm hath bound the restless wave . . .

The captain's voice was amazingly precise considering the wind. I responded by moving my valves. I wasn't sure just how long "Those in Peril" would go on, but I was certain that at its close I would come in, and somewhere after me, or maybe during me, the can would go over.

> Who bidd'st the mighty ocean deep
> Its own appointed limits keep:

My valves were clanking. . . . A sharp look from the captain's wife.

To reassure her, I coughed and opened the cornet's water key, shook forth some residue.

> O hear us when we cry to thee

There was an amazing amount of water in the pipes of the cold cornet.

> O hear us when we cry to thee.

Was that my cue? Under the lowering boom a hand struggled up. Waved.

That certainly had the look of a cue.

Perhaps it was for the helm, however. After all, if we did not even up the deck a bit there would be a ceremonial problem—to have us barreling along spewing sorrow just as in the farcical Ewell story.

There was, thank God, the distant relative, or executor, or graves committee man, or whoever. Wouldn't he actually have the final say? He was looking right at me, an expression of slight pain on his face, truly a committeeman's pain. Or was it the pinch of an unfamiliar hood he was endeavouring to strip in homage? The lurch of the untrustworthy deck?

Cold against my lips was the mouthpiece. We lifted upon a wave and there was the captain, head and all, and he was pointing at me with the flopping hymnal. Behind him, like a hunchback concertina player squeezing out the finale to "Lady of Spain," was Ed, struggling with the can.

"Of course," I thought, "he's got to open it. He's got to open it up. And to help him in his moment of need, I must play."

But what was this coming back to me in my face? Not ash certainly, but something more terrifying:

Notes.

Spits of "Taps," scraps of material more advanced.

Nearer my peril to thee? Those in Jesus on the sea? Was it going to be the old mandarin Reveille fiasco all over again? Was I going to go through the world on all solemn occasions with which I was trusted performing a cornet buffo?

Angrily now I fought against the past, all those stacks and stacks of bad notes that had not vanished, but had somehow been retained in the atmosphere. It was not now just a matter of doing something correctly. I had to blow away the foul contagion of the universe.

The captain was signaling again. Bernstein in parody. What did he understand of our customs? What did he understand of music, anyway? Even his wife was screaming at him. It looked as if he were fighting off bees. A cloud of them. The air thick. More like butterflies. Soft wings without proper hinges, their articulation provided only by the wind.

So here it was: ashes after all.

The literal taste of death on my lips, worse than even my own sour notes.

"For Christsakes, luv, ease your helm."

The captain pulled specks from his lips like an angry cigarette-smoker peeling wrapper dottle.

"For Christsakes, luv, you put us right into the wind."

"Well, luv," she shouted, "you're not the one with the bloody trumpet fahting in your ear, now are you?"

"What shall I do with this can?" Ed held the bottom in one hand, the top in the other, his eyes wind-bright as any percussionist who had waited out his overtures and scherzos for a crack at the triple forte finale.

"You, sir." The captain was looking right at me. "Have you quite concluded?"

I wiped a few dark things from my lips. At least his anger confirmed that I had actually been playing, that some sort of music had been escaping, as stifled Belle herself had billowed forth at last from her urn.

"Yes," I said. "It won't get any better."

"Then ready about," he cried. "Christ, we're damn near onto that bloody lighthouse."

His gesture of command had him facing the old man now toe to toe, and the old man still had the damn thing in his possession, one part in each hand, like a child that had taken apart something from the adult world and could not now put it back together. The captain was furious because without the object being fixed he could not go

on. His own hands trembled above the damned thing. Should he . . .
fix it, or fling it?

"I think we're supposed to Save-the-Can," said Ed. "Isn't that what
we're supposed to do now: Save-the-Can-for-the-Mantelpiece?"

With a single swipe the captain stripped the two parts of the urn
from Ed's hand and shot them into the water. "Hard-a-lee!"

The wife spun the helm, and the ship responded, the sails swing-
ing over our heads as we all ducked, our heads at last bowed.

PART FOUR

Winter

... Work while you can
his hopeless spirit thrived to him to say,
along those treacherous coasts.

—John Berryman, "Dream Song" #178

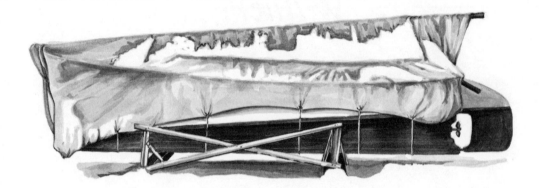

THE SEA IN WINTER

The smouldering enormous winter welkin!
—Gerard Manley Hopkins

THERE IS no help from the sky which is a lid without the comfort of a lid, but the winter sea is held out of the harbor except when the wind blows the wave over the wall. This does not happen on every wave or even every other one, so that as you sit on the bench in the lee of the diesel shack and listen to the fishermen on the rusty dragger across the pier, you are also searching half-consciously for the rhythm of the scene.

The dragger is not the type to end up in your average Mystic Summer Outdoor Art Festival painting. She is rather one of those designs that a dozen years ago were to be the hope of the offshore fishing industry. Her lines are more bloated than saucy, her stern broken down at her very conception to facilitate the demands of the new technology. But it is the texture of the hull that is most discouraging, her once-white steel soured to the yellow on some vile underrim. In the windows of her pilothouse are plastic curtains that might more likely bedeck the shower stall of a cheap motel. Perhaps like the jetty beyond, they have their role to play in keeping out the winter sea.

A clang of the forward scuttle, a head and shoulders emerge like a prairie dog. It is a large man in his mid-twenties holding a full-sized dresser mirror above in one hand. With the other he combs his moderately long, black hair. This occupation holds him for several minutes as measured by the spume raining just beyond the boat. He interrupts his toilet only to shout cheerful obscenities down the scuttle. His only problem is the wind fights him for the mirror.

His mates eventually come on deck through the pilothouse. There is one who is some twenty years older than the rest and he busies himself at the rail by checking the rig that holds the trawl door to the gallows frame when the net is not in use. There is a naked light bulb strapped to the gallows frame. The light bulb is more ominous than the great rusty cable on its drum or the heavy net doors. The fragile light bulb. They work the rig at night. Out there.

The other men lean up against the far bulkhead. It was what kept them from the sea, but now it might as well be any wall ashore. They are kidding the young man in the scuttle. He has ducked below to exchange the big mirror for a clean sweatshirt, all this a miracle of seamanship because of the mirror's size, the parry and flaw of the wind, and the tightness of the scuttle. There is nothing to do for him now but to swing over the inside bulkhead and step ashore.

Because of the wind he must shout into the outdoor phone on the diesel shack. He explains to his wife that he is flying off the island. He wants her to come to the mainland airport in an hour to pick him up. Yes, he knows the ferry boat is much cheaper, but it does not leave right away. Exactly when does it leave? She doesn't get the point, he says. It really doesn't matter when it leaves. It doesn't even matter how much cheaper it is. He is aware she was not expecting him home for dinner. He will take her out. Yes, that will be more expensive. No, it is not that they made all that much money on the trip. How much did they make? She doesn't get the point. He wants her there, at the airport in an hour. And how will he get to the island airport? He will get there. He will take a cab. Yes, a cab. That is why she should bring some money to the mainland airport, to pay for the plane, or part of it. It is all a very complicated idea in the wind, sending your voice home on a cable beneath the winter sea.

Twenty dollars.

If you have to know, baby.

Three weeks and I have twenty dollars to show.

And the hair-combing all undone by wind.

He goes below, and a station wagon pulls up to the pier. It is filled with women and children. It might well be headed for the shopping plaza if the island had one. What the island has is the harbor, beaten on by the sea. And this rusty dragger.

"Go ahead, talk to her."

The crew along the rail has singled out what seems to be one of their members, a big man, bushy in foul-weather gear. He indeed looks as if he's been three weeks offshore.

"Go ahead, talk to her. She's your wife."

They push him away from the comfort of the bulkhead. The older man at the gallows frame grins. This is going to be a good show. After three weeks at sea, this good show.

And the wife knows her part. Sticks her head out the station wagon jammed with curlers and kids and starts screaming that matches the saline content of the air. Straight into the wind go her words. No matter. They get where they're going and the big, bushy man deflates inside his foul-weather gear. His hands thrust out to compensate for the body's shrinkage. He is pleading not only to her and her packed car, but the crew behind him along the rail and to the gathering audience in the lee of the diesel shack.

"Hey, what do you want me to do, honey?"

"Get home and do something for me."

He turns to the crew, his hands out, you heard her, she wants me to get home, she wants me to . . .

The young man who is going home strides past him, his clean sweatshirt, his hair plastered, a gym bag in one hand.

"You want me to go fishing with these guys?" says the bushy man. He tugs at the man going home and shouts past to his wife. "Honey, you think I should have been aboard this tub fishing these weeks? Well, look at this guy."

The example obliges, adjusting his hair while the old man at the light bulb snickers.

"You see this guy. Three weeks. Out there." The busy man turns past his amused gallery to where the sea obliges with a great smack, fountain, and patter. "Out there three weeks for twenty bucks."

"Then get home and stop pretendin you-wah ah fish-i-min."

"But, honey, what do you want me to do at home?"

He gestures at the rigging, none of which, of course, is at home. "I mean, honey . . ." He rests his case.

"Take out the gah-bidge," she says. "Build me a shelf."

His knees buckle. His hands fly straight up. "Build a shelf?" He turns to the crew.

Hey, she's your wife.

"Build a shelf?"

Behind him the sea falls into the harbor.

Just how cold is the sea in winter? Professor Frank Bohlen of the University of Connecticut at Avery Point is interested in storm water. He bottles it just before and after a big wind and he does this all year. Just before a hurricane, when the boat ramp is clogged with fishermen trying to extract their boats from the oncoming blow, Professor Bohlen is shoving his small, wooden, flat-iron skiff the other way, into the water. In the bottom of the boat are two or three empty bottles. "I'm the only guy I know who goes to sea with empties and brings back full ones," he says, and off he goes. Out in all seasons, he often feels his way home at night by reading the subtle changes in the tide rips like a blind man navigating scuffs and chaffings in carpet texture no one else feels.

While he is interested in sediment transport, he also takes the temperature of the water.

Professor Bohlen's stations range all through Long Island Sound. He finds the coldest month to be February, from the middle toward the end, depending upon the year. "But there is little significant variation from year to year in sea-water temperature no matter what has been happening on land." In February lows it may get down to minus one degree centigrade. Sea water freezes at about two below (28.6 F). The average, however, for the coldest month is two degrees above freezing, an abyss reached after a smooth but steep decline beginning the first week in October. The sea stays pretty much the same from the middle of January through the last week in March, when it begins an upward climb at a little slower rate than the corresponding descent. The end of April matches the end of November.

There are variations, of course, depending upon the depth of the water, nearby influx of fresh water, and local configurations of land which may slow or accelerate the mix. "There is, however, a fairly constant horizontal diffusion throughout the Sound, and that mixture also corresponds pretty much with the water out on the continental shelf as far as winter temperature goes. There is a great deal of energy in the winter sea," says Professor Bohlen, smacking his lips, "and that gives us some rather nice events." He points to a chart showing the peaks of a sediment transport after just such a "winter event." "Thought with all those jars of water I was going to knock the bottom out of the boat on that one."

That energy is why the difference between the temperature at the top of the water and the bottom, a summer separation familiar to every diver, will close abruptly in mid-September and the water will be the same temperature from surface to floor until the middle of March, when a slight separation occurs that becomes significant the last weeks of April.

The large sheets of ice that occasionally seem to fill the Sound are not, however, Professor Bohlen says, the offshore water freezing, but ice produced in brackish and fresh water upstream flowing out to sea and rafting up, tenting and fusing at the low air temperatures. "That's why when you see dog footprints on the ice out by Seaflower Reef you needn't worry about where the animal went. He was probably chasing a squirrel ten miles up the Thames River a week ago."

When queried about survival equations tied to varying sea-water temperatures, Professor Bohlen shakes his head. "Academic," he says, "academic. You go over out there now and you're gone sooner or later. The sooner or later depends more on the shape you're in and a little bit on what you're wearing. The important thing to remember is that there's not apt to be a hell of a difference between the sooner and the later."

There have been people, of course, who have survived considerable immersion in the winter sea. Recently, off Alaska, a trawler started to go down, and among those who jumped were two who came ashore safety. They were dressed in the new, so-called "survival suits" that combine technique, learned from such unholy antecedents as the skiing, scuba-diving, and space industries. And the suits look like it, too, giving one the appearance of a moon man who isn't sure if he's been invited to slalom, snorkle, or schuhplatteltanz, a hard act to pull off for long while working the deck of a trawler where often not all the crew are dressed for the party.

"What are you supposed to do?" says one local fisherman, "stand there shining in your immortality suit while all your buddies who are going to die in their jeans and boots admire you?."

"We can't call them survival suits anymore," says a clerk in a place that sells everything for commercial fishermen from pelican hooks to wet notes. "They are helpful. They could be the difference between making it or not. But as for survival, no one can guarantee that. So we have to call them 'exposure suits.' That one we can guarantee."

Nevertheless sea traffic must move in winter as well as summer. As a lighthouse keeper stuck two and a half miles out to sea one winter, I do not recall a day when there was no ship working, and that included Christmas Eve gales and February sea smoke. There was even, to judge by the hilarity on the mid-watch radio, some enjoyment to it. The old skipper on the pilot boat would be growling admonitions to the apprentices in the small boats not to "get their toesies wet" while taking pilots off the freighters in fifty-knot winds. On calmer days the apprentices would put their more naive members off on ice cakes and return late than promised.

More practical, but still in the spirit of winter festival, was the day we were working a forty-foot utility craft out of a lifeboat station, our mission to transport an electronic technician, a notoriously indoor rating usually successful at finding impregnable, warm, closeted tasks for themselves. This time, however, the assignment was to adjust the blinking mechanism on a big sea bell. Had not the air been so classically winter clear, the buoy would have been out of sight of land. We could have stood by encouraging, or more likely jeering, him on, but instead left him there, to zoom even further offshore to have a leer at some folks we knew on the lightship who had recently acquired a considerable fame by almost having blown up the ship while trying to make a still in the boiler room.

As the bell and the technician shrunk together and then to nothing, we deck apes felt triumphant over our throbbing twin diesels, but when we returned an hour later to take our former simpering indoor man off and watched him step aboard with a new dignity, it occurred to me that his had been the interesting day—riding that deep bell with nothing at all in sight but a thin gray line on the horizon and it was all his: the immediate task in his hands, alone with his talent and his tools on a soft, crystal surge.

Some mariners actually do manage to make the most of going to sea in winter. Noank's Adrian Lane, who has skippered everything from his own hundred-year-old Crosby catboat to the Coast Guard's barque *Eagle*, once went down aboard a research vessel two hundred miles offshore in the January Atlantic. The ship took less than an hour to sink, but luckily Captain Lane had had the foresight to buy his own inflatable rubber raft. He and his crew spent a couple of days floating around before being picked up by a Norwegian freighter with a sharp lookout.

The freighter took the rescued crew the rest of the way across to Europe, where Captain Lane and men were wined and dined in fine style. "It's not exactly the way I'd plan a winter cruise," he says, "but it turned out to be a marvelous time and I still hear from the skipper who saved us."

Captain Lane spent last winter slowly traversing the Atlantic aboard a new research vessel. "Didn't see another ship sometimes in weeks. Frankly, I loved it. Of course, sometimes I'd relieve the watch and find the fellow staring at the rivets on the bulkhead. Young men brought up on television may find the winter sea boring, but I keep thinking, look, look, use your eyes. Somewhere out there in all that emptiness there might be someone just like I was."

Classically there is a respite in the winter sea. This is the two weeks framing the winter solstice when the halcyon breeds on water. The Greek poet Simonides explained this by strumming. "Whenever during the winter season Zeus brings a fortnight of calm, mortal men term the season windless, sacred to the brooding of the painted halcyon." Although modern birders have a tough time matching any of our birds with this calming creature, Aristotle in his *History of Animals* is happy to play Roger Tory Peterson:

The halcyon is not much larger than a sparrow. Its color is blue-green and inclined to red. The entire body, wings and in particular the neck parts, are a blend of such colors, though none are distinctly defined. Its beak is yellowish, long and thin.

John Pollard in *Birds in Greek Life and Myth* examines the halcyon literature carefully and concludes:

There seems little doubt from Aristotle's description that the bird he had in mind was the European kingfisher *(alcedo ispida)* which is not mentioned under any other Greek name ... It is in winter that it is seen in Greece and presumably the myth of its winter nesting was connected with this, since no Greek could have seen its nest in reality.

Certainly no Greek saw if offshore, for Hesiod has already warned the seafarer to "hang the well-wrought steering-oar over the smoke of the fireplace, and yourself wait for the time to come when a voyage is in season ... (for) it is an awful thing to die among the waves." Halcyon seasons may come, says the old wisdom, but one is best off not counting on a feathered friend to flatten a few tons of cascading sea.

The halcyon's nest, chief architectual product of this suspension of hydrostatic fury when it does come, has also, of course, been spotted by Aristotle:

Its color is reddish and its shape recalls that of long-necked gourds—there is a small opening just large enough to squeeze through, so that even if the nest is overturned the sea fails to get in.

Plutarch in *Oh the Cleverness of Animals* compares the halcyon nest to a fisherman's creel, closely woven so as to be waterproof. Indeed this is a clever animal, Plutarch says, when we consider that for bobbin and shuttle it possesses only a beak. He himself has seen many of these nests, as, of course, has most everyone. He has merely gone a little further in actually touching a number of them and in coming up with the business about the clever beak.

But it is the lyrical aspect of the halcyon that appeals most to me. Homer, in one of the backwaters of his military similes in the *Iliad,* tells us that Meleager's wife is named Alcyone, "because her mother wept with the plaintive cry of halcyon." The seventh-century B.C. poet Alcman says, "Would that I might be a kerylos, and flit over the wave-crest, in company with halycons, spring birds of the purple sea."

Perhaps what is really most admirable in this whole business of the halcyon is neither its cleverness nor its music, but its ability to maintain the one by means of the other in the face of the winter's sea, for while it is true that what we love in this bird is apparently mythical, and that even the waters and weather old *alcedo ispida* was imagined to contend with are Aegean, we still, in our northern waters, require some sort of plaintive cry as hot soup for the February soul.

Up-river with the ice nibbling the hull, Andy and Gunner are trying to crank over the old Palmer diesel on the lobster boat nestled between the two houseboats. The damp air is cut by woodsmoke from the stacks on either side. Members of the inshore fishing fleet, they do not intend to leave the slip, for in mid-winter the lobsters are, as Gunner says, "pretty well hunkered down." The few creatures that might blunder into their traps are not worth the great risk to the vessel.

A few weeks earlier a kid in a lobster boat lost power within hailing distance of the Groton shore and drifted all night to within less than a mile of the tip of Long Island. "That's fourteen miles as the crow flies," says Gunner, "with the next stop Spain."

With the big engine hatch open, the boat is exposed. You can look right down past Gunner and Andy into the unpainted bilge: heavy, rusting iron and damp wood. There is a big green keg, but it is not for beer; it is the hydraulic reservoir for the pot warp winch. Andy stands astraddle the engine like a man over a grave, unwilling to go down, but go down he must.

"Hey, it could be a submarine," says Gunner. "You know, Andy, it could always be a submarine."

"A submarine?" says Andy. "Hell, when I was on submarines in winter, it was a piece of cake. Goodbye mama and away we go. Come up in Bermuda or Miami or Spain."

"That's 'cause you was never on the old ones, Andy. You was never on the diesel jobs we had to come up to charge batteries come summer or winter. And in those days, remember, everyone was your enemy, so we had to pull the plug, be ready to pull the plug in less than thirty seconds. In winter the hatch rims would freeze right off the bat, freeze right up so we couldn't shut them. So you know what we did, Andy?"

"Goodbye mama and hello, Davy Jones."

"We had a bucket of glycerin handy. Painted the hatch rims with glycerin and the water'd hit and run right off. Then you could shut the damn hatch. That's what we did in winter on them submarines, a bucket of glycerin and you come up, look around, whip that brush all along the hatch and maybe, if you're lucky, that's all there is that day, just a bucket of glycerin and a quick brush."

After much foostering with glow plugs, battery charger, and a few ales, Andy and Gunner coach the engine into a black belch. It was hardly the plaintive cry of the ancient halcyon, but in its own way had the sharp, classic edge that on a cold day goes right through you to warm whatever it is we have these days for a soul. "Yessir," says Andy, "it's important to keep these fellows so they can kick over once in a while. After all, just because it's winter, you can't let everything die."

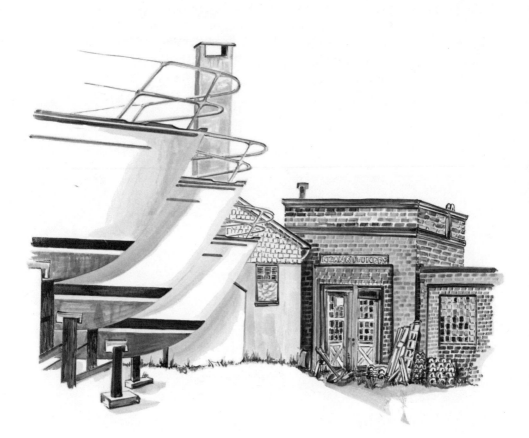

SONGS OF THE SEAHORSE

Nor shall winter storm obliterate our house of songs.
— After Pindar's "Ode for Xenocrates"

ONE OF THE BEST places to think about the sea during the winter is in the Seahorse Restaurant in Noank. In the off-season, hauled boats from the cove just over the hill crowd the low, white stucco building. "I don't understand why it's built that way," says Noank marine artist Jim Mitchell, "you'd think it was a fort, preparing for some kind of attack." High on their winter cradles, the sailboat hulls insure that The Horse is protected from direct confrontation with any view of the actual water, an item which is in evidence only by the sound of the bubblers working about the pilings to soften the harbor ice.

If you can see out of the tiny windows at all, beside the boats, you have looming across the narrow road the three-story Noank Foundry, a brick building that was once an auxiliary power station on the trolley line between Westerly, Rhode Island and New London.

It is a pleasantly integrated sort of industry; however, as among its activities the foundry casts the mushroom anchors that moor most of the local boats in summer. Lacking space and silence for such delicate operations as paper work and customer relations in the foundry itself, the owner uses the relatively quiet and soot-free Seahorse for his office, and after dark Seahorse parking overflows into the anchors and foundry sandpiles on up the old road to the missing bridge. Even in winter the great two-story foundry doors often stand open to vent the low fire inside. Snow falls on unsold anchors in front of the doors.

The air is laced with the smell of burning coal, wood smoke, and low tide. There is even more ripe mud than usual as a drag-line bucket has been working through the thin ice in the cove dredging up great gobs of the harbor bottom onto a mud barge behind the boat shed. On the unpainted building is a small sign:

> Bottom Cleaning
> Repairs
> Objects Retrieved

Mixed in with the nearby ice bubblers is the distant sound of North Dumpling Light, high and tinny, then what may be the deeper diaphone of New London Ledge.

The wood smoke comes from the fireplace inside the Seahorse. The smoke now goes out the new cinderblock chimney. The earlier tin stack often lost its draw, blocked by the looming hulls of the boats in the surrounding yard, so that in a damp east wind gasping patrons were to be seen in the street, drink in hand, shaking angry fists at sparless yawls and sloops. There were some experiments with a Franklin stove which not only reduced the drama of the back-draft, but alas, also that of the crackling fire.

Now even with the fire going, you can see the ceiling: what at first appears to be heavy trowel work, which artist Mitchell finds reminiscent of the Italian bars of the twenties built eastward down the line in Rhode Island. "I mean I may have made a living painting coal smoke at sea, but if I owned the place, even I'd put a big skylight in there."

Indeed it is dark in the Seahorse even in the day, as witness the recent Christmas Eve open house when the electricity failed in the afternoon. Half the village seemed to be in the place, though it was hard to tell until various neighbors brought in candles and flashlights.

However, according to Charlie Doughty, former owner, now resident accordianist, he "personally put the marks on the ceiling not to suggest anything at all in Westerly, but bluefish, the house specialty." On the paneled walls are more than the mere suggestions of fish. There are stuffed specimens—most of them look tropical. All have been actually hooked by Charlie and his cronies, many on January vacations down south.

The Doughtys are used to dispensing cheer. Charlie's family was in the ice cream-making business down the road across the river from Westerly in Pawcatuck before World War Two. "In those days, it was not unusual for each town to manufacture its own desserts." For years Roberta Doughty, who lives on Bright Acres, the oldest farm in the Fire District, made the Seahorse pies. "If a pie is four hours old," Roberta says, "that's an old pie to me." Charlie's daughters Eunice and Elsie grew up working at the Seahorse. After some rumors that the Seahorse would become a private yacht club, Charlie and his long-time partner Bruce Wakefield sold the business to two young men, John Hewes and Mark Swencer, who appreciate the Seahorse tradition and are running the business as usual. They have even rectified the Sea Horse's chief fault.

This difficulty was a problem Charlie suffered from that is known among the hardy folk who stay north as the "die-in-Floridas." Each

January he would head south and close the Seahorse a whole month. "Good God," said more than one patron, growing less hardy by the minute, "just when we needed the place the most."

As if in anticipation of this die-in-Florida syndrome, even the local stuffed fish such as blues and bass were embalmed by a famous Florida taxidermist so that they look to be iridescent, warm-water companions of the sailfish, dolphin, and barracuda which share the Seahorse walls. In summer and fall, when blues and stripers are in season, the stuffed fish on the wall come in for a certain amount of criticism by fishermen who may that very afternoon have landed the real thing, and even tried to sell a few still flopping at the back door.

"What's the story on that fish over there, Charlie?" some wag will say, pointing to a Floridized blue. "Catch that one off Fort Pierce? Must have been hard landing him without having the 'cudas take a chunk out of him."

"That fish," Charlie will explain, "was caught within a mile of where you are standing right now."

The comedian will then look at his feet to check the exact location. "Well, I was just out there, Charlie, and caught two dozen of them, but none of them looked like that. That must be a Fort Pierce special."

A number of people will now have gathered to compare the fish on the wall with fish they have personally known "out there." This allows folks to use non-Noank words like amberjack, grouper, and gulfweed.

To settle the issue, Charlie will finally say, "That fish on the wall there is a stuffed fish."

The fish which serves an important role in these arguments is the dolphin (dorado) near the kitchen door where it is flanked by other arbitrators: a wind-speed gauge, a wind-direction indicator, and a tide clock. Known primarily as a warm water inhabitant, this blunt-headed fish does make it up to Montauk and so can serve either as example of a local or an exotic. "Furthermore," says Charlie, "it changes colors rapidly when you catch it, so nobody can say we ain't got it correct up there on the wall."

In the private dining room, up in the back of the building, is the big government offshore chart. On it a patron has marked in felt pen the boundaries of the Mystic Marlin and Tuna Club which meets at the Seahorse. The line runs from the Hudson Canyon at the southwest to the Atlantis Canyon northeast and takes in the southern New England waters on out to the hundred-fathom curve. Considered along with the trout on the north wall, which Charlie caught in a pond a few miles inland, you might say the chart indicates the normal limits of Seahorse conversation.

There are, of course, exceptions to this provincialism, as represented by the southern fish and an even more tropic dream: a mural of grass-skirted maidens disporting on the interior stucco. The girls came out of the old South Sea syndrome to which coastal New England folk have been partial since the nineteenth century, a fantasy which received a boost at the close of World War Two when the Seahorse grew out of a hot dog stand. I remember the strange effect on my father, who'd just come back from the South Pacific. Family decisions to dine there the first year always seemed to involve the circumspection of a patrol planning a raid on a pillbox, an illusion enhanced by the building's bleak exterior masonry, though I think it was the maidens on the interior walls that might have been the real problem.

As lasting supper-room fresco, the girls were no Leonardo. They were crudely shaped, applauded by palm fronds more suited to the indoor theatrics of feathers and fans, leered over by the watery blues of a sea and sky never locally known. Their flesh was the hue of surgical tube, saved only by the plaster into which, even during the fifties, they were being absorbed. One wonders if by now, back of the paneling, they have not been sucked right through the surface of lime, sand, and water, drawn on out behind the lath to romp intramurally like great Brueghel rodents dancing in winter.

"Yup, those girls are still in there somewhere," says Charlie, "bopping their sweet little hearts out. We just wanted a bit more class to the place."

Class is also brought to the Seahorse by Charlie's Wednesday Nite Band, an amalgam of local talent that includes a cadre of a hot cornet, a tuba played by a man in the wrecking business, and Charlie's accordian, with various sit-ins on banjo, sax, trombone, clarinet, mandolin, etc. The band's style seems to vary between Polish Wedding and New Orleans Riverboat. For years the number one Wednesday man was the late Eli Schoonmaker, on loan from the German Club up-river in Mystic. "Yessir," says Charlie, "Eli sang and played banjo with such skill as to be considered almost in another league. Something like that could be dangerous."

Like eighteenth-century harpsichordists who knew they might have to fill in the part of a trollop-stricken woodwind or fevered violin, Charlie has become more versitile. "Through the years you'll notice I've added various state of the art apparatus to my accordian so that it doesn't matter if the others don't show up or leave early. I got a button that will more or less simulate the characteristic din of the departed."

Some of the most musical moments were not instrumental. I can recall people in Willimantic back in the fifties trying to get a party together to drive forty miles through a snowstorm to hear this "marvelous young telephone lineman who sang at the Seahorse." Actually a pioneer in computer programming, John Rathbun is the younger son of the late deacon of the Noank Baptist Church, Captain B. F. Rathbun. Local musicologists claim John inherited his fine choir-loft tenor from his father. In any case it was adapted to what one might call a more secular repertoire, which included "sea shanties."

There was also a singing barman, a scholar of what might be termed "Elizabethan song," with the appropriate name of Walt Hunsinger. Walt's show-stopper was a rousing, oak-thumping ballad that took up the better part of a round of drinks to detail the ambiguous amorous life of certain members of the benthic community.

Master Mariner Adrian Lane would come ashore with his concertina. His repertoire had been gathered the hard way: Scandinavian songs from the winter North Atlantic sinking; nights with dynamiting oceanographers when he skippered the sailing research vessel *Atlantis;* encounters with tugboatmen in World War Two in Vladivostok . . . "I'm still a believer, though, that a voyage should be as dull as possible," he says. "Leave the disasters for the songs in the Seahorse."

"We finally had to cut out the singing in the bar, and confine the music to the Wednesday night band in the dining room," says Charlie. "The state wanted us to charge entertainment tax every time Walter or John opened his mouth.

"These were strictly amateurs, mind you, singing their heads off spontaneously, but believe you me: they had rep-wa-twas. I mean they knew some songs, and all the way through, all the words. Make you laugh. Tunes, too. Wonderful ears, make you cry. When you think of what goes down for a singer's reputation now: a piece of a tune with half-a-dozen words and the rest electronics."

So with the fireplace under control in the bar and the ballgame mumbling overhead, what you have now is mainly talk, much of it about the sea. In summer the harbor has become the number one sailing port in the state, with most of the boat owners coming from inland. So congested has the water become that a special planning commission had to meet all winter up the hill in the Noank firehouse, where the talk is more official. "What is our jurisdiction? Who will get a mooring in the year 2000? What about houseboats? What about some guy who comes in summer from South Africa in an old ketch? You remember him; he stayed clear to winter and scattered ashes."

Down in the Seahorse, however, at least on this night, the conversation is about local winter business.

At one of the 1940 luncheonette-type tables near the fire, a solidly built man in a torn sweater is fighting the way the pedestal on the bottom of the central leg rocks unsteadily on the floor. His great Rasputin beard attacks the chrome edge of the table as he peers under. "Is it the table, the leg, the floor, or just me?" He has the deep voice of a man who has spent a lot of time under water.

"You're just fussy, Tom," says his female companion.

"Fussy?" His diving-bell baritone is down there with him under the table. "Me, fussy?"

"Maybe it's because you're a cabinetmaker." She has lots of wild hair like his beard, but softer in the firelight, and she swirls it around as if that might help him on his survey.

"Hey," he says, "I'm just grateful to be a cabinet-maker and not a diver anymore. I'm just grateful not to be out on that boat in this weather." He comes up for air and steadies the table with both hands.

"Why on earth would anyone ask you to go out diving in the ocean in this weather?"

"Hey, the professor needed his readings all year round. He didn't give a damn if it was in the sleet in January or February off Narragansett."

"And you really did that, you dove in that winter water?"

"Sure, it was . . . scientific to do that."

"You'd never get me off that boat."

"Actually the boat trip out was often the worst of it, what with the seas sticking to the windshield so you had to hang your head out to see. You had to be like one of those old-time locomotive drivers." He illustrates an old-time locomotive driver. "Christ, by the time we got to our buoy, we welcomed going overboard."

"I don't see how it could be a good thing," she says.

"It sure beat some summer dives I did."

"I wouldn't mind summer dives myself."

"Not when you have to clean jellyfish out of the water collant intakes over at the Millstone Reactor. You go up in those tubes like el spermo going for the egg. You just hope though you can come back."

"Well, you can forget that, then," she says. "But I still can't see . . . in winter . . . actually getting your foot over . . ." She sticks a well-booted leg out. "I don't see how . . ."

"Don't trip the waiter," he says.

"I'm all right," says the waiter. He holds his tray of John Courage draft on his shoulder. "Do a little diving myself."

"Your foot and then your whole . . ." She shivers. "It's bad enough at night ashore, just sticking my foot out into the dark."

"We found a way that would help, though."

"Extra thermal layerings?" says the waiter.

"You might put it that way. We peed in our wet suits."

"You what?"

"There was something about the stabilization process that was wonderful."

"You mean," says the waiter, "a thermal interchange modulation across the interface?"

"Something like that. You know, there you are out there with no land around. The water is coming down from the sky and it is cold water that is coming down from the sky. You are going into even more cold water. There just doesn't seem to be very much of you in all that."

"And peeing in your wet suit helps that?" says the waiter.

"Yes, it does."

The waiter looks at the girl.

"Sure," she says, and she gives her hair a toss so the firelight goes wild. "It helps set the universe at balance."

"That's right," says Tom. "You got a shim on you?"

The waiter is still thinking about the thermal exchange across the interface.

"That's OK," says Tom. "I got one." He holds a match box aloft, then ducks back under the table.

"If you say so," says the waiter.

"He does," she says. While she waits for Tom, she folds her hands on the table. It quivers anyway.

The waiter shrugs and moves on his rounds.

Two lobstermen stand by the bar. They have been talking about the cooling system in their new diesel engines for almost an hour. A cooling system in winter can indeed be a tricky thing. They both still have several dozen pots overboard and so rightly think of themselves as more serious than the summer people who pull a few traps in warm weather. They both work at other shore jobs, however, so they know they are not as serious as an acquaintance with a hundred pots who fishes "full time" and has a cooling system you could talk about for well over an hour.

"I know he thinks I'm a jerk," says the first lobsterman. "The other day when we were all down at Orion's dock, I was kidding him, hinting I was pulling his pots. I said his buoys were real pretty colors, made 'em easy to find, but that those three-pot trawls he'd rigged were sure hard to haul."

"I bet he didn't think that was so funny," said the other.

"I'll say. You know how it is down there ar Orion's. It was too cold to sit on the bench and boxes, the usual stuff, so everybody was standing up, leaning on my pickup. Well, I sighted down the side of the truck after a while and you know what? He wasn't leaning against my truck! Everybody else was, but not him. He wouldn't lean up against my truck. I sighted twice."

"I think I've figured it out," says Tom, and he surfaces. "It's a little bit of the table, a little bit of the leg . . ." Like his girlfriend, he puts his hands on the table and folds them. "A little bit on the floor and a little bit of me."

John Rathbun pulls on the collar of his white turtleneck and is into a story about an old relative of his, a fisherman who had been after cod off Wilderness Point, Fishers Island, only three or so miles south of Noank. The winter squall he was caught in is an old storm, but New England weather being what it is, the tempest could just as well be last night's howl. Hardly a winter goes by, it seems, but some Seahorse patron doesn't renew the yarn by a narrow escape of his own. Like some bit of ancient Pindaric awe, it is "a tale to run on the lips of men."

"They drove ashore on the back side of the island, the two of them: captain and crew. But the crew was hurt so the skipper had to drag him up through the surf. On the beach, he got the fellow to climb up on his back so he could carry him. Those cobbles back there on that shore are mean enough when they're dry. He lugged him like that up the island looking for a house. The sleet was in their face, but he kept on into it because that way was the one light he could see. He didn't have much extra breath, but he used some of it to keep up a kind of mumbling conversation with the guy hanging onto him. He had the illusion it was a two-way conversation, and for part of the way it might have been.

"After a while it didn't matter. Just one foot after the other. Somebody opened the door in the house, pushed the snow away, and started to let the two men in. Then had second thoughts. 'Leave him outside, Cap.' 'I can't do that. He'll freeze to death.' 'He already has.' And he had, somewhere along the way up from the sea. So they left him outside in the woodshed and that night the captain had a heart attack from the strain of all that lugging in the deep snow, and he died a week later."

"Why, John," says a bearded man in a duck coat, "that's damn near as epic as the winter night you drove your car into the harbor."

"I didn't drive it into the harbor. I drove it down Store Hill, that's where I drove it. The brakes did the rest."

"Well, John, all I know is I was sleeping in the corner house then; I woke up when your brakes went, a mighty squeak like a strangled rat, then heard you hit that log at the edge of the town beach and—"

"We hit that log all right, went right up in the air, never did touch the beach, went straight into the harbor. There I was behind the wheel going on down tide just like some fancy summer person in a Hatteras twin screw."

"I don't imagine she gave you much steerage way in that rig, John," says Captain Lane.

"None at all, Cap. Besides, I was too interested in getting out of the car to take navigation seriously."

"Well, you did rescue Bruce's wife at sea, so to speak."

"I'm not so sure. I did get clear of the car and I did see her and start to tow her ashore . . . just like my ancestor had done, I thought, but it was mighty tough towing. I said, 'Marion, what you got there you're dragging?' She said she had her pocketbook, you know that big satchel of hers, and the mouth of it had sprung open. It was like we were towing an otter trawl. Just like they towed from one of those draggers used to lay right there in that very spot before the hurricane. Only I didn't have a Perkins diesel and a big wheel. All I had was my feet and one free arm.

" 'Cast loose that satchel, Marion,' I said. 'I can't,' she sez, 'the whole night's receipts from the Seahorse is in it.' 'Well, then we're gonna drown,' I sez, thinking of my ancestor, "cause I can't make it up tide with that mouth gaping.' 'Well, I ain't letting it go,' she sez, 'I got the whole Seahorse in here.' So I let her go and relaxed, figuring it was all over but the heart attack. The minute I eased up, though, my feet hit bottom. By then we had somehow gotten ourselves into only waist-high water, but damn cold, I'll tell you.

" 'So,' says Marion, 'you see I saved the Seahorse after all,' and she holds up that damn bag."

"Oh, I love rides on the water in winter," says a lean blond woman. "Don and I . . ."

"But not in a car," says Don, whose distinguished gray sideburns indicate he may know just what is the proper way to go on water. "No, of course not in a car."

"Sorry," says John Rathbun, "thought I had a trend going there."

"In a launch," says the lean blond. "Don and I took the launch up river the other day when there was just that thin ice on the surface. There was no one else out there and it was ringing sounds all the way—just like sleigh bells."

"Yeah, and it's that thin ice'll cut a wooden boat open like a can opener," says the bearded man in the duck coat. "When they finished that off-shore dragger *Baby* II up in Mystic, the owner couldn't wait to take her out. All they did is go down to Noank and back and they cut three-quarters of an inch into that brand-new oak stem."

"Those off-shore guys," says the first lobsterman, "you see them come in with all that ice on their rigging. They got hunks this big." He makes his hands indicate diameters of grapefruit dimensions.

"Jingle-jingle," says the lean blond, "just like sleigh bells."

"Damn it," says Tom, "this table's still wobbly."

Outside, the ice bubblers slop and sigh, the two lighthouses snore, one high, one low. The flakes are thicker, falling harder. You can hardly see the fire inside the open foundry doors. Stronger than the wood smoke and the coal is the sharp smell of low tide. Snow covers the round flukes on the unsold mushroom moorings so that the anchors look under water, dug in on the bottom of the harbor.

HARK BRASS
Christmas in B♭

We are shown fair scenes in order that we may be tempted to inhabit them, and not simply to tell what we have seen.

—Thoreau, *Journal*, November 24, 1857

WALKING into a store a week before Thanksgiving, I was assaulted by Christmas music and, I'm afraid, fell to cursing, whereupon I was challenged by the proprietor. "What's the matter?" she said, "Don't you like Christmas carols?"

"No," I said. "At least not . . ." and I waved my hand toward the ubiquitous woofers and tweeters whence issued the violins of Montovani.

A few evenings later as I reached for the TV button, I heard a dismal cry from the street. Fumbling the curtains, I discovered an amalgam of what church groups call "young people." They were intoning what could have only been, by its lugubrious legato, the Franz Gruber tune about the night's being silent.

Their eyes were not, however, after the manner of Christmas-card figures, uplifted piously, but rather roamed furtively on what appeared to be mimeographed copies of the words. There was even one tall goop who held a flashlight which he cast about on the various scripts like a meter man in a strange cellar. As for the music itself, everyone was on the melody, more or less, so that the only harmony came in desperate lunges as someone fell far enough off the pitch to make a momentary, inadvertent third. The tone was heavily adenoidal with occasional thickenings brought on by a catarrh-stricken coloratura and a phlegmatic basso. Further tonal color was added by an abruptly descanting soprano in the back row whose boyfriend's idea of a Christmas goose seemed less Dickensian than Benny Hill.

After the one verse of "Silent Night," this Mimeo Chorale went on to "Jingle Bells," an arrangement which floundered during the "dashing through the snow" apparently owing to there not being enough copies of the words to go around. The grand finale, no doubt in the interests of the ecumenical spirit, was "Rudolph the Red-nosed

Reindeer" sung with unprecedented gusto and almost without assistance from the fellow with the flashlight.

Who knew, however, if there weren't additional words written down on those trembling papers? Recalling King George's problems with Handel during what appeared to be an even more obvious finale flourish, I opened the door and waved to release the chorale from any further sense of bondage to their public. When they moved off, their voices were improved by distance, and the flashlight seemed to take on the dignity of a lighthouse beam on a remote coast.

I lingered in the doorway, breathing the cool, fresh air. At least they had brought me thus far, so that it was not so much anger I felt this time at the Christmas music, but sadness. Better the Mimeo Chorale than nothing, but as an example of people's street culture, was this our last best alternative to shopping center music?

Perhaps it was just time having its revenge, for how many years, when I was myself a Young People, had I inflicted holy tunes upon an audience besieged in their very homes?

Could things have changed this much since the days when the most exciting time of the year was when I joined the brass choir that strolled our West Hartford neighborhood blatting out "Silent Night," "O Come All Ye Faithful," and a lungful of assorted favorites?

Some of my first memories were of the huge, tooting bodies indistinguishable from their brass bells and coils as they all lurched and hummed about our living room. They would begin coming in for an hour after supper in those final weeks before Christmas. Some of these shapes were identified to me as uncles, other trombones, some friends of my father, some trumpets. Others were merely big kids from the neighborhood. One, alarmingly enough, was a euphonium tangled in the family doctor.

Not only was the sanctioned din a marvel but this carnival of komik flubbs and outright phaffs was offen followed by most un-Christian bellows. Better yet was the rug-besotting employment of water keys, or as they were more familiarly called, "spit-letter-outers." But most astonishing was when my father's face contorted in emotion when playing the trumpet lead on "Silent Night." Was he unhappy beyond reach? Was he in some kind of puffing pain? (I had overheard stories about the tragic early deaths of trumpet players named Bix and Bunny and Bubber.) Or was he in some kind of happy place with his friends that was both in our living room, yet not in it?

In any case, on Christmas Eve they all went out into the night, and my mother and I listened as the sounds echoed off the houses, then faded. When my father came back alone hours later he usually had a Christmas wreath and an odd trombone or trumpet that he'd somehow picked up. But most of all, he had the look of glory in his eyes.

One night, he handed me one of the trumpets and did not stop me when I began to breathe through it.

He played first trumpet until I was old enough to carry the melody. This allowed him to go off into the more difficult second cornet part. It was then I realized something of the discipline that had been behind those raucous sessions in the living room. They practiced until they knew the notes, as the phrase was then, "by heart," and the notes included harmony which they felt was, after all, the main point.

This second cornet part was typical of my father's way with musical theory. It was never referred to as "a second part," or "an obbligato," or any of the other possible terms his noodling might have been called. The part had come from a fellow named Pete McCabe who had long ago played cornet on my father's old schooner, and so these notes were known ever after as "Pete McCabe's part," though most of us had never met the fellow.

Our arrangements were occasionally written out by my father, who used one of his thick carpenter's pencils to write out sol-fa notation on an old Portland Cement pad or the back of a Jones Builders envelope. We had two keys we played in: "open" and "the one-finger key." "Open" we more or less knew was "our C" or, more begrudgingly, "concert B flat." We played most of our stuff in this. The "one-finger key" was the key in which we played "Adeste Fideles," in order to allow Uncle Art full descant on trombone. It was called the "one-finger key" because one night the euphonium player looked up from his coils and keys and asked us quite simply, "Are we in the one-finger key or the other one?" Years later I discovered this was concert E flat.

None of this homemade theory was a problem unless we ran up against piano players. People who played this unwieldy instrument seemed to be female and to need music which required they locate and, what was apparently the real problem, actually don their glasses. Even with the music and the glasses, however, they always played in what they called "their C." Some of them even announced snobbishly that this key was, after all, "concert C," by which they seemed to imply, the "real C." As a result, I grew up thinking the main difference between men and women was that women needed music and played in C.

One Christmas, in those pre-ecumenical days, a Jewish friend of mine from up the street arrived with his clarinet.

"I've come to play Christmas carols," he announced. "The tune I do is 'O Come All Ye Faithful.' "

My father made an odd noise. I did not find this quite the "Abie's Irish Rose" situation that apparently my father did. After all, the kid had taught me his rolling hook-shot only that week. My father looked at the boy a moment as my friend nervously ran his fingers over all those keys. "You don't play that damn thing in concert C, do you?" he said.

"No sir," said the boy. "The clarinet is pitched just as the trumpet and trombone are, in concert B flat."

"Good," said my father, "come in."

As musical director of this street band, my father had an unorthodox background that in retrospect seems to have been just the right training to keep such a rag-tag outfit going for some ten years through the forties into the fifties. His father had earned money as a side-arming fiddle player out in Unionville, and his mother had played piano on what was known as the Elocution Circuit, sojourning to such then remote places as Collinsville and Farmington by horse or "steam cars."

Both folks taught him some of what music they knew. His father for instance seated him at the piano to play the "bear-paw" chordal accompaniment to Irish workman's tunes like "Drill Ye Tarriers Drill," smacking him on the head with the fiddle bow when it was time to change chords. More important than passing on such technical matters, his parents showed him music was something that had to be made by whatever means you damn well could.

To this background in violin and piano, my father, before being thrown out of the Boy Scouts, added bugle. Once freed from the limitations of military tooting, he picked up an old Conn trumpet and lugged it to New York speakeasys where he sat in with Red Nichols and His Five Pennies and the California Ramblers. Initially his performance was limited to the opening of "Bugle Call Rag," but as he mastered the three trumpet valves he went on, taking the more gruesome duties such as late-night requests for "Melancholy Baby."

Even more nocturnal, however, was my Uncle Art. There was a story about him atop a piling at Block Island at three in the morning tromboning "Stars and Stripes Forever." The point of the story varied through the years to illustrate his musicianship, stamina, or patriotism. In addition to his parents' advice, he had formal musical training, and even played in the Princeton marching band, which maybe ac-

counted for his parading about in our small living room on any occasion that gave him an opening such as "Adeste Fideles."

A large man made even larger with trombone, he seemed to me
a kind of raucous, silver elephant extending and withdrawing himself
in and out of the family by means of this noisy yet delighting trunk.
He had an ear-ripping staccato when he wanted it, ricocheting a bar-
rage of sixteenth notes off the big mirror in the living room. Once at
evening's end, on the way to his car, he blasted the house next door
which happened to be faced in stucco so that I grew up with an odd
association between stucco and staccato. He could also float you off
on the most amazing velvet pillows, so that a typical post mortem by
my father would run, "Well, your Uncle Art got a bit obstreperous
tonight." Pause. "But he had a good tone."

Like Uncle Art and the legendary second cornet Pete McCabe,
the euphonium-player, Roy Allen, was a member of the gang my father
took down the Connecticut River summer weekends. Roy had been
aboard the night my uncle'd stood tromboning on the piling at Block
Island and had vowed revenge. A veteran glee club singer, he ran-
sacked Hartford's second-hand shops to arm himself with the most
formidable piece of plumbing he could find. Commanding in size, the
euphonium was, however, as its Greek name suggests, a pleasant-
sounding instrument.

Roy spent some of those early voyages teaching himself the euphonium, and the doleful notes he discovered often seemed influenced by those emitted by major aids to navigation in thick weather.
In fairness it must be admitted that some of these acoustical effects
were brought on by what we would now call the "multiple use" of the
instrument. Space aboard the schooner was, after all, limited. This
meant that, as Roy was the cook, the capacious bell of the euphonium
served as receptacle for potato peels, coffee grounds, bottle caps, and
other culinary off-spewings, sometimes not of the cook's selection.

At all times, however, "the Horn," as it was now known, was a
gleaming object, devoutly polished. This was no small task, for there
were yards and yards of in-coiling tubing, to say nothing of ornamen-
tal knobs, baffling fistulas, and delicate water keys whose very where-
abouts could remain from year to year a mystery only revealed by odd
gurglings. As his wife was wont to comment, "You know, it's not the
greatest way to spend an evening. I mean sitting next to a big instrument that's being stroked with a fluffy cloth."

Roy read no music but had a good ear and a great love for harmony. We all assumed his horn was, like ours, in B flat, but there

surfaced from time to time nasty rumors that the euphonium was actually an E-flat instrument. Research was done on the matter which seemed to clear him, but someone made the mistake of investigating further. This research indicated there were some E-flat euphoniums. Close examination of Roy's horn revealed there was—tucked away among the more remote coilings—a fourth valve, an oddity in our three-valve realm that certainly smacked of deformity, if not heresy. But so long as it was not the hated concert C, no one worried, and besides, the notes actually played by "the Horn" were so low and so mellow and seemed to fit in so well, no one concerned themselves with such conservatory-bound questions as to what key Roy thought he was in. His part, like Pete McCabe's, was never known as baritone or bass or third or fourth, but simply "Roy's part."

It was, in fact, Roy's utter reliability through the years that kept the ritual going, and in later years he contributed the only female to the group, a clarinet-playing daughter.

"A woman?" said my father, opening the door.

"Don't worry," said Roy, "I brought her up right. She plays in B flat."

When we got together beforehand each year there would be the problem of who was in shape. Some people could be counted on to hit the note they aimed at a decent percentage of the time and even continue to do this throughout the repertoire. Others soon fell to an acoustical phenomenon known to us as "phaffing," which is to say the emitting of what is sometimes charitably called in jazz circles "ghost notes."

While these sounds did have their comic character, there was, as in all American muscular activity, always the lurking question of moral fiber. "Hey," my father'd shout to some lax-lipped lout in the corner, "you got anything coming out of that horn?" Or, "Have you been eating cookies again? . . . Clean the peanut butter out of those valves." To my mother, who was always hovering about with a popular tray, he'd say, "Don't give them any more of that peanut butter."

"But I don't give them peanut butter."

"Every year they get peanut butter in their valves."

To avoid being accused of having peanut butter in my performance, I frequently took my horn apart, carefully separating all the crooks, slides, springs, and valves in the bottom of a lukewarm tub. My cornet was a beautifully engraved Buescher, which we had bought from an FBI man who had suddenly lost all his front teeth. I thought its components lent an elegance to the bottom of the tub. Coming across these one time as she was preparing her own bath, my mother, however, let out a yelp, later explaining her alarm by saying, "I think he's going to be a plumber, not a musician."

My father merely said, "It's always a good idea to flush out your horn . . . in case an old guy died in there." (Bix, Bunny, Bubber?)

No matter; ultimately a player with a peanut butter lip would get better as the practice sessions went on, or if he didn't, he would find his way to a role in the harmony requiring less preliminary calisthenics. There were, through the years, as many as a dozen people out with us at one time blatting away. Some doubled the harmony, but most "helped out" on the melody, which produced a top-heavy performance as we moved away from the house. Further down the street, however, what with the aid of chill-gummed valves, cookie-clogged mouthpieces, bad lips, and general holiday confusion, many of those on melody had in actuality, if not spirit, dropped off the tune, so we became fairly well balanced, between Roy's part, Uncle Art's part, Pete McCabe's part and the lead.

After a while some of the piano players in the background decided that even if horns were in B flat, the youngsters coming up should have more formal notions of music than "the one-finger key" and "Pete McCabe's part." Some, like my cousin Russ on trumpet, were lucky enough to receive instruction in the public schools. Being a little older, neighbor trombonist Jon Belden and I resorted to a brass man who gave lessons downtown. We called him "Leaky Krantz" after the way air would escape from the side of his mouthpiece during demonstrations. Leaky gave his lessons in a stark little room nestled somewhere aloft in the eaves of the decaying, fin de siècle elegance of the Palace Theater.

On my way to his room I encountered a blonde woman in red velvet bathrobe standing in the hall smoking a cigarette. Behind her a half-open door gave onto a room in which lay a cot under a naked bulb. In Leaky's room there was also a cot and a naked bulb. We, however, also had a music stand. We sat side by side on the cot and looked at the music stand upon which perched my lesson. Leaky did not know about the one-finger key and insisted on what he called "real notes." I asked Leaky if the lady in the red bathrobe down the hall was perhaps giving singing lessons. He diverted my questions back onto dotted quarter notes. As I played away, a French cuff, brilliantly studded, would reach out with a gold pencil to annotate the real notes with "proper fingering."

When I reached the bottom of the page, Leaky would sigh, lean back, and snap the suspenders that held up his pinstripe pants. Then he would run his hand through thinning silver hair. Occasionally he'd pat his stomach and burp on ginger ale fetched from under the cot. "It's rough," he'd say, "the music business." Whenever my buddy Trombone Jon got home from his own Leaky Krantz lesson, his mother, a piano player, would have him take a mysterious "green pill."

Leaky was, however, an excellent musician who played brass in such Hartford events as the Shrine Circus. Meeting him on the street one day when the circus was in town, my father asked him how he'd found the show. "Terrible, just terrible," said Leaky.

"What," said my father, "no elephants? No acrobats? No clowns?"

"I don't know anything about elephants," said Leaky, "or clowns. All I know is it's *pft-pft* . . . all above high C."

"Silent Night" was our show stopper, one we could always manage no matter how cold or what players had managed to survive. "Play it in your sleep," said Pop, and some nights I think I almost did, wondering how many times we'd repeated the "round yon Virgin" phrase that began with two A's. Playing just notes it was disillusioning to discover the paucity of moves upon which many magical tunes were based, the repetition masked by the advancement of the words, which we did not, of course, employ. These repetitive phrases we worked hard to vary by shading of loud and soft, most dramatically on the close to "Adeste Fideles," where my uncle kept increasing his volume like an approaching freight train.

We usually began with "Joy to the World" because it was a free ride all the way down the scale and halfway up to see if all the valves were still working in the cold air. For some reason, however, late in the evening my father tended to confuse it with "Hark the Herald Angels Sing," and Pete McCabe's part suddenly would not fit.

One year we tried "We Three Kings," but Trombone Jon claimed he kept losing his part somewhere after "over moor and mountain" owing to the undulatory suggestion of the camel's gait, a bit of mal de mer from which no green pill could save him. "Angels We Have Heard On High," on the other hand, was dropped as we got older because we tended to rag it too much in the *Glor-or-ee-yore-ee-oar-ee-a* section. At the height of my powers I'd try "O Holy Night" and one Christmas Eve on Buena Vista did actually succeed in sustaining its demanding long notes that built over the pumping arpeggios of the trombones. At the climax I could either mellow down to a middle C or go for the high one. Bing! There it was. I had not known West Hartford held such beauties as the lights below sparkling all about my bell. Had the "old guy who'd died in there" come out to hit that note? My lip cracked and I turned around to see everyone had already mercifully been invited inside.

We usually went from place to place on foot, our mouthpieces in our hands shoved deep in our pockets. There had been a story about a boy who'd stuck his tongue onto an iron railing and we did not want the same thing to happen to our lips on the trumpet metal. Later some of the younger players used plastic mouthpieces, but we considered this sissy as it gave a mushy sound.

The politics of just who got serenaded were initially simple: whoever had relatives in the band, plus people who struck us at the moment as needing a serenade. Some were raucous party types or even more secular businessmen who, until we arrived, were celebrating Christmas Eve by getting their briefcases in shape before they used the holidays to depart for warmer zones. These we felt needed a little "holy-ing up," stressing "Silent Night," which we'd inflict through several verses. Others were old folks behind trembling curtains who needed a little jazz like "Adeste Fideles" or "Angels We Have Heard On High." Through the years these often arbitrary visits became ritualized, and the list of houses anxiously preparing everything from cookies and cocoa to gin became literally staggering.

So it came to pass we had to use cars, but this broke up the neighborly feel of the group so my father employed the company dump truck, filling it with hay and musicians and horns. The truck was a beat-up Chevrolet, a veteran of Balf's quarry and numerous clutch-popping trips up Morgan Street Hill. Understandably it had developed a habit of creeping into its dump mode when starting in low gear. At one stoplight we were all well out onto the hood of a trapped Volkswagen before my father noticed what was happening.

It was necessary to compose ourselves after this near-disaster. Although often invited in, we always played outside, so as to have, as my father put it, "the effect of music over open ground." Also it kept us away from any parlor pianists who might want to do something in concert C. At the next stop, the home of one of the about-to-depart businessmen, we were so cold from the truck ride that all the spit in our horns had frozen, so we allowed ourselves to be invited in first.

We set our horns by the fire while we had something hot to drink. There were business papers scattered all about the room, and attaché cases gaped like tuneless cherubs. There was no tree, so the only festive decoration was the arrangement of our brass warming before the open fire and the hostess with her cocoa and whisky.

"Well," the businessman looked at his watch. "How about something appropriate to justify this lavish outlay?"

Half expecting an eruption of obstreperous avuncular tromboning, I looked toward my uncle. He pumped his slide noiselessly and looked at my father, who wiggled his valves but looked at Roy half-buried under the bell of his euphonium. This deference made sense, for we were still a bit shaken from our truck dumping and Roy was not only ship's cook but, after all, a medical man.

From under the big bell of "the Horn" came his quiet voice. " 'Auralee.' " And then he added, in his best bedside manner, "Though not strictly a Christmas carol."

"Auralee" was, of course, from the summer repertoire, a song built for harbors when the sun has faded, and the hollow in the land made by the water holds the harmony in the final ripeness of its distillation. Ashore or afloat, however, it was our best tune and it was Roy who made it so because, as he always confessed with a wink, "I sneak in a sixth."

" 'Auralee,' then," he said, "though not strictly a Christmas carol."

"What's this 'not strictly' business?" said our paper-shuffling host. " 'Aur-a-lee' is simply not in any way a proper Christmas carol. As a matter of fact, it is an outright paean to secular love. Something, I believe, concerning 'a maid with golden hair.' "

For the sake of allowing room for Roy's part, "Auralee" was pitched in the one-finger key, and that night we played it the best ever, with Roy's part and Uncle Art's part and Pete McCabe's part and the lead part all in their right places.

When we were done, Roy removed "the Horn" from his lips, wiggled a bit of spit from the water key onto the host's Oriental, and said quietly, "Nevertheless, a holy tune."

BLUES FOR OLIVER

The Demise of the Corner Music Store

Lord, they closin down the corner music store
Lord, they is closin down the corner music
     store
I don't know where I'll get
My rainy weather lovin anymore.

   —Blind Jelly Falorp, "Music Store Blues"

THE MOON eclipse tides have caused the waters in the river
town to abandon the piers, and boats that usually have water
at their slips now slouch on the mud, exposing their keels thick
with cold molgulas, wisps of grass, whatever the summer has left. On
the corner a block from the drawbridge, low tide seems to have also
hit Oliver's Music Store, and what is left as the sun goes down on this
last day is what has been so far rejected by customers taking advantage of the going-out-of-business sale. Capricious as the inventory now
is, it is yet a selection which somehow seems essentially . . . well, Oliverian.

   The place is at the bottom of a steep hill so that stacked above it
is the bank with its Greek Revival pillars and above that a big house
with a huge widow's walk and above that the church. Down on the
same level are new stores that sell only kites or teddy bears. The busi-
nesses scheduled to replace the music store will also sell specialty items.

   Oliver's is not especially New England in style, and with its yellow
stucco and curved brick lintels on the second story it has a sunny look
even on rainy days. The front of the building is beveled off as it makes
the corner, like a railroad roundhouse or a lighthouse. All this architecture makes you realize how important that door is. It opens right
onto the busiest corner in town. This is the place where the louts would
gather if it weren't also the spot where the policeman stands and taps
his foot to the music coming from the speaker when the store is open.

   Though the door is unlocked, there is no music today coming out
under the big, round sign shaped like a record. The crudely pasted
red letters on the plate-glass windows proclaim the fatal sale. Inside

there is only the knock and cry of a hammer, not John Henry, but a man as much a victim of the times. Owner Ted Bessette bends, stripping the vertical tongue-in-groove siding that has served for thirty years as a low barricade around the inside of his two show windows. Oddly enough, he is humming, the first music I've heard issue from him personally in all the time I've known him.

"Well," he says, "it is better than just standing here." He straightens up from his work, suddenly a tall man, and his voice, usually hardly audible over the record player, almost booms out from under his thin mustache. "You gotta do something."

Oliver's is certainly not unique. There used to be a music store in every town as sure as a package store and a drugstore, and maybe more to the point, a church. For many, these music stores were not merely located in the town, they were what made the town.

Up until recently there was, for instance, Harry's, only ten miles away in New London on Bank Street. Harry's was an equally intriguing place with piles of sheet music, good records, and a variety of instruments. But rents go up; franchised "audio centers" cut each other's throats in malls, and Harry's has gone. And now, in Mystic, Oliver's.

It would be foolish, however, to overplay Ted's musical omniscience or make a cult zone out of the store. There were certainly those who saw Oliver's as a bit square. It was not like, say, William Russell ensconced in his Amercan Music Company store in the Vieux Carré with fifty violins on the floor of the back room, and four bins of the very best New Orleans music out front, much of which he'd recorded himself. It was not the old Commodore Record Store in New York with Jack Teagarden and the Dorsey brothers themselves dropping in. Nor was it even a musician-run shop like Harry's in New London or The Music Center in Norwich or the shop in West Hartford run by symphony players Harvey and Bill Goldstein. Nor did Oliver's have a gadget like the music store in downtown Westerly, there were no bellows to pre-wheeze your harmonica in a sanitary fashion. Ted was not even always necessarily the first guy on the block to discover someone like Pavarotti. He never carried "Rick Zitz with Trapped Gas," etc.

The thing was you never knew quite what would be in Oliver's. Though a typical small-town music store, it was yet rare for the mix of musical instruments and records; the wealth of musical accessories—not only the violin chin rests and valve oil, but guitar pics and Black Diamond violin strings in deep scarlet packages; earphones; flutes of wood, plastic, tin; jazz whistles; for trumpets or trombones, straight mutes, Harmon mutes; odd lyres for God knew what kind of twisted horn. (Even in better days you always had the feeling that you were buying not only Oliver's last bottle of valve oil or whatever, but the last bottle in the world!)

You expected to see one day hanging in the window a sackbut, or a viola da gamba.

As you never knew what would be in the store, you could never be sure what tune would be coming out of the speaker. Just as you were sure Ted was hopelessly mired in a kind of Herb Albert-Aker Bilk-Bert Kaempfert syndrome, he'd rinse the world with Caruso doing *La Forza del Destino:* "O tu che in seno agli angeli" or a Kansas City Seven with Lester Young on clarinet.

In any case, Oliver's public moods were never as bad as those twin anathemas of contemporary airs: shopping center glop or dormitory window din.

And you knew inside the door you'd find, if not the actual Count Basie or Pavarotti, at least something relevant to their world, even if it only be the faded scarlet packet of Black Diamond violin strings.

How many times over the years either my father or I would come back from Oliver's with some sort of odd instrument or bit of musical lore. Because my father makes music on many different instruments, he and Ted have had countless dealings. Recently he picked up some fiddle rosin, valve oil, and a guitar. Ted also threw in a black leather bass drum cover. The cover made sense because my father does have a bass drum in his living room, but the leather was a bit musty so my father put it out on the woodpile to air. My mother knew, of course, about the drum, but was not prepared for this new pelt sunning by her back door. After an initial shock, she said, "Oh, something from Oliver's. Usually they are louder."

People have been dropping in for two weeks or so since the announcement, some almost like mourners at a wake, to express their loss. Others don't seem to notice anything unusual. You'd expect them to say something like, "Do you have any alto reeds left?" But, apparently ignoring the desolation, they say, "You *carry* number two alto reeds?"

Ted looks about the store and shakes his head. He who carried everything from spit keys to valve springs and three stiffnesses of alto reeds has to say, "No. We don't . . . carry . . . alto reeds."

The bewildered alto player departs. In come two girls, one suffering from what at first looks like punk-rock make-up. Up close, however, they are genuine black eyes, the biggest, most violently col-

ored I've ever seen. "Do you, ah, carry Fleetwood Mac?" Ted's eyes
do not even shift to the three boxes by the window. There are maybe
fifty records over there. I try to remember if Oliver's ever did "carry"
Fleetwood Mac. It's quite possible he didn't and critics will see this
flaunting of obvious Economic Reality as the cause of his deserved
demise. Today in any case, he carries, well . . . The punched-out girl
sways for a moment before the depleted record rack. She would like
to oblige Ted. Not only is he tall, with mustache, but his blue eyes
have a way of lighting up that beats any arcade game. Her loyalty to
Fleetwood Mac, however, is pressing, and she is not a wealthy woman
who can at the moment afford eclecticism. Ted recommends the
shopping center.

A middle-aged woman with the look of a navy officer's wife ex-
presses sympathy for the store's closing. "But if it's as I read in the
paper that the rent here is now simply too high, why not merely move
down the road?'

As Ted begins to say the problem is that he likes it here, she
interrupts, "Do you have a tambourine? My daughter's in ballet. She
needs a tambourine."

There is one hanging on the wall where it partially covers a crack
in the plaster.

"But," says the mother, "is that the proper tambourine for a ballet? For one thing it doesn't seem to have a covering, a . . ."

"A head." Ted removes the frail ring of belled wood from the
wall and shows it to her.

"Yes, your tambourine has no head."

"There are several kinds of tambourines. Some have heads. Some
do not." Ted gestures expansively with the tambourine. "All kinds of
tambourines."

The woman scans the empty green walls for this stock.

"And this . . ." Ted gives the tambourine a little Esmarelda move,
"is one such . . . tambourine."

"But there is no way of knowing, is there?" says the woman. "No
way of knowing which one is for ballet?"

"There are different kinds of ballet." Ted, however, draws the
line here. There will be no Petrushka kicks or entrechats from dying
swans.

"Well, I suppose we'd better not get this one then if we're not
absolutely sure."

"Here," says Ted. "Take it . . . for nothing."

The woman is not sure now if she wants a headless tambourine for nothing, but she reaches out and it is in her hand now. "Ah, ballet." She gives it a shake more suitable for Major Barbara than Pavlova. Stuck for an exit line, she says again, "I'm sorry you are going to leave us."

"Hey, it's not my idea," says Ted. "I like it here."

The woman frowns. This is not the sort of thing she likes to hear. The sticky door also presents a problem. "But what will you do?"

"Take a trip," he says.

"That's the spirit." She attempts the tambourine again, then bolts, and I realize the reason I've never noticed the store had a fancy tin ceiling was because there used to be so many instruments hanging there.

What is left is an odd residue: on the shelf back of the counter are several upholstered violine chin rests. Bereft of the usual cheery company of red jazz whistles, bamboo flutes, and harmonicas, the chin rests look sinister as wasp's nests. Below them is a small jumble of flute lyres.

In the Main Street window, on a bed of sea pebbles, reposes a scattering of faded music for a hermaphrodite instrument called the "Mel-o-din." There are, however, no more Mel-o-dins. There are: three batons; two sets of bass drum sticks, one a combo hard and soft; a bass drum pedal. The most curious object lying in the window is what looks like a one-string Chinese lute.

At least that is my guess.

Ted laughs. "We had this in our other store when we closed it. This is just something we kept." He looks at it.

The other store was up in Danielson. It was his father's, the "actual Oliver," and the family closed the place when he died a few years ago. Ted looks up, and his eyes brighten. "No one could guess what it is."

"I can't."

"It's a wooden under-arm lyre holder."

Sure enough, the spoon is not for resonance, but for conforming to the rib cage under the arm, and the hole in the neck is not for the string but the lyre, which so located may now parade down the street before you. He shows me the few wire under-arm lyre holders left but they look like coat hangers. He tries to find more lyres in the huge catalogue he still keeps on the last section of the last counter, and sure enough, there are as he says pages and pages of lyres he could order.

In the Pearl Street window sprawl: three flute lyres; a Western-style violin made in China; a copper and brass trumpet with sticky valves in a beat-up case (an instrument that my father and I have cautiously discussed), and a couple of recorders that at first look like chair legs.

The furniture is in fact shockingly visible now that the old tongue-in-groove-half-wall between the customers and the office has been removed, and there stands exposed a rolltop desk painted here and there industrial gray. It is accompanied by a swivel, reclining, wooden, slat-back armchair with brass swivel and brass casters. Behind the chair is a narrow doorway leading into a room whose persistent mysteries can only be a blessing.

In the middle of the store, once a glass case for CBs and small radios, Ted has dumped all that is left of this side of the business: three cardboard boxes in which are heaved plastic grab bags of Morse code tickers (the Philmore Model No. B53 Telegraph Key); Duto-dusters, which "remove harmful record dust and foreign particles"; assorted jacks, wires, noise suppressors, collapsing aerials; single-ear headphones; lapel mikes; and even more directly musical oddments like viola bridges, guitar strings, and pitch pipes.

There is only one record table left, with three boxes the contents of which together would make up maybe one. Nevertheless the records run the full spectrum of Oliver's from Lester Bowie-Phillip Wilson "Duet" (half an hour divided up in three separate compositions in which a trumpet and percussion duel, on the Improvising Artist's label) to Alex Moore, "I just sit down and play them (the blues), unaware to any knowledge or idea or thoughts of them until I sit down at the keyboard and begin playing and making them up on the piano." I put these two under my arm.

Necessary too for someone at home is the instruction record *Blues Harp* by Tony "Little Sun" Glover from *Simple Rhythm Exercise to Transitional Bends*. Unfortunately there are no more blues harps left in the store and the instructions start with volume two.

Easier to pass up are the fourteen volumes of sound effects that range from "opening iron gate (un-oiled)" through "cash register (hand cranked)" to "machine gun fire (light caliber)" to "rocket (dart)." "I used to have a good business with these records," says Ted. "People who made their own home movies." Un-oiled gates and cash registers can, no doubt, be handled, but how, you wonder, will it go now with our people when their vacation films require a little spicing up with light machine gun fire?

The half-dozen polka albums present no temptation, though the three that follow are tough because they are the albums I most asso-

ciate with his outdoor speaker on slushy days: *The Best of Vaughan
Monroe, Billy Vaughan,* and what is perhaps the essential Oliver's al-
bum: *The Wonderland of Bert Kaempfert and His Orchestra, Including
"Tenderly," "Morgan," "Midnight Snack," "Auld Lang Syne" and "Plaisir
D'Amour."* The prices on this tattered album chart not only its life, but
Oliver's: Mfr.'s List Price $9.98, Our Low Price .93. On the back are
three prices: $4.98, $4.79 and .95. Peeping out from the price stickers
is the kind of little thing you can pick up at Oliver's, that the lush
trumpet solos are not by Bert Kaempfert himself, but a fellow named
Charly Tabor. At these prices I cannot resist a fantasy: I will buy the
three key records and, organ-grinder style, stand upon the street corner to churn forth the spirit of Oliver's into the dreary February morn.

On the floor, leaning against the wall right under where it used
to hang next to "The Story of the Trumpet," is a framed pen and ink
of a poignantly skinny girl. The patron spirit of the shop, she is stuck
in a moonlit field consoled only by her gawk-necked dulcimer, but
every blade of grass is attendant upon her, every flower's petal, every
fret. "You said you wanted that the other day," says Ted. "I'll make
that a contribution."

Already we have preserved at home the large, framed wall chart
"The Story of the Trumpet" featuring "Great Modern Trumpeters"
Mannie Klein, Louis Armstrong, W.C. Handy, Harry Glantz, Saul
Caston, and Rafael Mendez (no Leaky Krantz?). To our music book
collection have also been recently added an Oliverian fake book, a
Simplified Beatles, complete Judy Collins, Dolly Parton, Joan Baez,
and a real treasure, a youthful, if shopworn, 1967 Peggy Lee book of
her own compositions such as "Grain Belt Blues" and "Things Are
Swingin'."

For Christmas I gave my father a long brass herald's trumpet,
which Ted explained would come in handy if my father "ever finds
himself out on a castle wall." On the chance that it might fit my valve
trombone, I picked up an empty Selmer case. "Bring it here if it doesn't
fit," said Ted, "and I'll give you your five bucks back." It didn't and
neither did I. After all, in the case was not only a trombone lyre, but
a bass clef book with "Steamliner March," "Zephyrs Waltz," and "Cin-
derella Gavotte." Besides, the way things are these days you can never
tell when you might need an empty trombone case.

The second-hand "Clavioline" with Wow Lever and two dozen
stops from clavichord to bagpipe now stands in front of our wood
stove. Evidently a kind of harbinger to the Moog Synthesizer, the elec-
trified keyboard contraption was rented to a band that faced up to its

propensity for coming up one member short on each gig. "They never knew which member it would be," explained Ted, "but all you had to do was pull out the stop of whatever fellow didn't make it that night." As advertised, the Clavioline has at our home "stimulated young people to play." In fact I can only get a whack in after midnight when in the interests of family peace I must suppress the bagpipe stop in favor of the clavichord with no Wow at all.

Gone forever, though, are enough concertinas and accordions to populate every spile in town with shantymen intoning the necessity for Johnny to leave her. (Music for this and other shanties was always in the Pearl Street window, which is the view that looks toward the river.)

Gone is the old dark fiddle that was repaired in a New York shop in 1948 for a hundred dollars. (The tag that demonstrated this noble past was included in the case.) Gone the trombones, bugles, the alto sax, the mandolins and banjos and bongos that hung from the tin ceiling. Gone from the Pearl Street window is the Chinese moon banjo.

The case of the Chinese moon banjo is typical of how Ted built up his unique inventory. Most music stores these days, like most stores in other fields, merely take what the distributor's truck leaves. Ted, however, prided himself on hunting down interesting stuff. Through the years he had cultivated a number of unusual distributors and unusual ways of dealing with the usual ones. "You have to," he said, "if you're going to be able to get something for somebody in any reasonable time.

"I found the moon banjo at the World's Fair in the 1960s where I saw this guy with bamboo stuff—kites and flutes. He also made a thing that looked like a lute. He called it a 'moon banjo' so I ordered one. When I sold that I git five more. Through the years I got some more and sold 'em all. They were well made, all out of wood, but the strings I never could figure out. They weren't like anything I ever saw. They seemed like llama hair. You looked at 'em closely you could see somebody must have spent a long time in winding them."

His own favorite instrument? The sax. "When I got out of the service I saw Guy Lombardo in New York and Lombardo had nine different kinds of sax lined up on the stand. I know there are only usually four different kinds but there he had nine. I think I figured on fooling around long enough with the sax so I could find out about those other kinds."

Gone are all those wonderful records. He would feed the corner not only with Kaempfert and Vaughan but things like a reissue of

King Oliver: *The Great 1923 Gennetts:*" Chimes Blues," "Dipper Mouth Blues," "Working Man Blues," "Canal Street Blues." It might seem reasonable enough to find such a record in a music store, but when I was in New Orleans, only a few blocks from Canal Street, I could not find anyone in a music store who had ever heard of King Oliver, much less had a copy of his "Canal Street Blues."

Gone are Russ Morgan; Hoagy Carmichael; Bunny Berrigan; Glen Gray; *The Complete Caruso,* Vol. 6, 1909–1910, Vol. 7, 1910; Sydney Bechet, Muggsy Spanier, Jack Teagarden, Teddy Wilson Jazz Archives ("B-flat Swing"); *Memphis Slim & Willie Dixon at the Village Gate,* Fats Domino, Chuck Berry, *Nat Cole from the Very Beginning* ("Slow Down," "Stompin' at the Panama," "Gone with the Draft," "Hit That Jive Jack," "Sweet Larraine," "Early Morning Blues"); Albert Ammons ("Monday Struggle," "Baltimore Breakdown," "Boogie Woogie at the Civic Opera").

Not everything hanging in Oliver's window ended up at home. A grade-B Oliver's fantasy would find you plowing up the street one day and out of the corner of your eye appears, say, a gleaming alto sax on its bracket. There is a price tag on the bracket for $40 and you stop to think. Could that price be for the whole works? At Oliver's it just might, and even if what is coming out the speaker is Ray Conniff, you could imagine a more acrid Earl Bostick, or maybe a smoky Charlie Parker on a ballad. Your basic axe is trumpet, and that you only play publicly at Christmas time or on summer picnics to Flat Hammock. But twenty-five years ago you did a high-school rock 'n' roll gig on a C melody sax. So there you stand as the cars counterpoint slush, imagining yourself noddling Parker's "I'll Remember April," blowing down diminished sevenths till all gutters green and bloom.

Unfortunately the price is only for the bracket. OK, you slop on up the street, but now you're whistling.

An old draggerman is leaning against the last bit of counter. To my annoyance he's not talking about music or apparently even the store's demise. He's going right on as if this were a day like any other, and he's telling Ted about the eel holes and where the big bass lay so still you could spear them in the muddy cove below the railroad bridge in the thirties. I can see Ted likes this talk, though, and I remember he had an old Noank boat up on the marsh near where the fisherman is narratively mired. It was boats, in fact, that got this store in town in the first place.

Ted's father began by repairing radios at home in 1923. He started the Danielson store in the 1930s, where he repaired and sold radios and outboard motors. "Sold a lot of outboard motors, too," says Ted. "That's how we got interested in the boats. There was a lake up there, but it was full of stumps. One time I was going fast on the lake and the engine got out of control so I couldn't stop. Had to wait for the engine to run out of gas and the whole time the stumps kept flying past on either side."

His father decided to get a lobster boat out on "the real water." "He used to close the Danielson shop on Sunday and Wednesday to go fishing on this old Maine-style lobster boat. She leaked so badly that after each trip he and I would run her aground outside the harbor on the mud to keep her from sinking. He took her up in Noank's West Cove to recaulk her at Butson's yard, but when we hauled her out of the water she simply . . ." He opens his hands, and his fingers spill like so many splayed planks.

"You can't take an old boat out of the water," says the old drag-german. "I ought to know." He pats his ribs as if he's been out of the water too long himself.

"You're so right," says Ted. "So we started to build another boat, exactly like her, but a bit bigger, copied the lines right there. Straight stern, and that year they built one over at Eldridge's with a straight stern, too. She was real good in a big sea, just got up there and . . ." His eyes light up. "Went."

They kept the new boat tied to the movie theater that sat on the river by the bascule bridge. "I used to hear the music begin up there and I'd climb off the boat into the back window to see the movies," says Ted.

"Being next to the theater wasn't so handy, though, when the big fire came that burnt down half the town. I was here in the store and tried to get back to the boat because I was living on it at the time and everything I had was there. The whole middle of the town around the bridge was on fire, and the wind was really fanning the flames, so they wouldn't let me near the place. I went down the alley out back onto the pier and borrowed a rowboat and got across where I could see the wall of the theater on fire. That wall was leaning on the boat, right on the mast, heeling the boat way over. The wind was blowing like crazy, so I got up under the flames and cut the lines. She was a deep boat with a keel so she shook off the wall and came up OK.

"Only thing was she took off on the wind and I got confused with other boats and the light from the fire and the dark so I lost track of the boat. The current was going out the same as the wind, so the boat went a long way down by the railroad tracks before I caught up."

This corner location was not the first Mystic Oliver's store. They began over by the French cleaners on the other side of the river. The present location had been a restaurant. When it went out of business in 1952, Oliver and son moved in. Father and son were then mainly in the TV business. "It was the first days of TV," says Ted, "so we put up most of the first wave of aerials.

"My brother and me. But I got sick of working in the store all day, then making rooftop runs at night, so when my father went back to the Danielson store and left this one to me, I moved in the records and it seemed natural to bring in some instruments and the things that went with the instruments."

"I remember," says the old draggerman, "when they sold the first four Model T's across the street . . . Where the sporting goods store is now. It was the livery then."

"Well, I remember the horse trough they kept right over there at the turn-around," laughs Ted. "That was there even after the Second World War. They filled it with geraniums."

"That's right," says the old draggerman. "And now they're gonna fill your place with geraniums."

A week later, just as I think I have gotten used to the blacked-out store front, I am coming into town in a tricky winter twilight. In the river's pink air, the tide is brimming and the tall cranes working on the new railroad bridge seem, with only a small effort, to be giraffes grazing at the edge of some savannah lake. It is perhaps the one forgiving moment of a dreary day, and when I look over at the corner I am not surprised to see the music store again triumphantly alive. There are lights and gaudy goods beyond even moon banjos and auto harps. There is even someone inside, a customer or maybe Ted himself, parading about with a long, narrow, uptilted horn that looks like the very model Joshua used in trumpeting down the walls of Jericho.

I rush forward but find myself like a desert traveler before a mirage. Seen up close, Oliver's is still dark and empty. What I have fallen for is the reflection from the sporting goods store across the street, and my shofar player is merely a teenager holding a foreshortened hockey stick up to the artificial light, the better to assess how his future slap shots might be tuned.

UPLAND BREAKDOWN
Vehicular Collapse as Winter Festival

Walk to the sky
Even in this life
— Henry Vaughan, "Ascension Hymn"

I have this day put on my shoe . . .
— Samuel Johnson, letter to Mrs. Thrale, Jan. 26, 1773

I ONCE FLEW in a small plane with a man who told me that while focused on his destination he always kept track out of the corner of his eye for places he might land in an emergency. No potato field, pasture, ball park, or country road escaped his nod. Now, a little after noon, the road to Hartford up from the shore was clear and the sky above a clean, winter blue. Ahead there was only a sequence of houseless hills unrolling under a dust of snow. In summer's green or autumn's glory the sight of these hills had always charmed me since, as a boy, I had come over the first hill and my father'd shouted, "Ah, 'the crowded east!' " Since then I had always wanted·to wander here, but aside from some half-formulated plans for trout fishing had never found an excuse.

And yet there was also always a more sinister feeling I'd felt going inland. It was there my family always went to the hospital and there they were buried. In fact the only reason I was driving up there now was because my lady had been hit broadside at a stoplight the night before. Crunched into a big V, that car now lay sixty miles from home in a wrecker's yard. When I'd received the phone call late the night before, it hadn't surprised me; inland, after all, was where we went to die.

Fortunately, however, in this case the people had survived and it was my job to bring what remained home.

It was all very pleasant and warm in the cab of the pickup truck, so pleasant in fact that it did not surprise me a bit when the engine began coughing. Like my pilot friend, I even had the sward selected to receive my dying vehicle.

So there I sat, two horses shot out from under me.

Though there had been a feeling of finality to the way the power had blubbered and ebbed, I ran through the gauges and gave the engine a chance to start again out of politeness to 60,000 miles of past loyalty. Nothing.

There had been just enough momentum to get me up onto the shoulder. I could sit comfortably in the sun and think about the drama of having two horses shot out from under me and the wonderful hills all around me and the cozy irony of "the crowded east" still good after some forty years. From time to time I could allow the engine another chance. But the sparse traffic, when it appeared behind me, came with a rush that can perhaps only be appreciated by one who was recently in its midst, and soon hospital images of a friend who had been savaged into a vegetable in just such a situation impelled me out of the cab.

The thing to do now, of course, was to raise the hood and go through what little I knew, more in the form of benediction than any profound sense of mechanics: throttle, spark, straying wire. *State animo fixi, hostique sperinto sofras.* So be it.

Slam.

There were now snowy hills.

They were better than hospitals.

I locked up, pulled my scarf and coat about me. I was free. Or was I? I was not sure that this ought to be the day to roam blithely about the middle of Connecticut. Wasn't there, after all, some obligation, after the manner of officers taken prisoner, to escape? Surely I must get on with this, ah, escape.

There was, of course, the more straightforward obligation of picking up my lady in Hartford. The only question was which way to hike. I remembered some buildings a few miles back, and since the wind was coming out of those barren humps to the north, I lowered my earflaps and set forth south upon the broad highway. Thank God I had on my old hiking boots.

The north wind was crisp, but as it came from behind, I welcomed its strong push and shrugged off its ear-buzzing edge. The ground along the roadside was stiff, but dry. I studied the eyes of passing motorists to see how they were taking my truck and the widening distance between me and it. In a recent trip through New York I had seen near a dozen cars abandoned along the ten or so miles leading in and out of the city. In such moments one tends to look for instruction. What is the difference between fallen comrades and oneself? What did they do wrong? What am I (still) doing right? While there are many things that can cause a car to break down along the highway, and these were even all very different models, the amazing fact about every one of these New York vehicles was that they seemed to have suffered identically. It looked as if each of these cars had been going merrily along when they had shed all four tires, spewed all glass out of their windows, and burst into fire.

With such things in mind it became increasingly difficult for me to look back at the space between me and my beloved truck. From a hundred yards I congratulated myself on my progress, yet worried about the increasing difficulties in defense that distance meant. If, say, this blue van with the lout at the wheel were to pull over, could I sprint back, all tweed flying, to pull him off my darling's hub caps? And assuming I could handle him, what about the buddies he might have stored in the blind back of his rolling world, a race of super-oafs roused from the inner recesses of cut-pile carpet and stereo who would come yowling and blinking into the sunlight to live out a fantasy fed on Burt Reynolds flicks and NFL replays?

Could one expect help from passing traffic? In youth I had hitch-hiked some with fair success, but counted each ride as something survived rather than accomplished. The last occasion, I'd looked up to see a trailer truck head-on swapping lanes with us. Since then the nut-rate would hardly seem to have diminished, so I plowed on trying to leave the impression not of a wounded creature straggling further and further from the nest. Fortunately my truck is painted much like a state highway vehicle, so, as I strode on, I tried to create the image of a transportation engineer, some mid-management type impatient of delegated report who wanted to get out in the field to more precisely pace off the latest happy asphalt incursion.

In any case, the truck was nearly lost along a long, slow bend. To hell with the bloody tin box on wheels anyway. In these same ancient walking shoes I had once tramped from the Mystic River through the Great Swamp to Narragansett Bay in three glorious days. And wasn't everybody's kid sister now doing fifteen miles running before breakfast? How rediculous seemed the prisoners of the passing tin boxes, hunched over their steering wheels like heretics on the rack, most grimacing, some maniacally cackling at New York DJs and helicopter traffic reports.

There was a concrete highway crossover ahead and before it the few houses I had seen in the corner of my eye as I'd sped past. Now floating in sunlight halfway up along the side of the hill, they seem not so much strung out and suburban as composed like an island village. From a large, old-style house in the middle rose smoke from a wood fire.

I walked toward the village, trying to make it come into some sort of congruity with the highway, but as I got closer it became apparent that the settlement up there had nothing to do with the road down which I walked.

Because the traffic was light, I could cross my lane, but the median divider was a wide ditch gagging with water thinly and intermittently frozen. I followed the median ditch until I found a spot narrow enough for leaping. Beyond lay a dense band of briars and shurbs. Directly above me, the village might as well have been suspended in mist like some Shangri-la.

There was nothing to do but keep walking on past the village, hoping for a break in the briars. The brush remained impenetrable until I reached the overpass, where the highway scar served to allow a path up the steep, loose rock. I remembered trying to get up to the Plains of Abraham outside Quebec and having the bank come sliding down all about me as if I were climbing a mountain made of pennies. Here, after a preliminary uneasiness as we got used to each other, the bank, being composed of granite trap, held, and I found myself eye-level with a narrow road that wound back up into the village.

Up close, the place was hardly a Shangri-la. Snagged around a few old farmsteads were a half-dozen contemporary homes that looked as if they'd washed up from housing developments. Far below, no more disturbing than a trout stream, the highway hummed and bubbled. I rang the bell of a pink duplex and stared at the oblong plastic button that was lighted in the middle of the day. There was another bell button just like it on the other side, so I tried that. A dog barked at the house next door. I crossed the street, aware that perhaps the eyes of the villagers might be sizing me up.

And what indeed was I now? Not the knight on the horse come to save the fair maiden. Probably not the highway engineer impatient of report, either. Although for an American to be deprived in mid-passage of his wheels can lead to an identity crisis, it was not so much my own self-picture I was worried about as finding a *persona* that would get me help. After all, there had been much in the papers lately of dreadful breaches in civilization, men knocking down doors, shooting old women, raping young ones, pistol-whipping men, and even sitting about for hours in the breached homes dining on chair legs and the entrails of sofas.

What did I have to work with? Down on the highway I'd had my truck as costume. Now I was naked of all but what was a few inches out from me. Was I, for instance, "well-dressed"? One wanted to be,

of course, presentable, but not too . . . well-dressed. I considered the
matter not in reference to any current fashion, but that ageless Post
Office wall sense, as: "alias 'Rimp Vasqueeze,' drives late-model cars,
can forge several signatures, has mastered a variety of con games, is
armed and well-dressed."

My topcoat was last fall's model, a two-hundred-dollar Railroad
Salvage Harris tweed marked down, apparently for mere rumpled-
ness, to five. True, it had been ignored since and was probably mis-
tagged. ("Vasqueeze has been seen switching tags at discount clothing
outlets.") Under the Railroad Salvage Harris tweed poked those ancient hiking boots I had been so recently thanking God for. Would
Vasqueeze, surely a wing-tip man, let himself be betrayed by so mun-
dane a thing as a boot?

My cap, however, was a dark wool with the Ashton Club label
nearly faded from the interior. It had been my late uncle's, a con-
servative man who had worked for the Federal Housing Authority as
a mortgage consultant. Would I ingratiate myself in the community if
I seemed to be coming around, as had he for years? This was clearly
the sort of spot where he'd have his eye out for space heaters and
handrails on cellar stairs.

This, of course, raised the key question. Exactly what sort of fed-
eration was this community in? I didn't even know its name or the
name of the nearest "big town." Was it like any of the shoreline towns
from which I had just come? Was it more like a suburban "Capitol
area" bedroom? Was there a difference any more that might matter
in such cases? My sixth-grade teacher at Beach Park School in West
Hartford had always stressed "When in Rome, do as the Romans do."
But was this Rome or Brundisium?

Perhaps this place was one of those pockets of religious fanati-
cism one hears about within our borders? Would it then be best to
appear to be a man of the cloth? One of the Apocalypse salesmen who
come out with the jonquils in the spring? Or would this be the precise
heresy that ended one in the pot, so to speak?

Across the street, down which no vehicle had yet come, was a
house with a faded sign on the lamp post. At first I thought the pass-
ers-by were being offered African Violence, but up closer the deal
seemed to be about flowers. Perhaps this would be a good place to test
this business of "well-dressed."

While I waited for the violet person to verify my respectability, a
big black dog stalked me stiff-legged from all the way across the street.
Were dogs in these parts like dogs in my parts? Indeed, the beast

looked very much like the one I'd left behind to stalk stiff-legged any unfortunate itinerants. Could this dog be made to appreciate the situation?

"Nice dog."

Not necessarily, Vasqueeze.

The uneasy language of the dog did bring forth its owner from across the street, a young woman apologizing in a recognizable dialect for the dog's rudeness.

"Not at all," I said generously. "He's only doing his job, just what in fact I'd want my own dog to do at my own personal home, which is broken down—electrical malfunction no doubt, you know these new-fangled cars these days, a pickup actually, but you can't see it, ma'am, as it's just around a bend in the highway below where I was going to pickup another car that was wrecked, incidently a dog very much like this, part Labrador, right? . . ."

This speech, which began to sound to both me and the dog more and more like vintage Vasqueeze, seemed amazingly enough to set the heart of the maid at ease, a fact I took with mixed feelings. Praising the dog's continued integrity, I followed its mistress as she led me to her house. ". . . and the irony was, here I was going to pick up a lady who'd had her own little accident."

"Yes," she said, "usually the house next door gets all the highway people."

Ah, I thought, a village of moon-cussers who savage the wrecks of innocent navigators.

She insisted I come in, though I was willing to settle for a cap-in-hand, front-stoop wait while she phoned the agency of her choice. Vacillating between seeing myself as the victim of her moon-cussing and my own potential as the pillager, I wanted to cry out, "No, no, don't let me in—I am Vasqueeze, the con man, and at the very least I'll switch tags on all your interiors."

Her interior featured a wood stove which gave off a cozy air, and the dining room table gleamed so that I thought of old traveler's tales in which the weary always "partook of their fill."

The garage she recommended would be down with a wrecker in a few minutes. The interval gave me a chance to run my eye over the library, chiefly paperback romances. Out the back window, the highway ran at the bottom of its valley. Competing with it for what thin sound the sun-stained air permitted, the TV struggled to hold its soap opera. "I'm sorry," she said, "the reception isn't so good in the daytime, especially a pretty day like this, but I'm hooked on this show."

"G.H.?" I said, feeling more Vasqueezian.

"Oh, no. This is 'One Life to Live.' G.H. is not until another hour."

She went to the table and pulled out a bottle which she set on the gleaming surface. As the sun hit the liquid the yellow tint looked like an Italian liqueur, the one in which they put the twig and let it writhe the slow, vegetative dance. By the wood stove stood an axe with a head-to-handle ratio that would have taken a brawny man to drive.

"Thank you," I said. "I'll wait outside."

As I turned at the door to wave good-bye, I saw she was not drinking the stuff in the bottle, but spreading it out over the table and rubbing it with a light rag.

The big garage to which I had been towed was socked up against the bank made for the highway exit. The truck started up immediately and ran until the mechanic and I got bored listening and turned it off. While the traffic roared overhead, I began to feel I'd made up the whole thing just to get a walk out of the Marlborough hills. The mechanic, however, assured me that it was probably all the fault of the snodnel inverter's intermittent malfunctioning. To clarify, he slapped the evil part, a box of plastic gourmet pasta stuck on the inside of the fender ahead of the ballast resister.

"What does it do?" I said, "that is, when it is not malfunctioning."

"It works," he said.

"Yes, but doing what?"

"It's like this thing." He pointed to the ballast resister. "It does something you didn't used to need, but now that you do, you can't go without it."

The snodnel inverter, of course, could not be fixed, even though we were in a huge garage, with a large, obviously competent crew, all equipped with racks and benches of sophisticated equipment. It had to be replaced from the reserve of snodnel inverters in the nearest major city, which turned out to be Middletown. Such a quest would take the rest of the afternoon.

I made my phone calls. "I'm glad the highway didn't get you," she said.

"I'm glad it didn't get you either."

While I waited I asked to be shown a place in the garage where I might be out of the way. From the tiny closet where the bookkeeping was done, I was presented with a green vinyl chair with clean, steel arms. This impressive chair was placed about eight feet from the wall upon which hung a Currier & Ives calendar. It was an area relatively free of pneumatic wrench and tire iron fire. There was a soda machine, from which I bought a can of orange-flavored liquid. I removed my Railroad Salvage tweed and folded it carefully, sat on it, sipped the orange, and thought about lunch. Most of the mechanics managed to avoid my bloated throne.

One that didn't dropped a plastic "organizer" containing little boxes of fuses down the back of my neck. When the organizer hit the floor it became very disorganized and all the little fuses fled in various directions radiating out from my chair. The young man spent the next half hour on his hands and knees chasing down the various sizes and trying them in the organizer. A number of people knelt on down to the task from time to time, until it looked like a crap game.

Eventually everyone left the young man to mutter and organize alone. I took the opportunity to lean over and ask him if he knew of some place I could get lunch. Was the old Marlborough Tavern open, for instance? He said no, that had been closed for years, but there was another place that was "pretty good, except . . ."

"Yes?"

"It's way down the road."

"Oh." I sat on my throne and watched him grovel for the fuses while the sun poured in the plate glass and the pneumatic wrenches rattled and the tire irons clanged. I stared at the Currier & Ives, which was of an inn on a snowy day, and I soon found myself walking down a country road past a waterfall where white ducks bobbed and splashed.

The noise of the ducks and the waterfall drowned out the harsh din of the garage, and even after I was up the hill away from the pond, there was yet a country stillness all about, for the highway, which was parallel, but out of sight, could easily be the lingering sound of the waterfall. There was even a slight smell of earth and leaf mold under the crisp ground.

At the top of a gentle rise was a big, old clapboard house for sale, and as I maintained my pace it was an easy matter to tour the house in my mind, moving through kitchen and dining room and even climbing the stairs to my bed for the night.

With the house behind I had a down-hill with a scuffed water opening up on the left. The water was far beyond the dimensions of the pond with the white ducks. Indeed, there had been something faintly familiar about the road, but now it came back to me: the lake with the long, funny name we'd count on to get us halfway down to the shore in the 1940s. As we'd drive up over the hill I'd think we were "there," at the shore, that is. At first there would almost seem to be enough water in the lake to support that illusion, but there was always the absence of tide line manifest in the way the cottages perched tight to the mild edge. "Maybe we should stop here," my mother'd say. "And could you get a schooner in there?" my father'd say. Now walking along its edge, I felt the lake seemed to almost hold more water than I could, schoonerless, handle. Between me and it, however, there were the same ramshackle summer cottages with their screen porches and low swaybacked roofs, I remembered, and the sound of the far-off highway was easily the wind off the lake.

There was a narrow strip of land between the lake and the road, and under great trees were some boats laid up for the winter. One was a big, flat-iron skiff just like what you'd expect to see on such a lake in the forties. The other lay under a clear plastic cover. From the road the line of the sheer and the depth of the skeg were striking. Deep-water stuff. Attracted by the sea-kindly features of this little ship, I stepped over the guard rail and peered down through the plastic. Lapstreak, double-ended with stern-sheets and a sailing rig, she lay like a Sleeping Beauty awaiting her prince. I looked into her full bilge and even stooped to search for a name where the plastic skirts gathered at the stern to opaqueness. The sun was getting low and the air cold, and the sound of the far-off highway was easily the wind in the trees.

Up the road two human beauties approached, rubbing their nostrils with the back of their gloves and blowing bubbles. Feeling a bit like the Man from La Mancha, I asked them if I were on the right road to the tavern. After a struggle with the language, they confirmed my route.

"All ya gotta do is jus keep go-win."

They, of course, had no idea how long it was "by walking," though they had come that way. I began to be concerned about getting back to the garage in time to greet my lady, who'd be getting a ride down from Hartford, but I was also hungry enough not to want to face the fuse organizer and pneumatic wrenches lightheaded on an empty stomach.

The road began to climb, and behind me the lake in the late sun had shifted. I remembered coming up this same hill. It had been in summer, some thirty years before, when there had been no other highway. Going very slowly we had been . . . much like now . . . but the trees in foliage overhead. We were riding roofless in a low-slung, home-made contraption, part jeep, part roadster, and were towing on a small trailer the main spar of a gaff sloop. It was to be the last voyage for that ancient rig, as the boat had been modernized. The gaff simply could not sail to windward in light air with the new Marconis and

not carry a luff, so here it was on its way to the final resting place
where it was to live out its life as a flag pole, there to suffer the igno-
miny of perpetual luffing. If we drove in third gear, or even second,
the trailer would begin to gallop, and the tip of the mast would flick
the tar. The only solution was to stay in low, and in the monotony of
that grind we were lulled into illusions of the sea, dangling our hands
over the easy sides of the roadster, like lovers in a canoe.

As the light lengthened and the trees close to the shoulder soft-
ened, it came to me now that on and off since that summer of the gaff
rig, in dreams, I had traveled that stretch of road walking or sometimes driving in the roadster at a walker's tempo. Lately, however, as
I found myself vicariously displaced, caught between the inland jobs
some members of our family had had to take and the shore where we
wanted to be, floating out there between the sea where we most felt
alive and the city where we all seemed to go to die, climbing this hill
had become the major occupation of my nights.

The odd thing now was, I didn't feel it was some sort of dèjá vu
nightmare. What was happening was simply the way to handle things—
you just keep on walking.

The tavern was on the back of the next hill and at first I thought
it was just a colonial house. The way in, as I was on foot, also bewildered me, and I found myself at the front corner window peering
into a room where several tables were set with silverware and linen
over a floor of wide boards. Through the windowpanes I could smell
fresh baked bread. The walls were light blue, a shade paler than the
lake behind me now, and I saw a man at a table against the far wall
eating stew and drinking dark beer and blotting his lips.

Inside, while I awaited my own stew and black beer, I munched
on the fresh bread and looked out at the lake, which was now harsh
under the wind that had come up at dusk. According to the menu,
the tavern was based on an "ordinary" which functioned as a way
station in the 1600s on the Monhege Path in what was then Glaston-
bury. The path served as an alternate to the Connecticut River, which
in those days was undredged so that travel was "slow and hazardous."

The man eating next to the wall turned out to be the tavern keeper
and he said they recieved many people who were glad to be in off the
highway, but most of them had not had two horses shot out from
under them on the same journey.

The stew was excellent and I sopped up the last drop with the
fresh biscuits, paid my modest bill, and set forth again. The air was
chill and the wind against me, but I was fortified and boomed back

up the road, grabbing a stick alongside the road as a walking staff to propel me.

In the gathering dark, I had to duck more traffic on the narrow road and became acquainted with a number of mailboxes and newspaper holders that had been sideswiped into twisted figures that loomed like tormented gnomes. I passed the flat-iron forties-like skiff and the Sleeping Beauty boat with hardly a nod. The big house I'd imagined buying was dark and did not look inviting. Under the waterfall the white ducks jerked and squeaked like targets in a carnival ring toss. The car behind me was the mechanic, who told me the snodnel was in and offered me a ride the last few hundred yards. I tossed aside my walking stick and got in.

"I used to come through on this same old road when I was a kid," I said.

"Well, you know, he said, "I guess this is a nice town. Hell, I bomb in and out of here all day and half the night pulling people off that highway out there—people who are gunning up and down to Hartford who never even know this little town exists until something bad happens."

My lady had arrived at the garage. We inspected the snodnel, paid the bill, and rode the few minutes back to the tavern. "You probably walk further from the parking lot to the job," I said.

"I think I do."

"Well, I'm glad the highway didn't get you."

"I'm glad it didn't get you."

The dining room was crowded now and we got the last table. I had another beer and some salad and watched her eat a quiche in the candlelight. Past her, out the window, the lake was invisible in the dark, but I thought I could hear above the murmur of the room the rumble of the highway, undredged and hazardous.

"I'm really glad that it didn't get you," I said.

She raised her glass.

On the way out we saw a sign that offered us the highway or the old road, and we came home on the worn round-top where there was no traffic and the earth rose and fell gently beneath us.

PART FIVE

Spring

Soon as the weather permitted, I made a tour around the shores of the island, and afterwards crossed over every farm of the interior, examining first its geological structure and then its agricultural resources. I had occasion to stop frequently at the houses of the inhabitants, and was every where received with kindness and hospitality.

— Charles Jackson, M.D. *Report on the Geological and Agricultural Survey of the State of Rhode Island,* "Block-Island, or New Shoreham," 1840.

The first day in the spring, you know, after the winter has kept you out of there, I'm just a bit leery of looking into last summer's places.

— Tony Fasceon, Blue Diamond Shellfish Company

BLOCK ISLAND
MEMORIES I

Let's go to Tahiti.

— Dr. Roy Allen

Perhaps your doctor has prescribed a sea trip, but through fear of seasickness you do not take it. Come to Block Island and enjoy a sea trip without any of its inconveniences!

— *The Book of Rhode Island, 1930*

I REMEMBER being deep in the middle of the state some twenty years ago to help carry a coffin up a back-breaking knoll just as a sleet storm was edging in. After the custom of our times we were supposedly merely honorary pall-bearers, but this particular plot was in such lumpy terrain and the footing so insecure that the usual mortician's machinery was helpless, and we had been pressed into serious service. A sad crew it was, too, a handful of middle-aged men picked for their dignity and me as a token young buck. The man next to me, known for his heart condition—cocktail parties always found him early sagging onto his hosts' banister—asked me between gasps to shift in a little closer to him so that I could assume more of his load. He needed, he puffed, he needed a hand free to pop another nitro pill. I took a bigger bite of the coffin; he took his pill and we groaned the corpse closer to the raw hole. The priest signaled for us to ease our burden down, and the heart patient looked around. The land fell away below us in startling lumps and waves, the heaving ground spindrifted with frost and sleet. The priest coughed softly and opened his mouth to begin. What came out, however, was a stage whisper from the heart patient. "Jesus," he said, and I grabbed the back of his coat, "Jesus, but doesn't it look just like Block Island."

For my fellow pallbearer, Block Island not only was a sustaining dream while literally tottering at the edge of a winter grave, but had been in healthier summer a place of weekly pilgrimage. Each Friday he would leave his office job up in Hartford and out he would go from an eastern Connecticut port. It was twenty-five miles, the last twenty in unprotected water, his pre-war wooden motorboat banging into the seas off Watch Hill passage, his stumpy signal mast beating the vast sky as the old round-bottomed girl wallowed down the swells that even on calm days rolled in from the open Atlantic.

He would usually stay in Block Island's Great Salt Pond harbor, rafted at the end of Pier 76 as it was then known. Evidently inspired by a vision of some cross-eyed, drunken yurt-maker, he would expand his small, leaky cabin so that it might provide a more gracious setting for his wife, rigging a series of canvas roofs and side walls, the design, erection, and maintenance of which would occupy him most of the weekend. There might be a half-dozen boats tied snugly on either side of him but he would always hoist a barn lantern up through the canvas roof, where it would dangle from the top of his mast. "You've got to have an anchor light at night," he'd say, "whether you're moored at a pier or way out by yourself in the roadstead."

For him, apparently, Block Island was always a case of being way out by yourself in the roadstead. "I don't know why I have a boat," he'd say, "and I don't know why I must always go out there. I get seasick every single time and I am always deathly afraid."

The pallbearer's lament was familiar, for as I was growing up, getting to Block Island as often as possible, no matter the peril, seemed to be what one lived for. There was what you might even call a medical imperative, for dressed in shorts and a straw hat and carrying a bunch of bananas and a stone crock of rum, the family doctor would come aboard whatever boat we had, put the crock under the bunk, hang the bananas in the skylight, and shout, "Let's go to Tahiti!"

By which he meant, of course, Block Island.

"A man's work," writes Albert Camus, "is nothing but this slow trek to rediscover, through the detours of art, those two or three great and simple images in whose presence his heart first opened." Even as my horizons expanded, I found I had been imprinted with Block Island, and years later when I was dozing in a drizzle aboard the ferry going from Galway to Inishmore, I woke up thinking I was on the Block Island ferry. Or going from Piraeus to Poros on a blazing summer day, I blinked in the famous Greek glare for a moment and found myself back on the Block Island boat.

There are a number of different men who handle the various ferry boats running in and out of Block Island's harbors, but the local favorite is young Matty Rooney, now still only in his mid-twenties. Matty was a Block Island waif who fell in love with life around the ferry slip and did odd jobs, grabbing a dock line here and there or

carrying some freight when the crew was caught shorthanded. At six-
teen he became part of the crew.

The legendary Captain Dan took a liking to Matty and brought
him up in the pilothouse on the run between Old Harbor and Galilee
on the mainland. In that privileged spot Captain Dan shared how to
lay out a course, how to keep up the charts, how to spill a bad following sea. Most awe-inspiring is how in a strong March wind shifting
across the roofs of the fish factories at Galilee, Captain Dan's protégé
goes aft on the bridge to his outside control box and like a kid in an
arcade shooting planets manages to jockey the very real and very high-
sided *Quonset* into the narrow hole among very real rafting draggers
that every day present a different configuration.

Though presently sporting a huge Mexican sombrero on the
Quonset, Matty will be on the Block Island run only through August
when he will work oil-rig runs in the North Atlantic in the fall and
tow boats down around Hackensack in winter.

Ferry boats are all right, but the idea used to be that you had to
earn your way out. In the late 1920s, Frank Jo Raymond, who was
keeper at Latimer's Light in Fishers Island Sound, took one of his
liberty days and, instead of rowing the half-hour into Stonington, used
the fourteen-foot, round-bottomed boat and its eight-foot oars to row
to Block Island. Frank is still around, a lean man with white hair and
a white beard. Though his lighthouse is on automatic, he is not. "That
day I decided to row to Block it was thick fog, but that was my liberty
day, so I went anyway. Five and a half hours later the fog broke and
there was Block, those big bluffs under the Southwest Lighthouse. I'd
miscalculated my tides a bit, and it took me an extra hour to get around
inside the New Harbor, not exactly what you want on the end of a
trip like that, but I was just glad to see the island at all.

"Just a few years ago, two other local fellows, Ambrose Burrows
of Quambaug and Peter Tripp of Stonington, they each rowed out.
Ambrose's wife was already out there, so that was the way he joined
her, and Peter, he was supposed to meet a fellow who had a boat out
there but the transportation schedule got so complicated he said 'the
hell with it' and simply rowed out."

Usually it was enough merely to sail. Of the many who make sailing pilgrimages to the island, one of the most interesting in terms of
the island's continuity is Captain Adrain Lane of Noank. Captain Adrian is the namesake and descendant of Dutchman Adriaen Block,
who landed on the island in 1614 and changed the map-happy da
Verrazano's name of the place from "Claudia." In designating the

island after his sponsoring king's mother, Verrazano, of course, had ignored the Narragansett tribe's pious evocation of Manisses ("Little God"). "Block not only landed on the island," says Captain Adrian, "but stayed long enough for his son Peter to marry one of the native girls. By then it was known as 'Adriaen's Eyland."

The present Captain Adrian takes a busman's holiday each summer in his ninety-year-old catboat *Dolphin*. "Somehow we always seem to manage to wind up out at Block." Right where his ancestor managed to wind up 371 years ago.

In summer on most pleasant days the wind is southwest so that from Connecticut it is easy to let your boom out and roll downhill to Great Salt Pond, a long-afternoon's sail. Coming back from Block Island, however, you often get what Captain Adrian calls "a good muzzler" and "have to pay the piper."

The puritan morality indeed has its way in most concrete terms: if the weather is still good, that same fair wind that brought you out for nothing is not only on the nose, but always seems somehow nastier. If the wind has shifted out of the east, it will give you another ride back, but lest you think the trip is without price, the easterly will usually bring fog. In either case, the hole to hit coming in at Watch Hill can be elusive.

The reefs have a history of wrecks and only a few years ago, in just such a boat as my father and I used to make the same passage, a father and son disappeared somewhere in there where the sea curls over the granite and the squat sea bell clanks its requiem.

That the piper has been indeed playing, is, of course, part of the Block Island myth. Sometimes a particular boat will build up a reputation that survives down to its present crew. A man I know well once bought an old schooner, partially I think because the vessel had, as the former owner bragged, "learned her way to Block Island all by herself." Unfortunately, when the new owner sailed into Great Salt Pond the first time, with his wife aboard, he was greeted on the pier by a chorus of what might euphemistically be called chorus girls. "Hi, fellas! We saw your boat come in from the hill." Bottles in hand, they were all set to board when the captain's wife emerged from below.

An afternoon at one of the piers will demonstrate how some of these reputations are built. While two sun-dazzled girls in bikinis cavort, glass in hand, about the fighting chairs in the cockpit, here is a fellow up on his flying bridge, dark glasses on against the glare, bellowing into his radio, which he's got hooked up so that the entire harbor is his party. "Hi, dear. Yes, we're out here tuna fishing at Block, but we're pretty well socked in, you know. What? No fog at home?"

There is a roar of laughter, catcalls, and advice from all the surrounding boats.

"Well, this much be a case of local conditions, dear. I can assure you we're some socked in."

Informing the harbor life from the top of each surrounding rise but providing a more old-fashioned, elegant tone are the hotels, big wooden turn-of-the-century buildings with mansard roofs and wide verandas. Through the years these places ran the range from the always-elegant Spring House to the now-defunct New Vasqueeze House. After the 1938 hurricane put the final disastrous touches on the Depression many of these hotels went to ruin, but the remaining ones are coming back, as epitomized by the Manisses House restoration into a hotel which combines the best of the new, such as Jacuzzis in private baths, with the old atmosphere.

Old promos for the "health resort" even parsed exactly what was in sea air: "Doctors knew of the health-giving qualities of breezes laden with sulphates of magnesium and potassium, chloride of sodium, bromine, iodine and other of nature's remedies distilled fresh from the ocean laboratories."

Visitors were asked to "think of those long sleepless nights when you have prayed for a breath of cool air, when you could have enjoyed a refreshing night's sleep at Block Island! The soothing and restful quality of this balmy air, and the ceaseless music of breakers on the beaches, have a magic influence upon overworked brains and the nervously prostrated; while the stimulating influence of the tonic air compels the dyspeptic to forget the remorse of his guilty stomach."

I have indeed enjoyed restful nights' sleep at Block Island. Though at the moment I'm hard put to remember when. Rafting at Pier 76 there were feet over one's bunk all night, or, more pleasantly, avuncular tromboning from atop the nearby dock piling, or long narratives all middle and no ends by another uncle hanging upside down in the open hatch like a demented tree sloth. Away from the dock, far from all uncles narrating and tailgating, alone out on the anchor in the vastness of Great Salt Pond Harbor, there was always the worry that one of Block Island's "balmy airs" would crank up a midnight willie-waught and send you dragging on across the pond either into another boat or maybe (this a 3:00 A.M. fantasy) right on out of the harbor—*dérade*, as Rimbaud has it in "The Drunken Boat," ". . . dragged out of the harbor by winds."

Ashore, of course, one did not worry about *dérade*, or at least so I thought when I made my reservations at the New Vasqueeze House. As an example of what the Block Island hotel often was in the long degenerate phase between the era of the turn-of-the-century health spa and the present restoration, this ramshackle jumble of mansard and veranda might serve *exempli gratia*. Alas, the New Vasqueeze House has been razed to make room for a parking lot, a fact that will deprive future generations of this in some ways quintessential Block Island experience.

A typical overnight at the New Vasqueeze House began when you ascended the steps to the third floor. You have your key in one hand, and your unplugged electric fan in the other. Although your door does not shut tight enough to lock, you go through the furtive charade of opening it with your key. This scene has comic overtones when two or more strange couples back out of their rooms into the hall at once, each pretending to "lock" their doors while checking over their shoulders to see how the act is going. If the other couple catches you and they laugh, you are both apt to give up the show and go down to the bar and buy each other a drink.

"And what's in our room really worth stealing? A straw hat? A summer novel? A beach towel?

"What's worth stealing is the fan. And don't you forget it."

For indeed at the upper back of the New Vasqueeze House, one prayed on long, sleepless nights for a breath of cool air. To insure that no fellow guest preyed upon our fan we used to stash it in the car and carry it each night aloft to bed like a candle.

Even with the fan on, what one had for the "ceaseless music of breakers on the beaches" was the ceaseless music from the bar, which seemed to seep up through the floor. "Performing in the lounge" was someone like Al Frimillo or Danny McLoomie, artists locked in some cultural never-never land between music hall bellow canto and 1950s Catskills. There certainly was a "period flavor" to this, but what period was hard to say. Perhaps, like much of the post fin de siècle architecture of the place, the music can best be summed up by calling it simply "Block Island."

In any case, one soon discovered that Al Frimillo or Danny McLoomie suffered from an acute case of arpeggiosis. Not a bar of music had been penned by Cole Porter, Frank Loesser, E. Y. Harburg, Jerome Kern, Irving Berlin, Hoagy Carmichael, or Chauncey

Olcott but these pianists felt compelled to fill it out with the same run in the same key:

> Anda nun canna cum-pare *(diddle-diddle-diddle-ding)*
> With mya why-auld *(diddle-diddle-diddle-ding)*
> Eye-rush *(diddle-diddle-diddle-ding)*
> Rose *(diddle-diddle-diddle-DING).*

After a while you did not hear the tunes; all you heard was the ceaseless music of the fills, trapped apparently forever in the stairwells, so that as you lay on your back in the dark, hour after ceaseless hour, the effect was of having the "stimulating influence" of herd upon herd of bugs fingering their way all over you:

Diddle-diddle-diddle-ding.

At some point, of course, this "tonic air compels the dyspeptic" to attend to "the remorse of his guilty stomach."

You must begin looking for the bathroom.

In the interests of marital bliss, you cannot turn on the room light, a single naked bulb overhead, fit for major surgery, or in the "improved era" the "indirect lighting," which is so entirely oblique as to be digressive beyond all hope of illumination. You have not used your bathrobe on the mainland for the last two months, so it is not with you now.

You find your pants and put them on wondering if you should take your wallet down the lurching corridor or leave it with your defenseless sleeping mate behind the unlockable door. Which raises the question of the defenseless sleeping mate. (How about those five roughnecks bunking direcly across the hall, or that shifty-eyed dyspeptic coughing through the partition next door?)

Down the worn carpet of the hall you go. Or in the improved era, down the new carpet, which you can feel is laid over the old carpet. At least with just the worn carpet you knew what was underfoot. This feels like beach towels softly stretched over yawning voids, and you try to recall what kitchen cauldrons, what pianos, might lurk directly below. Also you keep checking over your shoulder at your door and the roughnecks' door and seedy-dyspeptic's door, all of which soon merge and are gone as up and down levels, around corners you plod, lit by lurid exit lights and the odd blast from a tantalizing door crack. At last you arrive at the bathroom door and are greeted by the sound of someone retching his guts out.

Anda nun canna cum-pare *(diddle-diddle-diddle-ding).*

When you finally return to your room after having found an unused bathroom on a different floor, you feel like Odysseus returning to Penelope. Unlike Homer's epic, however, your return merely wakens Penelope into realizing she must go on her own voyage. A discussion follows in which you promise to escort her (What, and leave the room with its fan, wallets, and wine unguarded?). When all this is worked out and you are lying back, your head on a New Vasqueeze House pillow, and realize someone has performed an arpeggioctomy on Al McLoomie in the lounge (an operation which only serves to remind you of how late it must be), the people in the room directly upstairs begin moving the furniture.

At sunrise, just outside the window, as part of the new Block Island improvement program, the diesel compressor for the sewer construction project is lit off.

On the other end of the scale, creating perhaps the aura off which the New Vasqueeze House and other hotels sought to live, is the Spring House. Famous continually since the turn of the century, the Spring House still commands its own green wave of a hill overlooking Old Harbor with a dizzy sweep of road down to salt ponds and the open sea beyond.

The Spring House itself is three white wooden stories layered by red shingled roofs capped by an ornate cupola. Surrounding the main building are red and white annexes, and assorted outbuildings, and whenever I see the girls up there on the long lawns, moving in and out of the white planked outbuildings full of sea air and assignation, I think of my grandmother, who before she was married went out to the Spring House to a teacher's convention around 1900 and liked it so much she stayed on several weeks.

There she was courted by a suave gentleman, a master at cards and conversation and comments about the sea below the lawn, a cut-glass salesman who moved through the more elegant corners of the world. One imagines the veranda, his straw boater, the movement of his mustache as he shapes and smooths, blowing long translucent balloons out of the day's sand . . . and his wink. "Something heavily prunted on the stem, my dear, with perhaps a foot rim gadrooned." At the end of the summer, he anneals their rigaree in a final, cooling lehr: "I am, my dear, you see, a married man."

On the great green roll of the Spring House's front lawn stand an oversize iron mastiff and nearby an iron deer. It is part of the magic of the air about the Spring House that these inanimate figures take on life. The deer strolls, and the dog, though still, seems to have discovered something across the grass, an illusion that works somehow strongest in bright noon light.

One such summer morning, after a night at the New Vasqueeze House, I was walking cautiously up past the iron dog, seduced by a snatch of Mozart drifting across the wide veranda of the Spring House. Inside the front parlor, empty chairs stood spaced discreetly so that I felt one could derive the precise social relationships among any who had ever reposed in this room for the past eighty years just by knowing where they had sat.

The Mozart grew louder, drawing me across the vast parlor where sea-light and health-giving breezes laden with sulphates of magnesium and potassium, chloride of sodium, bromine, iodine, and other of nature's remedies soaked the carpet from a dozen windows. Were there hallways to cross? Cadenzas where staircases descended from some high interior chromatically? There were French doors and these I gently opened. In a sun-room were four people seated in a circle before music stands: two violins, a viola, and cello. I stood open-mouthed.

The leader glanced up. He was a white-haired man who looked just like Isaac Stern. The sunlight drenched the horsehair on his Tourte bow, and as he began a cadenza, his grin flattened on the hard-rubber chin rest of his violin. I waved and backed out, closing the French doors behind me . . . floated across the parlor on the Mozart and out the wide veranda to the lawn, where above the sea, the iron dog trembled on point.

BLOCK ISLAND
MEMORIES II

". . . but it would afford a safe asylum for passing vessels if over-
taken by storm or by contrary winds."

—Frederick J. Benson, "Block Island Harbors," *Research,*
Reflection and Recollections of Block Island

A 1911 POSTCARD shows the "Block Island Jail," an ediface
that looks more like a fruitstand. Set in the sand, with a minimum of beach grass about, the shack can't be more than fifty
yards from the sea. Out front are three men holding up a two-post
veranda. The uniformed pair to the left would seem to be the law, the
overalled lounger to the right, the lawbreaker, though the uniforms
are so rag-taggle they may not be uniforms at all and so the situation
may be reversed. Or maybe on the day the photographer happened
by, there was no prisoner and the gentleman in overalls is the janitor.
It is a typical Block Island ambiguity.

In the late twenties when my father started visiting along the docks,
that jail no longer seemed to be around, but there was a resident state
trooper who improvised his own version of what we would today call
"restraining methods."

"If anyone got too far out of line in a bar, the trooper would
handcuff him and drive him out to the end of the island. The trooper'd take the guy's shoes off and uncuff him and leave him there while
he drove back to town with the shoes.

"In those days it was pretty much uninhabited out there and the
guy could bay into Rodman's Hollow all he wanted without bothering
anybody but the rabbits and deer. By the time he'd walked down all
those dirt roads back to town, it would be dawn and he'd be more or
less sober, or at least too footsore to raise any more hell for a while,
so the policeman would hand him back his shoes and that would be
that."

Even as late as after World War II, the offending drunk might
merely be tied to the piano leg at Pier 76. My father relates how one
misty dawn, while rafting at the pier, he was awakened by a terrible

whooping and hollering. " 'Cast off! For God's sakes, cast off! They're after me!'

"And here came this fellow in red pants running down from the bar on the hill. He's running the whole way waving a piano leg to which he's still handcuffed, and before anyone can even blink, much less adjust a rope or fiddle an engine, he's sailed on over two boats and into the harbor.

" 'Damn it,' he said, floundering about in the water, brandishing the piano leg, 'I told you guys to cast off!' "

The notion that Block Island is a place to carry on in ways the mainland might not condone began way back with Ben Franklin. There is a tradition among some people I know that the old kite man did a bit of high flying at Block, and since he also was "good for the country" ("Use venery only for health or off-spring, never to dullness nor excess"), his example provides the precedence for what Rhode Island laws still call, in a rather charming eighteenth-century fashion, "reveling."

The tradition is that Ben Franklin used to stop off at the island on his way between Boston and Philadelphia to get warm by a peat fire, where presumably there was also some grog and, of course, an island wench most anxious to sit on the lap of a young printer with electricity on his mind. The story is given weight by the fact that there are islanders named after the great man, and some of their off-island descendants like to wink when they tell you how they got their name.

Much of the excuse for Franklin's Block Island escapades comes from the famous passage in the Autobiography where he is being chatted up by "two strumpets" who got on at Newport. Somewhere before they land in New York (there is no reference to Block Island), the young Ben is given "kind advice" by a "sensible, matron-like Quaker lady," to whom he "had shown an obliging disposition." Witnessing "the daily growing familiarity between the young women" and Franklin, the matron takes him aside to inform him, "These are very bad women; I can see it by their actions; and if thee art not upon thy guard, they will draw thee into some danger." (A conversation no doubt conducted away from the table, at the ship's rail, where no doubt Block Island was indeed, after all this daily dallying against a muzzling sou'wester, yet to windward.)

When the ship arrives in New York, Franklin confesses the strumpets "told me where they lived, and invited me to come." Following the sensible lady's advice, however, he "avoided" taking them up. It was well he did, he decides, for the captain was missing "a silver spoon and some other things . . . and knowing that these were a couple of strumpets, he got a warrant to search their lodgings, found the stolen goods and had the thieves punished."

Franklin concludes his account of his "Block Island adventure" with a characteristic bit of navigational moralizing. "So, though we had escaped a sunken rock, which we scraped upon in the passage, I thought this escape of rather more importance to me."

In the latest biography of Franklin there is a tantalizing reference to him and a young woman and Block Island. Closer inspection reveals he is merely "inspecting" something—a post office, I believe, in Newport, and he continues gazing into the mail slots or whatever, while she takes a boat to "lonely, windswept Block Island," without him.

Whether Franklin succeeded ashore at Block Island or not, one of the stories in mainland boatyards about Block Island in the 1950s was about the fate of a man caught Franklinizing with a woman out there. The husband, with some local help, tied the offending fellow to the back bumper and dragged him about the island Black-and-Tan style until the heel's heels wore out. This was one of those stories no one I knew ever cared to challenge, but I did recently ask Island historian Frederick J. Benson about the yarn. Not only has Mr. Benson lived on the island since September of 1903, but he ran the Square-Deal Garage starting in 1917, is still the official Island Fence Viewer and Director of Civil Defense, and, most important to this evidence, is the sole local representative of the State of Rhode Island's Division of Motor Vehicles on the island. "If they towed everyone around the island with their heels dragging every time somebody took up with somebody they shouldn't have out here, why, these roads would be in a heck of a lot worse shape than they are."

On a grander scale of vice, since the island's "Dead Period" in the late fifties and sixties, the Mafia has been constantly rumored to be "taking an interest in Block Island." There was to be legalized gambling, and legalized ancillary activities. Mr. Benson laughs, "Well, yes, there was a time when indeed half the island could have been bought for a song. People say the islanders got together and withstood the Mafia. It makes a pretty story, but have you ever heard of anybody getting together and withstanding the Mafia? It's just that the Mafia found other places to go with that sort of thing."

"Why?"

"Apparently there's something about the island itself which just by nature discourages that kind of operation."

Block Island may have been run down; it may have been old-fashioned, obsolete, even, but it has not quite yet ever been tacky in a Vegas way. It could be the climate, those ever-nagging sea breezes, the often-difficult boat trip over. It is not that Block Island has not seen sin. It is just that, by God, people who come to Block Island have had to earn their sin.

The temptation to do things on Block Island that you would not do ashore is indeed great, and it should be pointed out that even on Block Island there are things you should probably not do. Indeed you may now obtain from the town hall a list of things you are not allowed to do, some of which might surprise you. For instance, there is a place where you can park illegally and be arrested almost instantly. Granted the zone is a small place to find with consistency, but it can be done and success will always be rewarded.

There is nothing quite like being brought up short like this on a place like Block Island where you think you are "free." A good place to sulk afterwards is up in the hills by the shingled cottage named "Smilin' Through" after the song that was was penned there in 1915, a tune to which is affixed rather insipid lyrics, but which nevertheless contains a rather nice move in the penultimate stanza. The whole atmosphere up there will, as they say in the ads, "remind you of Ireland."

Why people must be seduced to Block Island by being reminded of someplace else escapes me. Now that Atlantic City has taken over being "the Vegas of the Atlantic," there is a proliferation of "Block Island, Bermuda of the North" bumper stickers. I don't know what the connection is unless it is through Bishop Berkeley, an Irishman who established a college in Bermuda and went to Newport to try to convert the Indians, but who is more known for his philosophy in which "qualities, not things, are perceived," and, most important here, "that the perception of qualities is relative to the perceiver."

In the thirties, promoters were wistful about Block Island being the "Helgoland of the New World." Since there are not many Helgoland bumper stickers these days, it is perhaps necessary to remind ourselves that Helgoland is an island in the North Sea which was a fishing port / tourist resort, later taken over by German army and navy tacticians with such success that the British were forced to level it twice, once after World War I and once after World War II, the place having proven impregnable during the wars themselves.

You feel more impregnable than any dream of Helgoland, walking up in the "Pots and Kettles" hills and ponds above the harbor. In the spring or fall you think you could wander forever up there in the dirt roads that are protected from the winds by the hedges. On the high, south half of the island you keep coming across what used to be called "prospects of the sea," but you are so far above it here, mollified by bayberry, that you can afford to flirt with the anticipation of the ride back to the mainland, and let the whole island go canting along in the clouds with just enough turns in the road to lead you on. What startles you and brings your stomach up short is not the sea so delight-fully distanced, but the sudden encounter with the mansard of one of the great hotels, heaved up from an unexpected angle only to be lost like a passing ship in a full gale sea.

In summer, however, there are ticks and little shade; the roads seem endless mazes and you thing of the drunks plodding back shoe-less in the old days.

And there are more houses every year. Some seem to fit in with the roll of the land. Others fight it. Something stirs in the hedge: a hawk? The raptor is more apt these days to be a shard of building paper, and those little pink flocks perched on yon fence are tufts of insulation.

Beside building paper, what is around the next turn? A combi-nation unisex salon and blacksmith shop. Granted the blacksmith shop is not in the main house where the unisex salon is, but out back in the barn . . . Lobster pots and a few old, wooden boats . . . a big Coke machine isolated surrealistically against pond . . . black berries and bikes . . . birds . . . without even trying you can have pheasants pump-ing behind the hedges, flocks of indigo buntings, bitterns, hawks, shrike, obscene-looking local ducks that Audubon doesn't seem to want to know about with their turkey-gobble eye pouches, and a lawn full of cattle egret with plumage that looks like mattress stains in the New Vasqueeze House.

Here is a stone wall where, some thirty years ago, I watched two men try to fit a cow, one pushing, the other pulling, in slow local-color comedy. There is a farmhouse where once I bought a blackberry pie from an old woman and took it down the road a hundred yards to eat it still hot off the blade of my pocket knife.

Now, wind in the wires . . .

At one junction a sign gives you a choice:

Payne Road

Mohegan Bluffs

Doctor's Office (as if there were those too eager to choose the lemmings' cure).

Indeed lately the island has become famous for its Moped Controversy. In summer the island's volunteer rescue squad has been kept in a constant ferment just scraping up visitors careening about the once-charming lanes. The agencies who rent these nattering vehicles, however, do a business in six figures. The Rhode Island legislature has been loath to endorse local ordinances controlling the motorized bikes, and there have been town meetings where secession to a more sympathetic Connecticut has been bruited.

If you do go over the bluffs (slowly, one hopes, under one's own power, gathering handfuls of clay), there is often good beachcombing: more beautiful stones than you can lug back up, and sometimes an iron gooseneck from an old schooner or, less romantically, part of a brake shoe from a trawler winch, once the carapace of a blue lobster . . . oil filters . . . shattered lobster pots . . . and always a gnarled staff upon which to lean and whisper Prospero . . . or if you're feeling more youthful, to fungo pebbles a few innings of Red Sox versus Yanks.

When you get back to town you will want to drink, and since not everybody is continually liquored up on Block, it might pay to say something about the water. Block Island is the only place I know where if you don't like the water, you can have a chance of having it adjusted. We were sitting in a restaurant one night with a cranky old man whose hat I'd admired when we were coming over on the ferry. (Of such things are made Block Island friendships.) "I can't touch this water," he kept saying. "I just can't touch it."

Finally a man from the next booth said, "Well, sir, I'm the director of the water works, and if you'd be a little more specific as to your complaint, I'll be glad to fix it for you on my way home by the reservoir."

Midday, the sun is blasting the docks at Old Harbor, but it is dark inside the restaurant and so noisy with amplified rock that it takes a few moments to find the bar, which is an island in the middle of the room, and another moment to discover the bartender in his island and the three men sitting at the edge, their backs to the harbor. It takes half a beer to recognize that moments ago it was these three men who were out there laying chain along the pier, measuring it carefully with a carpenter's tape and nipping it with a long-handled bolt cutter. Now they seem as if they have been sitting at the bar forever staring into their beer.

The oldest looks like a Yankee, the youngest Hispanic, and the middle one could be Manual as played by Spencer Tracy. Behind them, out the plate glass, their nets and rigging make a seascape beyond the dreams of any restaurateur cultivating the nautical motif. The three men look only into their drink, as if it is the pool out of which floats all this modern music.

The noise, however, seems to come from the ocean side of the circular bar, an area that just has to be filled with laughing youth.

But there are no windows that way, and it takes the rest of your beer to realize there is no one at all there, that it is but a vast bay of empty chairs, crossed only occasionally by a silent young man or a young woman in cut-offs and sweatshirt supported by a college name. Behind these tentative travelers, breaking through in door-slamming bursts of sun and music, is the beach, the actual scene, apparently, of a joyous, communal frolic. As they grope their way in out of the sun and the music, each confronts not only the sudden, empty furniture, but an unlooked-for sense of desolation.

Each carries, however, an obligatory Bud. Some pause and sagely sip, surveying the layout. Some continue under way, stuffing their lips with the bottle and gulping as they go. Some do not seem to remember that this heavy burden which they hold in both hands is their own bottle for which they have already paid. Some, like Diogenes carrying his lamp, lift their vessel out ahead of them to fend off the gloom. Judging by the door they eventually find, the object of their quest is the restroom. As a parade, it is a brave sight, for out of the collective din, they continue to come individually, knowing that this which they seek to accomplish, like dying, is something that even youth must do for itself.

At the other side of the bar, Manuel is picking food off the Hispanic's plate. Both laugh and so does the old Yankee, who steals some of Manuel's when he himself is occupied raiding his neighbor. One of the girls comes to the bar. She has not only a college shirt and an empty bottle, but a black eye. It is not clear if this is a punk affectation or not, until she asks for a cold, wet towel. I think of my grandmother at the Spring House in 1900, hurt by her glass salesman.

Manuel is alone in the midst of the three ravaged plates now and is leaning over the counter to talk to the bartender. Because of the din it is impossible to hear him, but in the pauses between numbers he seems to be describing something that happened at sea. By the earnestness with which the bartender receives the news, it must be a recent event. "So he called the Coast Guard," says Manuel, "and they told him to just keep going, but keep going slowly and they would send a team out to dismantle it."

Manuel makes his hand into the boat that is "to just keep going slowly" and he and the bartender laugh. The girl wants more ice.

Outside the other two are back measuring and cutting the chain.

Now the whole town is alive so you hardly know which way to turn. There is a picnic table at the water's edge. At your back are the old wooden hotels with their wide verandas and awnings beneath which sits a beautiful girl in a wide-brimmed hat. Nearby, his Panama now just visible above the terrace hedge, sits the huge man in the pin-striped suit who has been watching you. He might be merely a lonely fruit peddler from Providence, or one sustained on passions more sinister than anything ever assigned to Sidney Greenstreet. Above him, the mansard roofs and open dormers float away to the green moors.

In front of you, off to the side, are the fishing boats, and at your feet, on a lip of sand bleeding out from the bulkhead, a skate, pale claspers extended like thalidomide feet, lies decomposing among cups and Kleenex. There is a deafening toot and all eyes swing to the ferry slip.

The Point Judith boat is about to depart. This is usually considered the rowdier way off and on Block; the "element" that comes to Block Island from this direction has not been tempered by the longer sea voyage that the New London boat inflicts, or perhaps this is just Connecticut prejudice.

In any case, as it stands at the pier, the boat's three decks are dense with shouting, waving passengers. They might well be the gallery in a steep-banked theater such as the Old Parson's in Hartford, or that more famous O in England that saw the rant and bombast of the great tragedians. The suggestion is strong enough for a man to step out onto the pier, which in preparation for the boat's departure is momentarily clear.

In floppy brown suit and porkpie, he dances a few steps to his right, doffs the hat, and demurs at the request from the upper deck to speak. A few steps to the left, doff and demur.

He bows.

The boat is leaning way over toward the pier so that it looks like Shakespeare's audience has rushed into the Tower of Pisa.

"Ladies and gentlemen . . ."

By now the entire gallery is rocking, crying out for a show.

"Hey, ladiers and gennermun."

The three tiers roar back.

"Hey, booo!"

"Hey, ladiers'n 'lermun. Ronald Reagan is a . . . a . . . a . . ."

Various fillers are supplied.

"Toby or not toby!"

More catcalls.

"I jus' wanna say . . ."

Cheers cascade upon cheers. Kisses and thumbs and fingers. Besides, what else can they do? The boat is going to leave when it is going to leave, and when it does, the boat will get smaller and smaller; and one day it will be your turn, and then it shall be the island that gets smaller and that will be the summer you just had, getting smaller and smaller until one raw, overcast day someone says, "Block Island," and there is the floppy drunk blowing his chance on the pier, or the gull wing-deep in styrofoam whacking the gut of the fly-blown skate, or even the beautiful girl under the awning, and the fat man in the Panama, the wide verandas, the mansard roofs and the moors above.

A more subdued coda to this ferryboat performance occurred recently on a blustery, late spring day.

Outward bound for Block from New London, there appeared on the upper deck of the ferry a bent old man. He depended upon his canes and the aid of a middle-aged fellow, who, though perhaps twenty years his junior, did not look any too well himself. After some struggle they had edged to the windward rail. There they struck up a conversation with a friend of mine.

The old man's speech was blurred by the stroke that had crippled him, but he managed to get out that he was going over to the island. He was going out there . . . because he had been, of all things, one of those who had been paid to play piano at the New Vasqueeze. "And . . . this . . . ," he stammered, indicating his companion, "is the . . . bastard I used to . . . work for."

His pale companion nodded that this was indeed true.

"He," said the old piano man, "had the foolish idea this . . . morning . . . to take me out of the rest home . . . for the entire day. . . . To . . . put me back . . . for a . . . day . . . on the goddamn island of . . . Block." A sea hit the windward side and sent spray onto the deck. The piano man blotted his face and heaped abuse on his old boss.

"Well, damn it," said the boss, "let's move to leeward."

"I . . . don't want to move to leeward," said the piano man. "I . . . can't . . . move . . . to . . . leeward. I can hardly even . . . stand . . . here."

A chubby girl sitting nearby on the life preserver box said, "Sure, you can make it."

The piano man looked at her. "No, I can't."

"Yes, you can," she said.

He tried moving his feet. Another sea hit and the spray soaked him from behind.

"At least," said the girl, "I hope you can make it."

He glared at her and began to move his feet. He was at last under way, but another wave sprayed him before he was out of range.

There in mid-deck he asked the way to the ship's toilet. The ship was moving, but he had his own counter beat going, a jagged flail and totter. His companion stood behind him, paralyzed by the pitch of the deck, the vastness of the sea, and the old man's cry.

Temporarily abandoned by his companion, he was just an old man waving his canes, shouting and searching the faces of those ringed about him. He was repeating himself now, growing into a white fury, but it was not at the chubby girl, nor my friend, nor at his boss or even at the ferry company.

It was a pure rage that such things . . . such things as bodily functions and a narrow room should on a day like this . . . that such things yet must be.

So then, where was this narrow room to which he was banished? Where was the solitary zone in which he was condemned with his sourness?

He used the old Anglo-Saxon, so that everyone caught the full stink and splatter.

Later, it was time for the passengers to press forward and capture the first glimpse of the island. Behind them, the piano man had emerged from his exile back out onto the deck.

The air was fresh. Around his wrists hung his canes, leaving the old musical hands free for the rail. He watched the lee bow meet the sea and his eyes were wet.

There was the island.

He had not seen it in years, nor had he ever hoped to lay eyes on it again.

Yet it could be no other place.

He could smell it.

His stroke-numbed lips began to mumble, "Bu'full! Bu'full!"

The movement was now all in the ship. The chording hands had merely to follow the rise and fall, and the rhythms were deeper than any New Vasqueeze night.